All That Bull

OTHER BOOKS BY MR. LOWE

I Scream: A Brief Expose on the Romance of Ice Cream (2004)

The Commodore (2008)

An Asylum of Sorts: American Menagerie (2017)

Pickles and Honey: Ruby's Song (2019)

Colorado Blue (2020)

All That Bull

A Life with Wall Street

John D. Lowe

JackRabbit Publications

All That Bull

Library of Congress Control Number: 2021908707

ISBN: 978-0-9914818-5-9

Cover photograph (public domain): Watusi cattle in the Thoiry zoo.

For:
Anne Chisolm duBois, from "Raunchy"
And to the memory of The White Rose, who stood up against tyranny,
1942-1943

All That Bull

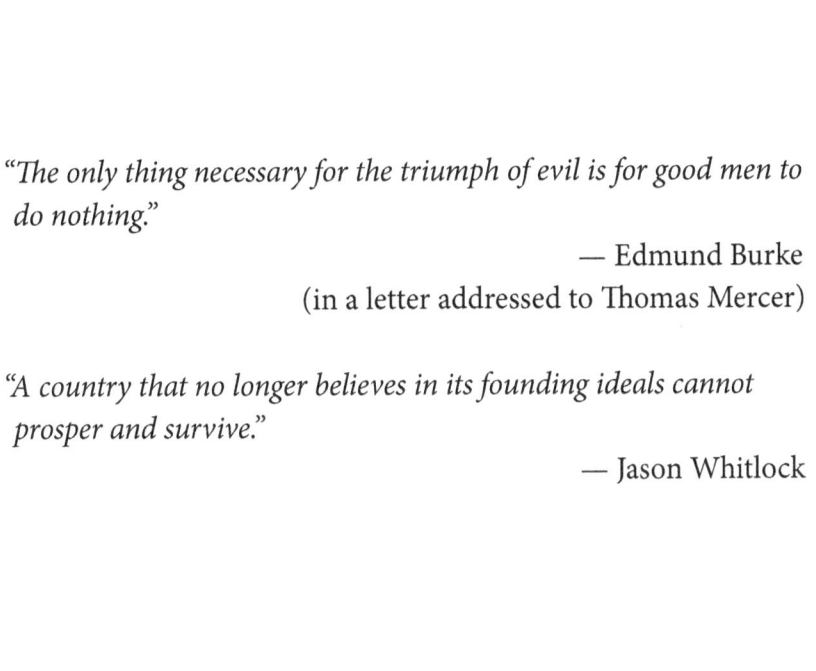

"*The only thing necessary for the triumph of evil is for good men to do nothing.*"

— Edmund Burke
(in a letter addressed to Thomas Mercer)

"*A country that no longer believes in its founding ideals cannot prosper and survive.*"

— Jason Whitlock

CHAPTER 1

A TRUE TEAM

They let him know that she was going to replace him as head of compliance, the woman who had collapsed drunk in an embarrassing heap at the last regional meeting. They knew he was the best they had in the East but, 'You see, we had to reduce two senior positions. Hers was one of them and she wanted to come back East, and chose your office as the one to take over. You can work as her assistant.'

"Stick the assistant, I have this team running like a clock and you're going to screw it up because you don't know what to do with a statistical hire," he had replied. They had hired her for her original position because they needed a woman but no one was saying a thing, except him.

They sent him a note later that week and told him to meet two representatives from the company at the local Hyatt.

When he got there, he met a Human Resources executive, 'yeah right', and a psychologist.

The psychologist was just out of undergraduate school and she started to cry when they told him what he already knew: he was being replaced with a statistic. He also knew that his team knew this and they were upset. He had made them work through all sorts of hell until they became the best in the system and didn't take anything from anyone. Two of them had even had a fist fight in front of him during one of his team building meetings but that made them tougher when they did come together. The same eight women who used to fight and backstab each other would now fight anyone who threatened any of them. They had become that rare team. They had become the best they could be and they knew it. He was their leader, their mentor, the boss who trusted them and who had their backs, and they knew that too. The psychologist was really becoming a mess and he had to keep telling her that it was all right.

He started to comfort the psychologist as she started to cry even more and say how sorry she was.

"Don't worry, you didn't do anything. I'll be okay. Stuff like this happens all the time; I'll be all right," he lied.

The company was a national name in 'financial planning' and they had him sign all sorts of things to prove that they didn't 'let him go' for his age, his sex or his race and that he really wanted to go on his own. What a crock that was. He grinned as he signed it all to be done with it and walk away with what little package they were giving him.

He would miss 'the team' more than anything else. He had had an open-door policy with them which he had been warned not to do but he did and on occasion he would have a team member enter his office in tears or completely frustrated with their relationship with other team members, but it worked in the end. He had a team meeting every Thursday morning, in the beginning, that he was also warned not to do, but he did. The fist fight was the worst of the meetings and he could do nothing but stand back in the corner and let it play out. It did and the rest of the team partially bonded when they broke up the fight as a team. It did scare him, he admitted to friends, but what came of it was a miracle of sorts.

They had combined three separate offices with two 'chiefs' or office managers, and that was what he had inherited. They had had one 'spy' and one 'disrupter' and they had found them out and neutralized them both so they were down to the eight. Then one of the former chiefs was going to rock the boat. She had been cracking semi-dirty jokes around him with innuendos attached and he thought the best way to deal with it was to ignore it although it made him extremely uncomfortable. It got to the point where he was avoiding her so he wouldn't have to listen until one of the team came to him and told him, 'she is going to report you for sexual harassment because you won't respond to her.'

"What do you mean, '... respond to her'?" he had asked really knowing the answer but avoiding the reality of it.

"What do you think I mean," said the other team member, who was concerned about her boss.

If he reported it, he took the chance of destroying or, at the least, disrupting his team. If he did nothing, which he had been doing, he would be falsely accused and possibly hurt the team. He was stuck until the woman on the team who had warned him reported the potential accuser and sexual harasser of her boss. What a team. He would never have imagined. They stepped in and knocked out one of their own to protect him. He did not want to give them up. They were so good that they were called upon for help from other offices of the firm. He had given them all top evaluations on their second year-end review and he received a phone call for that, 'you can't give them all top evals!'

"Why not, they earned it; and they deserve the raise!"

"You need to change them," came the voice at the other end.

"I won't, they earned it and they deserve it." The phone hung up on him.

He entered the blacklist for this and for having discovered the money laundering of oil money from Azerbaijan using life insurance policies to layer it into the system. How ironic, for doing his job.

He felt as though he was being ripped from his child when he thought of leaving his team and the team felt that they were being orphaned, all for a statistic.

He received thoughtful gifts from team members with even more thoughtful notes, which he kept. He received a grey marble egg and, at first, wished she had not spent the money on him until he read the note, 'You let me do my job, you trusted me to do my job and when I needed help you were there to give me the answers and help. No one ever did that before. Thank you.' It was simple but it was so much. The egg was symbolic for her being trusted for her talent and for him it meant a whole lot more and he would always keep that egg.

The statistic made it for four months and then collapsed in her office. They had to bring a team in to pull her out of the office without making too much of a scene. He didn't know how she had made it that far when he was told. They had found unsigned portfolio approvals going back four months in her office, which opened the company up to liability. In the end the statistic was just that: a statistic with no ability, 'an empty suit' as one of his former team told him.

It was too late, he was with another firm and, anyway, he was on their blacklist now. Team members would call him now and again over the ensuing years because that was the way it was. They had the best team any of them would ever experience at one time in their lives and they all knew it, including him.

Jake still had a future in front of him and he would take them wherever he went.

CHAPTER 2

IN THE BEGINNING – ELEPHANTS

Jake Bowen had started as a stockbroker at the end of 1980, in Manhattan, with one of the big brokerage houses of the day. He had to give up a career in journalism as he could not pay the bill for it and he had given up a childhood desire to fly, for other reasons. Several years before becoming a broker he was offered an internship out of college as an assistant writer for Harry Reasoner. It was the biggest mistake he had made, not taking it, but he had a student loan he needed to pay back. He was stuck with a decision after meeting Harry, but he had that loan and it was a non-paying internship. He knew Harry Reasoner was a great writer and that his head news writer was also the best. They wanted him to work with them because they had been given his name by one of their journalism friends who knew of the young budding journalist. But he made the wrong decision over money. He worked for a couple of 'rag' newspapers to pay the bills. He worked for these papers for more than a couple of years and eventually looked for more money. It's easy to look back on something like this and shake one's head but...

He sat for most of a day taking his Series 7 General Securities licensing exam on paper in a building on Whitehall Street, down by Wall Street. This license would allow him to sell stocks and bonds. He learned three weeks later that he passed, which was good. They would have let him go if he hadn't. They only gave you one chance to pass the exam back then.

He was in a large office over the old Penn Station, long after it was torn down, and he experienced everything, which gave him a good vantage point for compliance oversight years later down the road.

From the start he went after the elephants, the big clients that most were either afraid to go near or smart enough not to waste their time trying. Jake was different. He liked talking with these people, or their accountants.

He got lists of tax-shelter investors and started calling. He'd get into the office at 7:30 in the morning and set up, then start calling at 9 AM. He would work the phone until 9 PM with a break for dinner, which was free hors d'oeuvres with the purchase of a coke at Toots Shor's across the street. Free 'hors d'oeuvres' he'd laugh: chicken wings and mini meatballs, but it kept him going. Saturday was cleanup day and setting everything up for Monday. Sunday was his day of rest.

"Jake, do you ever leave this place?" asked Chris Dowling who sat in the cubicle next to him.

They sat on a floor with twenty cubicles called the Bullpen. Encircling the Bullpen were private offices which had large windows facing the street. One of those offices was his goal.

He grinned, "Sundays."

"Better man than me Gunga Din."

"I figure, I throw enough up against the wall it'll start to stick."

"Well, if anyone can bag an elephant it would be you; you have the talk."

"Ah, it's the oil conversion deal that's getting them to listen."

The firm was offering stock in a new oil and gas company in exchange for limited partnerships and private placements in oil and gas deals. These were tax-shelters that offered tax-sheltering by writing off the exploratory and development costs of procuring oil and gas. Once they were producing a revenue stream, they trickled return and were illiquid. Jake was offering these high-end investors liquidity and the firm was taking ownership of the producing wells owned by the tax-shelters in order to form the new company. 'Slick and easy' was the motto in his head as he spoke with these investors who, of course, were high net worth individuals or 'elephants'.

"This business is like chipping away at granite with an ice pick as far as I'm concerned," said Chris shaking his head.

"O ye, of little faith."

"Ah, you just know this stuff better than me Jake; I have nothing yet to have faith in."

"You'll do okay Chris, like your dad."

"Yeah, I guess."

Chris Dowling was the son of one of the top producers in the firm who was located in an office on Lexington Avenue. He really wanted to be an art teacher. He knew he wasn't good enough to be a successful artist but he knew he was good enough to teach. He lacked the self-confidence to be a good artist and he lacked the self-confidence to stand up to his father and tell him that he actually wanted to be a teacher. He was now stuck in the cubicle next to Jake, getting some of his father's crumbs or the smaller clients in his father's book of business.

In the process of calling on tax-shelter owners, Jake became an expert on the tax-shelter limited partnerships and private placements that he was calling on along with the same types of tax-shelter investments that his firm offered, especially oil and gas. In his talks with the accountants of the 'elephants', he also developed new clients by helping these same accountants with their other clients' tax-shelter needs. He became not only knowledgeable about different aspects of oil and gas drilling, through tax-shelters, but he also learned how to calculate the future value of oil reserves held by companies and therefore the value of the smaller oil companies. In addition to oil and gas shelters he became proficient at using aircraft leasing investments to defer taxes to leaner years, for clients who would be experiencing huge profits in the near term.

He became the tax-shelter expert in the office and started to share business when he was able to help another broker secure a big client through proper tax-shelter advice.

Then he started to get commitments from the elephants he was talking with, either directly or indirectly. They started signing over their oil and gas holdings to gain shares of stock in the new oil company, called USOIL, and the hope for good liquidity.

Even before the oil conversion deal was complete, he started buying and selling positions in the markets for some of these elephants because, as one of them said, "I trust you." It was that simple.

Jake would admit when he didn't have the answer but then get the correct answer quickly, and these larger clients found this refreshing. He would get the right answer and offer the correct advice every time. Their accountants felt comfortable that their clients would be kept safe by Jake and his client base started to grow. He had two presidents of banks, and several presidents of medium to large sized American companies. The markets were lackluster so he became inventive. He'd let his clients know what he was up to in the markets and engage them according to risk and need, making sure that he over exaggerated the risk, so that when things went against them it would be more acceptable.

He started leveraging bonds in margin accounts, besides taking in premiums for clients through selling calls against their stock positions, on stock that was never called away. When he leveraged bonds, he would put up thirty percent of the cost of either 'junk bonds', or discounted bonds short in maturity and with a high coupon rate. With an eleven percent margin cost he was still getting a double digit return to his clients in interest. With discount bonds, of companies in trouble, he not only returned a leveraged rate of interest but a capital gain on top of it. He bought 30-year paper, on depressed companies, with a couple of years left until maturity. As they were in deep discount, they grew in value with every month gained towards maturity. The bonds' increase in value gave his clients this added capital gain on top of interest. He was taking advantage of a very good leveraged yield-to-maturity environment.

It was all starting to work solidly for him within six months of getting his license when he decided to take a gamble. He rolled the dice and went off his guarantee salary that December, after producing a twenty-two-thousand-dollar month, in order to get a higher payout on commissions.

Chris was struggling next to him, until the day he told Jake of a sure deal.

"My dad has a client who is president of WaterFall Paper and one of the big card manufacturers is going to buy them. He had my dad buy more of his stock for his secretary and him. I'm buying some for everyone in my book. You ought to buy some Jake."

"Chris, that's insider trading."

"Nah, it's my father's client."

"Yeah, and the guy is breaking the law by telling your father."

"It's no big deal; you gonna buy any?"

"No and I advise you not to."

Chris bought WaterFall Paper for his book and within a week of the takeover he received a questionnaire from the SEC that had to be answered within 48 hours. A week later Jake came in on Monday to find that Chris was gone and that his desk had been cleaned out on Sunday, because he himself had been there on Saturday and the man's things were still on his desk.

"Man, those guys are good," he said to no one that morning. He was impressed.

On Tuesday Tim Clinton took over Chris's desk. Tim came over from E.F. Hutton where he traded options. The firm had paid him one hundred and fifty thousand dollars up front to come over and bring his book. He had to prove himself before he got an office, and then a lesser producer would be moved to the Bullpen to accommodate him.

Every time Tim wrote an options ticket, which was constantly, he'd chuckle to himself tight lipped before getting up to get it to the wire desk for transmission to the floor of the Exchange.

"Why do you chuckle every time you write a ticket?" asked Jake finally.

Tim chuckled, "Because they're suckers, it's just gambling."

When Tim had a particularly good day of chuckling the small birthmark on his forehead near his right temple would turn crimson.

Near the end of Tim's second week at the firm one of his clients, a Mr. Papper or just 'Papper,' showed up and sat next to Tim. He watched the market and had Tim put orders in for him but Tim would have Papper himself walk his own order ticket up to the window while he chuckled under his breath. Papper worked nearby and he would become a lunchtime fixture and every time he left, Tim would snort chuckle. Papper was the constant gambler who never seemed to win.

———

Jake's book of higher-end clients was starting to grow as he was given clients from the 'sleeper' who used to have an office but was now in the Bullpen winding his career down. He dosed a lot in his cubicle and now and again he'd fart in his sleep disturbing it enough that he would grumble and go back to sleep. Jake had to get a private office, and soon. He remembered an old-time broker that he had met downtown during his training who wore a green visor and smoked a cigar. He remembered his words, 'don't worry about it kid, you'll do fine, I've seen enough of 'em in my day and you'll be good; just remember that most of your clients, or the good ones, are going to have something in common with you and feel good about that.'

Jake wasn't worried about getting that office, the question was just when. He was gaining good clients he could identify with and that old timer's words had come back to him. Jake had always had a great deal of comfort with every level he had achieved since the four-hour psychological test he had taken before he was accepted. They had told him not to outthink it as the test would catch him doing that. But he found a pattern quickly and remembered the repeated questions put in different contexts with such repetitive answers like 'or would you rather run around the block naked?'; he particularly liked that one. He figured the test out and gave them what they wanted and had the highest achievement score they had ever seen.

So he was now inheriting some of the 'sleeper's' clients. He was getting the important ones but one made him nervous and, like most clients, he never met the guy. He'd call Jake and put in an order and then hang up. That same voice came in on two different accounts and every time the voice came up and bought or sold the same casino stocks, it made Jake uneasy.

"Ok, five hundred shares of Resorts, buy at the market!"

Then he'd hang up.

"That guy again?" asked Tim and then he snorted and chuckled.

This guy knew about Jake and Jake didn't know how or why and the 'sleeper' didn't know the guy who had two accounts under two different names and two different Social Security numbers. At least he thought it was the same guy. It became a mystery call. He started to feel as though he was being set up but maybe he had just seen too many movies. The guy sounded like Sal Tessio in The Godfather and every time he called and heard that voice come up he would visualize the character in a dark room someplace.

Jake clicked with Lisa, Dennis and Steve in the office. They were all in their twenties. Steve had his nose in the air on occasion and thought that he was a little better than the rest as he came from Kidder Peabody and the state of Connecticut. But when one of them caught him being an ass he got a smile on his face admitting that he was caught, and to an extent it was all a put on. Lisa was married to a big-time commodities broker. She was smart and beautiful and she had a mischievous side to her which fit into the group. She was devoted to her husband but the group gave her the mad relief she needed as he was the rock, the more conservative side of the relationship. He also appreciated how important this little group was to his wife, and so by extension was part of the group.

Dennis was like a leprechaun. He was short with a rapid wit and a mathematical mind second to none in the office. If all four were missing from the office at once, during the day, Jim knew where to find them. Toots Shor's place was their place. Jim was their manager; they called him 'Lumpy' because he had a lump on the left side of his forehead from a 'bump' on the head he received while flying for the Navy, and his last name was Lummond. They pushed back on him and gave him grief but they wouldn't trade him. To the last of them, if Jim left and asked them to come, they would go with him. He had only once come into Toots to collect his Young Turks and bring them back to the office and then stopped short of doing it. He would stop in on them in the future to check on them but never to pull them out, that was up to them. They were his budding core. They would all eventually have a private office so short of dragging them back to the office that first day, he left them alone and they understood why. From then on, they understood each other and Lumpy became fair game for practical jokes, as subtle as they might be. He on the other hand had their backs. He let them push the envelope.

CHAPTER 3

LUMPY AND THE NEED FOR AN OFFICE

One day, as Jake was sitting at his desk on the phone and thinking of his office, a man walked up to the side of his cubicle as Jake forgot about his office for a moment and watched with nervous curiosity. The man had tin foil wrapped around his head and his eyes were bulging. He wasn't dressed like a bum but close to it and, somehow, he had snuck past their excuse for security in the name of Florence, their receptionist located by the elevator.

'Crap,' was Jake's first thought. 'Florence must be on one of her coffee breaks.'

"You're interfering with my investment waves man!" almost screeched the man as he pushed up on his toes tilting his head a little to the left and pointing the index finger and middle finger of his right hand to his right temple as Jake excused himself to the client on the other end of the line and then covered his mouthpiece.

"What?"

"You heard me man, you're screwing with my vibes, my investment vibes," he said coming down off his toes and lowering his hand as he stared at Jake and ready to speak again.

'Must be one of Clinton's guys,' thought Jake a second before the man spoke again.

"Whaddaya gonna do man? You're messin' up my communications?" and he put his right index finger and middle finger against his right temple again.

"Geez, I'll get off the phone and restore your communications by turning my screen off and then back on. It'll reset everything," said Jake voicing his first thought.

"Ok."

Jake excused himself and hung up the phone, then turned off his GTE quote screen and the man all-of-a-sudden settled and smiled.

"Cool," he said as he tapped his forehead twice with his right index finger along with the middle finger and turned to leave.

"Jeeesus, I've gotta get that office now," he said for no one to hear as the cubes next to him were now empty for lunchtime and he was alone. But he saw Dennis staring at him from across the room with a big cat's grin.

"Real funny," he mouthed to Dennis who started to laugh.

———

Just before Jake moved into his new office, three offices away from Lumpy's large fishbowl office, Lisa hired a stripper.

Lumpy's birthday was coming up on the third Monday that July in 1981 so Lisa hired a stripper and filled the office in on it one-by-one as they pitched in. Lumpy's office was four times the size of the standard office and was surrounded by glass so he could see everyone in the Bullpen, and they could see him.

Lisa's stripper was actually quite beautiful and sophisticated in appearance; and Lumpy had a weakness for beautiful woman, his second wife being one and fifteen years younger than him. She came dressed in a business suit and looked to be in her late twenties. Where Lisa found her, no one knew but the beauty of it was that she was set up for an interview with Jim and her 'resume' was on the tape recorder she carried into the office.

Jim was sitting with someone from the headquarters downtown but it didn't matter, it was his birthday when the interviewee was led into his office. They all glanced in the direction of Jim and saw that his eyes had picked up her beauty as he, and his guest, stood and Jim offered her a seat and introduced her to his guest. They could see but not hear; but it didn't matter, they knew what she was saying. She was telling Jim that she wanted to be a broker more than anything she had ever considered and she kept her resume on recording tape. They saw Jim's face change a bit when she said this and he nodded. Then she stood up as the office started to slowly gather outside his fishbowl, which he did not notice as she turned on the tape recorder and her music started to play, and her jacket came off.

By the time he noticed them her bra was off and his lump had turned crimson red with the rest of his face. Jake was laughing to the point that it hurt and Lisa was not far behind him.

He just shook his head when he realized he had been had and saw the four laughing together front and center, surrounded by the rest of the office, as the stripper wished him a happy birthday, kissed him on the cheek, and made a hasty retreat to the ladies' room.

They were his for better or for worse. That's who they were and that's why they would be successful; they were smart, self-confident, young and full of life with a need to succeed. When he had interviewed Jake, he had thought 'the guy should apply to the Naval Aviator program' but he didn't say anything, he wanted him. That told him how important Jake was to him. Naval Aviation was important to Jim, even though he got out of it himself after eight years, and the fact that he kept Jake, instead of helping the Navy with an outstanding candidate, was telling. After Jim had interviewed Jake and Jake left the office, he reminisced about Navy flying for a brief moment as Jake made him think about it. He remembered the Jones Beach flight. He flew a Grumman S-2 Tracker for the Navy and he was temporally stationed at Naval Air Station Brunswick in Maine. He was out drinking with his co-pilot the night before because they knew they wouldn't be on the flight roster the next day but things change. The next day brought them an S-2 that had a repaired oil leak in the starboard engine and they were on the roster board and tasked to fly it down the coast to Floyd Bennett and then turn it around and bring it home. They had chalked up the cowling so they could see the slightest oil leak before it was lost in the slip stream.

God where they hung over. On the flight line a young man, with an Airman's rating, came up to them as they were fumbling with their gear in semi-stupors and asked if he could go along for the test hop, he also had flight gear and a helmet with him and a great deal of enthusiasm.

"Lieutenant, sir; you mind if I take a ride with you?"

"Sure kid, get geared up and hop in the back."

The kid got in and they forgot he was back there by the time that the plane was flying down along the south coast of Long Island. Jim was sleeping in the left seat while Bob Langford had the controls in the co-pilot seat. Jim remembered he was having a good dream and had his head and stomach where he wanted them when Bob started shaking him.

"Hey Jim, hey Jim, get up."

"What, what the hell?"

"We got some oil tracking back from that damned starboard engine, geez."

Jim leaned over and looked, "It doesn't look that bad." Just as he said this, flame came out of the inside of the cowling and the fire light and alarm went off.

"Christ," said Jim as he hit Bob on the shoulder and said, "let's get it out."

Then he didn't remember much other than that they started arguing and pushing each other back and forth over what to do because they were really hung over. The kid in back was not hooked up to the intercom and he could only see two lieutenants pushing each other back and forth in the front cockpit with the alarm going off.

They came up alongside Jones Beach and thought of putting the plane down in the water and then called an emergency for Kennedy International because it was closer and bigger than Floyd Bennett.

They were given immediate clearance and they put the S-2 down and turned off the runway two thirds down its length after touchdown, and moved quickly to the apron with the fire trucks coming to meet them, sirens blaring.

They had the wing foamed down in no time while they were still shutting down the port engine and making sure all switches were off.

They had forgotten about the kid in the back, entirely, as they exited the starboard side and went around the tail and walked out on the tarmac behind the port wing. They had walked right past him as they left.

While staring at the plane still in the stupor of their hangovers and thinking, 'oh shit', they saw two legs drop from the other side of the plane to the tarmac and then start to walk up towards the tail and they stared.

"What the hell is that?" Jim remembers having said and then he started laughing to himself in the office as people looked into his fishbowl at him doing so, and not seeing anyone else there.

Then they had remembered as the kid came around the tail.

He came up to Jim and, looking a little distraught, said, "Thanks for the ride lieutenant, that was my first time in a plane."

"You're welcome kid," Jim had said and then he and Langford had started laughing like idiots as the minds of two hungover guys with a smoking plane had no place else to go. The sailor had just looked at them, just the way the three brokers were watching him through the glass of his office as he went back in time laughing almost as hard as he did then. Jake was already gone and hadn't seen Jim having a good time laughing with himself.

So, Jake became his and not the Navy's. What Jim did not know was that Jake loved airplanes and had dreamed of flying for the Navy as a kid. Jim would not find out about Jake's love of airplanes until he soloed a year later on his way to getting his private pilot's license. Jake, himself, had also thought he was getting too old for Naval Aviation at twenty-five going on twenty-six, although he had wanted it at one point; and, anyway, his father had said he'd have a rough time taking orders from anyone. His father had told him this with respect in his voice, knowing that Jake had an independent drive in him that made him take chances and confront things head on with a minor disregard for authority. He also knew that his son could not change that, nor would he want him to.

Jake was the fourth of four sons and was an afterthought at best. His father called him the Vassar Graduate as he came as a result of International Night at Vassar College for women where his mother was attending post-graduate classes. There was a special bond between he and his parents and his father lived a bit vicariously through Jake's adventures and chance taking as he was similar. His father was similar but having married in his early twenties he needed to be more responsible early on, whereas Jake hadn't yet married, nor even considered it.

His father had been a pilot and had sworn it off like a bad gambler would gambling as Jake's mother did not want the family breadwinner inadvertently making a smoking hole in the ground, although he was known to be an excellent pilot; 'a great stick' as an old flying buddy had said. Jake had the bug, and Jim and he were inches apart from changing the path of his life in that interview.

Jake was 'full steam ahead…', but not 'damn the torpedoes'. He was thorough and fully aware of what he was doing before he moved forward with anything. He was anything but reckless and the clients he would acquire, and grow with, knew this. He was a risk taker but a creative and thinking risk taker. He was a broker who understood each of his clients with a clear understanding as to what extent he could be creative with them individually. They came first, on an individual basis, and word would get around about him to a stratum of clients that the average broker would never even get the chance to speak with.

Simply: Jake was true to himself, true to his client and never had cloudy vision on anything. He wasn't black and white but he didn't waste time determining grey areas. He could see them clearly and always moved in the right direction. He was energetic but only to the point of being fully alert and aware, and engaged. He did not wear people out and he was honest and fair.

CHAPTER 4

THE OFFICE

Jake was arranging his new office when Lisa walked in. The office was three down from Lumpy's office with a window facing 7th Avenue directly behind him. You could see part of Macy's from his office.

She looked in the direction of Jim's office and then back at Jake and laughed that throaty laugh of hers that got other people to laugh, "Lumpy's keeping an eye on his trouble-maker."

Looking up at her, from moving the blotter on his desk, he grinned, "Yup, and it's to protect me from you; he knows where the trouble comes from."

"He's smarter than that, I hope," she said with a chuckle.

"Yeah, he is. I'm not looking but look across the other offices into his office right now. I bet he's looking at us and you in particular."

She looked in the direction of Jim's office and laughed and smiled, and then waved at Jim who smiled back with some restrain. They were his and they were good, but they also made him a little nervous.

"Well, keep em' close."

"Now what's that mean?" asked Jake while still fidgeting with things on his desk as he removed them from a box on his chair.

"Keep your friends close and your enemies closer."

"We're not his enemies," he said looking up at her.

"No, but we make him nervous," and she laughed and looked over at Jim again, and waved and smiled, which put Jim on edge as he smiled back weakly, thinking, 'now what's up with them.'

Turning back to Jake and laughing again, "It is just too easy to get him nervous."

Jake stopped what he was doing and looked to the side of his office and into Jim's down at the end, and at Jim now looking right at them. He then put on the biggest Cheshire Cat grin he could and he could swear Jim's lump started to glow.

Turning back to his desk and Lisa, "Geez, it is too easy, I think his lump is glowing, we're going to have to do something."

"Let's call Dennis and Steve in and see what he does. Tell them to 'sneak' in."

Jake grinned again and picked up the phone, they were both in the office.

They both got up from their desks in cubicles at the same time and started to skulk around the office so Jim would eventually notice them and notice that they were getting progressively closer to Jake's office.

When they were both within ten yards of each other they stopped and made sure they had Jim's attention. Once they did, they looked at each other, smiled and then ran to Jake's office and through the open door, one to each side of the door hugging the glass walls as though hiding from someone although everyone could see them.

Lisa could see Jim shake his head and then head to his desk and his GTE machine and telephone, and then pick up the phone.

The phone rang in Jake's office while Lisa was looking at Jim and grinning.

Jake picked it up and heard, "Very funny," from the other end as Lisa watched Jim mouth the words into the phone.

"We thought you'd like that, just keeping you on your toes."

"Ah Geez, why the hell did I ever get into this business!"

"For people like us. What would you do without us?"

"Sleep peacefully at night."

"Now that's no fun and you know that."

"Now that you have that office, I expect the other three juveniles to make the grade and get theirs."

"Ah, then you'll really be asking for it."

"It only gets worse when it gets better!"

"You said it," and Jake laughed and then hung up the phone.

"Lumpy?" asked Dennis.

"Of course," said Steve.

"I was watching him the whole time he was talking with you so he could see me, that got him too," said Lisa, "He's just really too easy."

"He wants to know when you're all getting your offices."

"He wants to get us away from the masses, we're a bad influence. He reminds me of my parish priest Father Slattery, one of those old Irish priests who came over on the boat."

"How's that?" asked Jake with a laugh in his voice.

"When I was an alter boy I'd pour the wine for Communion and I'd pour just a little more than was needed just to get him to react."

"What's that have to do with Lumpy?"

"I'd pour just enough with a drop more and start pulling the wine flagon away and he'd start to sweat and mumble in a heavy Irish accent, 'Keep pourin' it O'Neil, you're not payin' for it'. I'd just about die every time he did it and couldn't wait to do it every time. He had to drink the wine that was left in the chalice and wanted to make sure he got his share."

"So?" said Steve.

"He was fun to bait and he put up with me to get what he wanted, sorta like Lumpy," and they all looked over at Lumpy on his phone standing by his desk to see if he looked like a priest as he looked back and again shook his head while his lump started to glow once more."

"Yeah, I see the resemblance," said Lisa.

"He'd look good dressed as a priest," said Steve rubbing his chin and contemplating Jim.

"I think maybe a Cardinal's biretta, he'd look good in red," added Jake as he moved up next to Steve who was now to the far side of Jake's office facing Jim's office while Jim was standing trying to talk on his phone.

"What's a biretta?" asked Steve.

"You're an idiot," said Dennis.

"It's a hat," said Jake watching Jim.

"No, No," said Lisa as she came up and joined them, as they were all now standing in a row facing Jim and discussing him while he watched them, "White robes, he'd look great in white robes with that big red lump glowing."

"Geezus, a Pope, that's it, he would make a great Pope," agreed Dennis.

"I could really see him being carried around on that big 'ol thrown with his staff in his left hand nodding to the crowds," said Jake with a serious voice and then they started to laugh. No reason, just the visualization that they all had at once of seeing Jim as the Pope with that big white tiara being carried about in a thrown and getting nervous about it with his lump glowing.

Jim, watching them, made the sign of the cross satirically and shook his head not realizing what he was doing or what they were talking about other than that it was about him.

With this they lost it. They started laughing so hard they were leaning on each other or against the glass. Each man, and woman, to his own and it was so loud the rumble could be heard from behind the glass as everyone in the Bullpen started to turn to look at Jake's office emitting this muted, rumbling laughter with four people in different states of leaning support as they were losing their collective breath.

'Idiots,' thought Jim as he turned to face 7th Avenue while still on the phone listening to his young wife complain about being bored. They had a three-month-old at home along with Jim's teenage son from his first marriage.

Starting to collect themselves and their breath Jake, between gasps, said, "Let's...let's get outta here. Toots!"

"Good i... good idea," stumbled Lisa with the end of a laugh.

"Yeah, let's," said Steve as Jake started to lean into the glass door to his office to open it.

Dennis could not say a word as he was crying and trying desperately to gag his laughter and get it under control.

As the door pushed open the reduced laughter came clearly out of the office and hit the Bullpen as they started to head out.

Jim was too busy to notice their departure while he stared at the old Pennsylvania Hotel across the street and mindlessly watched the pedestrians on 7th Avenue as he listened to his bored wife. He didn't notice, or hear, them leave. By the time he turned around they were gone, "Oh, crap!"

"What?" came from the other end of the line in Connecticut.

"Oh, nothing honey, just my wise guys, they're gone."

"Oh," was all she said as she picked up from where she had left off as Jim moved with the phone line to his window overlooking 33nd Street to see the four of them cross the street and head into Toots Shor's at 11:00.

Toots' was cool and semi lit with a bar to the right and to the left booth seating. The walls were covered with celebrity photos taken with Toots Shor. They headed off to the left and a booth, and a waitress followed them as they came in.

"Geez, it's only eleven," said Steve.

"So what; you people in Connecticut have special hours for things?" Dennis sneered.

"I'll have a vodka martini, one olive," said Jake before anyone noticed that the waitress was standing right next to them.

"Make that two," said Lisa.

"Three," added Dennis.

"Oh, crap...four," said Steve, giving in.

"They say 'crap' in Connecticut Missa Steve?" asked Jake.

"Oh, cute."

"Well, geez, you're the one who has frostbite of the nose from the angle you carry that thing," grinned Dennis starring closely at Steve's nose sitting right next to him.

"Until he gets caught," added Lisa.

"Caught, what?" and then he couldn't help himself and gave the giveaway grin that he was full of it and got caught again.

"Hey, ya think the Lumpster noticed us leave?" asked Lisa with a gleam in her eyes.

"Ha, we were there and then we weren't," said Dennis.

As the martinis came, along with the short-skirted waitress, Jim stuck his head in the door of Toots and looked long enough to find his crew and see Jake raise his martini glass to him; then he came in the whole way.

"Who are you toasting?" asked Steve with his back to the door as Lisa raised her glass too, looking in the direction of the front door.

Steve and Dennis turned. "Ah geez," said Steve as Jim headed to the table.

"Good God, it's just after eleven," said Jim as he moved up quickly to the side of their booth.

"That's what I said," added Steve as he took a sip of his martini.

"Geez Steve," said Dennis looking at him, "did you bring an apple to class every Monday in grade school?"

"What?"

"Forget it."

"You're not going to spend the day in here?" asked Jim.

"No Jim; just time for a martini, moving is strenuous. Want one?"

"Geez no," said Jim looking at Jake with mixed feelings knowing this guy was going to be his best and, really, he was just the way Jake was at that age, "I tell ya, you're going to kill me, keep it light and I'll see you back in the office."

"You love us Jim," said Lisa.

"Yeah, like a truck driver loves hemorrhoids."

"Ah, geez," said Steve.

"Now what?" followed Dennis.

"Hemorrhoids?"

"Ya know what they are Mr. Shine?" asked Dennis

"Now what does that mean?" returned Steve while Jim and Jake and Lisa watched.

"God, you're like the four stooges sometimes," said Jim when nothing more came from Steve.

"Yeah, but we're all yours," grinned Jake.

Jim shook his head and turned, heading for the door with a departing, "Do yourselves a favor and don't stay long," over his shoulder.

They watched as he left, not saying anything, and then Jake laughed, "We really do scare him."

"Like the clown at the circus," said Steve from nowhere.

"What the hell does that mean?" asked Dennis turning and looking right at Steve's nose again.

"Do you have to stare at me like that?"

"Yeah, when your nose in the air says something stupid. I don't get the clown."

"The clown at the circus scares kids with half a brain but they're also curious and know the clown is needed to make a circus."

"Christ, did you come up with that on your own?"

"I hate clowns," said Lisa.

"Yeah, they're not my favorite either. Are you comparing us to those nightmares of small children?" asked Jake staring at Steve with a false appearance of looking serious.

"Yeah, well you know what I mean."

"Yeah, Stevie, we know," said Dennis with a grin.

"Ah, don't call me that."

"Well, for a while I know I'm going to start visualizing myself with a clown nose and clown hair like Bozo, when I speak with Jim. Thanks Steve," said Jake.

Lisa started to laugh, "That's good, maybe you ought to come in dressed like Bozo."

Dennis started to laugh to the side and to himself.

"What's so funny?" Lisa asked through her laugh.

"Just thinking of the live Bozo show without a delay, years ago," and he started to laugh again.

"What about it?" asked Steve.

"Bozo was talking with the 'boys and girls' in the stands at the beginning of the show, after singing that stupid Bozo song, and….it was perfect," laughed Dennis, "he went up to some kid and leaned over and asked, 'and what's your name little boy?' and the kid reached up and pulled his nose off and said, 'fuck you clowny.'"

They started to laugh again.

"Think of all those kids in the stands over the years, they have to have had twisted scary dreams of that clown, and one Bozo had a southern accent," said Jake, "sure don't wanna give Lumpy bad dreams," he grinned.

"One more martini before going back?" asked Lisa.

They had another round before heading back, and when they entered the Bullpen they could see Jim back in his office starring at them with a subdued grin. Jake thought about driving him crazy and he didn't want to do it too much. They all liked and respected Jim to the point of wanting to not only be successful for themselves but as well to help make Jim become more successful. He was just that type of guy. You liked messing with him but you did it with respect. Jake felt Jim probably knew this but they still made him nervous. Jake knew he needed to get back to work with his elephants on the oil deal. USOIL had a big payday attached to it as well as giving him some great clients.

As Jake was finishing his office move and getting settled in to work at his desk in his new swivel chair, Dennis walked in.

"How's it going?"

"Same as it was a half hour ago, what's up?"

"Look at Dexter and Dickhead, or Freddie and Flossie the Bobbsey Twins, over in the corner," Dennis nodded to the far side corner of the Bullpen and Dexter Bridgeway and Dick Morris.

Jake looked over to see Dexter and Dick standing up in front of Dick's GTE machine, which displayed the markets and individual stocks. They were looking at it like they were watching a football game, jumping up and down and laughing and cheering.

"What the hell; what have they piped into their GTE machine?"

"I don't know unless someone finally put something in their water."

Dexter and Dick were joined at the hip and looked and acted alike. They both looked like nerds, wore thick black rimmed glasses and had pen protectors in the front pockets of their always white shirts. They got excited about everything but now they looked like they were discovering the cure for cancer and watching the winning run for the New York Yankees final game of the World Series all in one.

"Christ, maybe they hotwired the tube for something other than the markets; shall we take a looksee?" asked Jake.

"We have no choice; these idiots have been doing this on and off since I got back from Toots and I keep seeing them outta the corner of my eye."

Jake pushed himself up out of his swivel chair as Dennis led the way out of his office and headed to the other side of the Bullpen, but to the opposite side from that of Dexter and Dick. The two were so busy jumping up and down and laughing in front of Dick's GTE machine that they wouldn't have noticed Jake and Dennis, even if they had walked right up to them. They made it to the far corner and watched. As they were watching Dick wrote out an order ticket and ran across the front of the office to the wire window and Marc the wire operator. They watched as Dick handed Marc the wire order. Marc was no fool and shook his head all day long at some of the stupidity that came across his desk. Jake and Marc would have lunch together every once and awhile as they both understood that they both understood.

They watched as Marc looked down at the ticket and Dick became animated. Marc was efficient and wouldn't delay inputting a ticket to the floor of an exchange but he would make sure it was right before it went. He showed the ticket to Dick from the other side of the window pointing something out and they could see Dick mouth, 'Oh Shit' just before Marc passed the ticket back to him and Dick corrected something with his pen and then pushed it back through again. Marc had his wire operator put it in and then handed the yellow trade receipt back to Dick, who held it up and pumped his fist in the air while Marc shook his head. The trade ticket, or order ticket, was made up of three copies: the white, to be kept time-stamped by the order room; and the yellow as a receipt, also time-stamped for the broker; and the pink, which went into the brokers box with the execution price once the trade was executed, and it would be time-stamped again with the time of trade.

Dick waited for the completed execution copy and pumped his fist in the air again and ran back to Dexter who was jumping up and down now, more than he had been earlier. When Dick got back, they kept their eyes glued to the GTE and then, all of a sudden, in less than a minute, they jumped up and down again in unison, as though someone on the screen had scored a goal. They then slapped each other on the back and shook hands like idiots in an over exaggerated manner.

They just could not wait anymore, they had to find out what these two were up to.

Jake followed Dennis as they walked to the corner that housed both Dexter and Dick, and as they came up to them, bending over Dick's GTE and pointing at the screen and laughing and cheering, they almost went unnoticed. The two barely recognized the presence of the two new arrivals to their inner sanctum.

Jake and Dennis looked over the shoulders of the two, expecting to see something that should not be on a GTE machine, and the only thing they could see was the trading status of a stock with bid and ask.

"What the hell are you two up to?" asked Dennis.

"Did ya see it, did ya see it; it moved, it moved again," proclaimed Dexter

"We did it, we did it," added Dick as he pumped his fist back and forth in front of the GTE machine like he was imitating the crank shaft and connecting rod of a steam locomotive that was chugging along at high speed.

"What are you idiots doing?" asked Jake now getting an idea.

"Holy crap, we did it, we did," laughed Dexter, laughing like a donkey inhaling and exhaling each laugh.

"Look," said Dick moving out of the way, "it's TERMOLINE!"

"What the hell's termoline?" asked Dennis.

"I don't know, some cancer cure company or some crap like that," answered Dexter excitedly.

"It's a penny stock, I know the stock," said Jake now looking closely at the GTE screen.

"Yeah," replied Dick with a grin from ear to ear.

"Geez, that used to be traded thin and in teenies," added Jake.

"Yeah, yeah, yeah," yelled Dexter in continued excitement.

"Boy that was one big trade that just hit. It's not thinly traded anymore," said Jake seeing a large block that had gone by about the time that the two were cheering as though someone made a big score.

"You guys manipulating trading on this thing?" asked Dennis.

"Yeah, yeah, ain't it cool," said Dick not taking his eyes off the stock as more volume came in and started to push the penny up. "Come on baby, come on keep buying, yeah, yeah, yeah."

Jake watched as the bid noticeably popped up.

"Okay, okay, okay," said Dexter as Dick picked up a ticket already filled out, "sell at market, sell at market, hurry up."

Dick ran with the ticket to the order window again and Jake knew that Marc was really shaking his head now.

"How long have you guys been doing this?"

"All morning, all morning," said Dexter too excited to look back at Jake as Dick started running back to them from the order window. Jake could also see a buy ticket sitting on the desk all made out.

"You two are idiots," said Dennis.

"I'm surprised Marc hasn't put a freeze on your trades but he will.

You are manipulating the market."

"Yeah, yeah, ain't it cool," said Dexter again fixated on the GTE screen.

While the two were jumping up and down Marc had Jim on the phone. This had been the second in-and-out.

Jake could see Jim's door open out of the corner of his eye, "Well boys the proverbial shit is about to hit the fan," and then looking at Dennis, "Shall we 'partir' mon frar?"

Hearing Jake's voice come from the direction of facing Jim's office Dennis looked up from the GTE and towards the office and saw Jim coming with a face he hadn't seen before. "Absolument," then looking at Dexter and Dick, "You two are so screwed."

Jake then grabbed Dennis by the arm but it was too late, Jim was already on them.

As Jim came up, "Lookie, lookie, what we have here fans," said Jake to no one in particular. "Hey Jim, these boys seem to be confused on how a stock gets traded, they buy and then they panic. They are really confused."

"They're cafokted, that's what they are," said Dennis quietly out of the side of his mouth to Jake only.

"Geez, Jake, are you helping these guys to be idiots?" asked Jim.

"You know better than that," grinned Jake.

"Yeah, yeah step aside so I can deal with these two morons."

"Look, look," said Dexter still excited while Dick was quiet, finally realizing the morning's game was over.

Jake and Dennis stepped back and started to walk way.

"Geez," said Jake, halfway back to his office.

"Leave it to Dexter and Dickhead, I figured they'd do something dumb at some point but this was better than I expected."

"Yeah," laughed Jake.

Almost back to Jake's office Lisa stood up, as her cubicle was close to his office, and looked at them quizzically.

Dennis looked at her then flipped his head in the direction of

Dexter and Dick and then shook his head and grinned.

She came up to them and they explained, and she looked over at the two 'recalcitrants' on the other side of the Bullpen being chewed out by Jim. "Poor Lumpy, the day is going to be a long one for him."

"Yeah, well who knows what's going to happen to Dexter and dumbass. Bad combination, like gunpowder and flame," said Jake.

"Ya know, they probably thought it was a harmless game. Man, they're probably done," added Dennis.

"What's up?" asked Steve walking up to them.

"Always a dollar short and a day late," said Dennis.

"Now what does that mean?"

"It's all over," said Jake nodding towards the corner holding Jim and the two traders, "The Bobbsey Twins just got busted for stock manipulation."

"You're kidding!" said Steve as he stared over at Jim with the two in the corner.

"Those guys are from Connecticut, aren't they?" asked Dennis with a grin.

"No," said Steve.

"Actually, they're both from Stamford and came in together. I guess they used to ride trikes together and swap Tonka toys as kids," said Jake.

"Ah, Stamford, well!" said Steve.

"It is Connecticut, isn't it?" asked Dennis.

"Well technically..."

"Technically, it is Connecticut. Man, you have some weird folks from that state."

"Yeah, like who?"

"Besides you, and Dexter and Dickhead, try Benedict Arnold," said Dennis with a big grin.

"Geez, what the hell's that!"

"You two are like two, two-year-olds," said Lisa as she laughed.

"You can't help it when you're around this guy," said Dennis looking at Lisa and ignoring Steve.

"Well, who's the two-year-old?" stated Steve looking in Dennis's direction.

"See, there you go," said Lisa.

What they all knew is that if Dennis were in trouble Steve would be the first to jump in to help him and vice versa.

"Well, that might highlight this office for downtown once more...I would hate to lose Jim."

"Why would that happen?" asked Lisa now concerned, as Jake's voice was serious.

"He had two guys manipulating a penny stock in his office. You know they should get approval before they buy a penny these days with what's going on. And even though it's an honor system, they will blame Jim."

"Hell, with John Muir slingin' this new issue stuff to everyone out there new to the Market like it's the next sure thing to come along since IBM, the powers that be are a little uptight; so, these guys will stick out like a sore thumb. It's not gonna be good," added Dennis.

"Yeah, well Jim's good, they know that," said Lisa.

"It doesn't matter," concluded Jake.

"Those idiots," said Steve looking over at Jim talking with them.

"Yeah, nutty Nutmeggers," smiled Dennis.

"Oh, that's good," said Steve.

"Yeah, well I've got to get to work on this USOIL deal; I'm behind. That could be big for both Jim and me."

"Yeah, I gotta get going too, it's been fun," said Dennis as they broke up and headed to their individual desks.

As Jake turned to head to his office, he caught Sheila O'Brien looking at him from her cubicle, just outside of Jim's office. He winked and she blushed and looked back down at her desk.

CHAPTER 5

SHEILA FROM THE SOUTH

Sheila was a year, or two, younger than Jake. She was a tall red-head, or one might say she had auburn hair leaning towards red as it was long and silken, and beautiful. She was slim and attractive with an athletic figure and Jake was more than curious about her because she was such an enigma, other than a couple of basic facts that he did know about her. She bought her clients Ginnie Mae funds only, which was sort of the office joke and quietly kept. She wasn't the brightest broker he'd ever met but in many cases that wasn't saying much. The one time that he did get to talk with her he found out that her favorite singer was Pat Boone and she loved Bob Hope. Now, Bob Hope he understood but when you put that together with Pat Boone you have a whole other thing going on. Talk from the women in the office was that the only items she carried in her purse, outside of a bill fold, was a small pocket Bible, a tooth brush and a pair of fresh panties. That would all be an eye-opener when he realized the validity of it but for now her head was down with the remains of a blush starting to fade as Jake headed to the door of his office.

As he opened the door, he turned slightly and caught Sheila once again looking at him and she blushed again and put her head back down.

He smiled to himself. She was interesting and quite attractive but he needed to get his juices flowing in the right direction, and that was USOIL.

He sat and just looked at his desk for a moment, calmed and then pulled his call book out for the USOIL clients. He had every conversation catalogued with each client and for a large group of twelve he had one central contact, as they were represented by their investment advisor who was their accountant as well. Eventually he would talk with each of the twelve individually. He looked at the book for a moment then, for some reason, looked up again. Standing at the Standard & Poor's book shelf, across the Bullpen form him, was Sheila holding a red Standard & Poor's binder open to some company that she was not looking at. She was looking at him and she smiled demurely in a way that he had only seen in the movies. He felt a warmth run up the back of his neck as though he had been caught looking at something he was not supposed to be looking at.

She was beautiful and she knew it and for some reason this woman, who was perceived to be shy, had full control of the distance between the two of them. USOIL disappeared as he was enticed and she knew it, it was plain to see in her eyes.

Before he had realized it, he was pushing his chair back on its rollers and pushing himself up to head to the Standard & Poor's bookshelf. As he moved forward her eyes went back to the opened page of the binder she was holding, and Dennis noticed and let out a very low 'bird whistle,' which Jake could hear.

He glanced over at Dennis, as he headed towards the S&P library, and gave him a helpless look that said, 'what else can I do.' He knew that Lisa would really give him grief, like a sister might, once he struck up a conversation with Sheila, which would obviously be more than just business to anyone watching.

"Now I'm curious," he said as he walked up to her. He looked her right in those green eyes of hers, at his level, and knew he was done, "what company are you looking at that has you so enraptured?"

"I don't know, you tell me," she said, shyly revealing a different Sheila.

That night Jake struggled away from his friends by sneaking out with Sheila to a place of her choice. It was called the Sugar Mill and the walls held framed drawings of sugar mills in the Caribbean and in Hawaii. The decor was tropical with touches of bamboo here and there and you stepped up to your table, one of ten that occupied both sides of an alley that went down one side of the bar. Sheila ordered a gin martini, very dry with two olives and Jake followed suit.

"You like gin martinis," he said as the waitress walked away with their order.

"Well, yes. What would you think, a Shirley Temple?" she said with full command of the situation as though she was now in her secret realm.

By the third martini, which were larger than normal, Sheila had her shoes off under the table and was caressing his left shin with her right foot. It took him completely by surprise as the martinis were starting to take effect on him with that special effect gin seemed to have.

She tilted her head slightly and grinned at him while putting her right hand up to get the waitress's attention. She ordered another round of martini's and became a Sheila he would never have imagined.

One more martini after that round and they were out front hailing a Checker Cab. She was on a mission with Jake in tow. He just followed, and for a brief moment he thought that he worked with the woman and this was not really a good idea and that he should have thought about this before going out for drinks with her. It was too late.

Once in the cab Sheila gave the driver the address and wasted no more time as she embraced Jake and kissed him tenderly, at first, before it turned into an erotic kiss; and this from a woman who loved Pat Boone and Bob Hope equally and carried a pocket Bible in her purse.

The cab stopped in front of a brownstone on the Upper East Side, in the eighties, and the cabby had to remind them that they were there, as Sheila was someplace else with Jake along for the ride.

As they walked up the steps and headed for her apartment, Jake asked, "What about your roommates?" Everyone, at their age, had roommates in Manhattan.

"They're not in tonight," and as it was past one in the morning the building was relatively quiet, and so was the apartment as they entered.

The door barely closed before Sheila was on Jake talking to him in a seductive southern accent that he had never heard come from her before. Admittedly he did not know her that well but well enough and they were quite inebriated, so he just accepted it as normal after a minute instead of being startled. It actually became somewhat erotic and before he knew it, they were on the sofa, against the wall, on the floor, on a kitchen table and it all started to blend together until the first rays of the morning sun touched his face.

As he felt the warmth on his face start to grow, he heard a door on the other side of the room open followed by a muffled gasp, and the door slamming shut again. This opened Jake's eyes and he thought for a minute, 'Where am I ... oh, crap'.

He looked over at Sheila next to him on the floor and they were both stark naked.

Another door opened on the other side of the room and once again he heard a reaction, this time a low screech from a woman as the door closed again.

"Oh, God, roommates!"

"What?" said a groggy Sheila as she started to stir, looked over at Jake and then realized where she was and that they were both as naked as jaybirds. "Oh, my God!"

"Yeah, that's what I said. I think you have roommates."

"Uh-oh."

"Yeah, I thought that too. I think we better get while the gettin's good." At least for him he thought.

One could hear a pin drop in that apartment as they dressed in their business best, which had been left arrayed around the room. It was somewhat comical as they helped each other locate items of their garments like two kids on an Easter egg hunt. The roommates were no doubt holding their collective breaths until they heard the apartment door close and the deadbolt snap into place as Sheila and Jake left.

They were dressed and out in a hurry, and once again on the street headed downtown towards the office.

"Did anything happen?" asked Sheila three blocks later. They were on the same page.

"No, nothing really."

They walked in agreed silence until they could hail a cab to the office and then entered separately in case anyone else was in that early.

It would always remain their secret and they never went out for drinks again. Jake allowed himself a brief moment to think what the roommates might have seen as he sat at his desk and laughed and shook his head. Sheila would later go to Lehman Brothers and fall perfectly into their method of calling a list of names and selling a new issue then going back around and selling them out on a cyclical basis. It was the Lehman process and it was the job that a 'monkey could do,' they all said, but Sheila would make an upper six figure income in a year after leaving a book of business behind that only contained Ginnie Mae funds. She had left a book of people who would need to be properly assessed, qualified for proper suitability and then fixed accordingly. It was a mess.

CHAPTER 6

JENNY AND JODY

"Where were you last night, you look like hell?" came Lisa's cheery voice from the direction of his open office door. Raising his head from the USOIL tracking book, "I was lost but now I'm found."

"How profound. Well, I hope you didn't leave any breadcrumbs leading back here, whatever it was."

"Cute."

"I'm known for that," and she grinned. "Just heard we have two new brokers coming in from Merrill Lynch today and one is getting an office."

"He's buying more brokers, doesn't he trust us to bring the numbers up in time," he said half joking.

"Certainly not with people who look like you right now."

With a grin he asked, "Any idea what they cost to bring over?"

"Nope, but I hear they both have good books, although they are coming in from Long Island."

"Is the office giving any formal introduction?"

"Not that I've heard. Thinking about it I think he wants to sneak them in and intimidate everyone to be more productive."

"Ah, good wholesome competition."

"Yeah, I think Lumpy secretly likes to shake things up. Two brokers from the same Merrill office."

"He is shaking things up then isn't he," he said as he glanced over to his right in the direction of Jim's office to see Jim staring right at him by chance.

Jake gave him a big exaggerated grin as Lisa turned to look at Jim and see him shake his head and look down at some papers he was standing over on his desk.

"Maybe he heard about what you did last night and this is curtains for you."

"Curtains? What've you been watching Philip Marlowe movies or Sam Spade?"

"Sam Spade?" she asked as she turned her attention to Jake.

"Yeah, The Maltese Falcon, Dashiell Hammett. 'The stuff that dreams are made of.'"

"What was it, martinis? You are out there this morning. I wouldn't talk to too many people in this state if I were you."

"Can't help it, it's just all this stupid stuff in my head."

"Yeah, and it comes out after you've been drinking martinis. I'm not going to ask if it's anyone I know."

"Yeah, don't."

"Oh, geez, someone in this office! Well, that's a limited choice and it wasn't me."

"That's funny."

She started to look to the Bullpen as Jake thought, 'oh, no.'

Her eyes stopped at Sheila who had her head down in her client book like she was still trying to figure out where she was. "Oh, no, don't tell me," she said as she turned back to Jake with humor written on her face.

"Tell you what?" he searched for a way to avoid what was coming.

"You had martinis with Miss travel purse."

"Oh clever," was all he could say as his head went back down to his book turning crimson red even though he was wrapped in a hangover.

"I am not going to repeat what I think."

"That sounds good," he said as he looked up at her sheepishly.

"I will only ask one thing: Pat Boone? It must've been interesting conversation."

"You don't know the half of it."

"These ears probably couldn't take it. I'd get cleaned up for the two Merrill women who are coming later this morning."

"Both women? Ah, now you're gonna gang up on me."

"But it's so much fun," she grinned and headed out the door.

Jenny and Jody arrived by 11 that morning and Jim met them at the small elevator in their reception area. He led them into the Bullpen area as Jake looked up from his work. Jim was pointing areas of the office out to them as they had come in blindly. It was one of those quiet deals where phone calls were made, money offered to move to an office sight unseen and then the move; a move which was made initially in stealth to retain one's clients before the firm they were leaving tried to retain those same clients.

Jim pointed at offices and then pointed at Jake and the two Merrill woman looked right at him as he grinned sheepishly with his full-blown hangover. He felt that he must have looked demented as they lingered on his office for a second before moving onto something else that Jim was pointing out.

Jim took them to the vacant office at the end of the line of offices. It had been vacant for a couple of days now as one of the two remaining older reps, like the farting 'sleeper', had been moved to the Bullpen to finish out his days telling stories to the young bucks as he transferred what was left of his book of business.

They walked into the office and Jim pointed to the vacant cubicle, just in front of the office.

The older broker was Jenny and she had the office. Her friend and mentee, Jody, took the cubicle in front of the office. It would turn out that Jody was a high producer as well but would have to wait for an office to open up; but as they had some large clients together, they came as a package. A very expensive package as it would turn out, but a welcomed addition as Jake and the others got to know them.

———

"I didn't know what to think when Jim pointed out your office and I saw death warmed over," said Jenny to Jake and Lisa a week later in her new office.

"Oh, you'll get used to him; he grows on you," said Lisa to Jenny.

"I'm standing right here you know," said Jake.

"And you're the tax-shelter guru," said Jenny changing the subject.

"Well, guru's pretty strong."

"He knows them better than some of the people downtown," said Lisa to a woman who quickly had become one of them although older and, they would both agree, wiser.

"Good, I have some rather large clients that I want to bring you in on. They need the help."

"Sure, of course."

"I also heard that you have some unique ways of bringing income and growth quickly."

"Yeah, bonds. With the market up and down and flooded with new issues I've been able to use the instability of the bond market and margin to my clients' benefit."

"Are you a cowboy?"

"No one's ever said that."

"He's a cowboy in lots of things," laughed Lisa.

"Thanks."

"Ah, need to watch out for you then," followed Jenny with a combination of humor and respect.

"I'm harmless."

"I hope not, I need you to take some productive chances with a few of my clients. I'd like to go over them with you when you get a chance."

"Now's as good a time as any."

"I'll leave you to it. I have to chase down Dennis and make sure he's staying in line," said Lisa as she headed out the door.

Jake sat down with Jenny and they went through a list of twenty clients, four of whom were having current tax concerns. The others would be clients who could benefit from leveraging bonds. They were all high net worth and older. They needed to talk with the young 'turk' who knew what he was doing, who was fresh and smart, and a 'cowboy'.

Jenny, from that day on, would only address him by the moniker 'cowboy'. He found it embarrassing but at the same time it was an honor coming from Jenny, who he came to appreciate as a mentor much in the way Jody appreciated her. She would also become somewhat protective of him in a different way than Lisa was protective. With Jenny and Jody as part of the mix, the client base started to grow and expand and their production started to increase. 'Lumpy' was stupid smart and knew exactly what he was doing, and what he had paid for.

Sometimes it was the simple things that just generated energy and intrigue. He noticed that Jody had a mirror on her desk and every time she was on the phone, she was looking into it. It had Jake perplexed until he asked her, "Why the mirror?"

She looked at him behind her in the mirror and without turning to address him she said, "They can hear you smiling."

"Geez, I never thought of that."

"Make sure you are every time you speak with your clients, it's contagious with them and they will listen more closely."

It was the simple stuff. It was paying attention to detail, it was listening and knowing what you were talking about. It was also taking joy in his clients. The old guy in the green visor was right. He started to have clients that were similar to him in many ways and they became close. He had one high net worth woman, who was a senior executive with a major airline, want to introduce him to her daughter. He had a tough client who he had made money for who was head of a bank try to hide his emotion on the other end of the line the day that Jake told him he was leaving the firm to get more involved with tax-shelters, but that was yet to come. When it did come Jake would miss them all: the clients he had grown to love in a way like his family, warts and all.

CHAPTER 7

USOIL: THE TIP OF THE FLAME

The USOIL deal was still his central focus while he worked with other clients along with those he had lined up for the oil holdings conversion to stock in this new company. The conversion targets had become clients as well during the period of time that it took to evaluate their illiquid oil holdings and put a stock swap offer together.

His group of twelve was the apple in the entire group of clients he was helping to convert. The numbers had come back and he was expected to get a commission of $435,000 just from this group alone, which would be the bulk of his commissions from the USOIL deal. It was such a large sum at once that the firm had put together a commodities-rolling program for him in order to reduce his tax exposure.

The head of the USOIL program, in the home office downtown, was constantly in touch with Jake as they looked forward to completing the deal. They had all of the paperwork in place and were in the process of collecting the signatures. As the group of twelve were in constant motion as CEO's, one being in Hong Kong overseeing his firm's building project and communicating by TELEX, they had to have their accountant, who had power of attorney to sign as their investment advisor, sign for them.

With one day to go, after the advisor signed a specially prepared document for his group, the head of the USOIL exchange program showed up at Jake's office.

There was a problem. The legal structure of the USOIL exchange did not allow for a single appointed signee for any of the limited partnership and private placement holders. There was no way to get around the needed documentation to satisfy the legal requirements under the deal. They had been working long hours with the legal department to see if there was a way to get around it and there simply was none. They were going to send representatives to the group's accountant to see if they could corral the needed signatures. It had turned into a mess because the people in charge had not been intimate with the legalities of the exchange for the company they were putting together. They were product developers out of touch with their legal group. How could they have not known this? But in the end, it was okay for the group of twelve as EF Hutton had a similar conversion going forward. The Hutton program had copied the one he was working with and it was done in hopes of catching some of the fallout from USOIL, which it did in this case. The "broker of the day" at a Manhattan office of EF Hutton would make himself almost half a million dollars because their paperwork was set up to handle an investment advisor with a power of attorney when time had run out at USOIL. 'C'est la vie' was all that Jake could think of, knowing that nothing in the financial business was in the bank until it was in the bank. What are you going to do? You just have to move forward, and he did now have those twelve as clients, as they would stay with him.

The Monday morning after the deal with the twelve died, Jake came in late and as he went to take his chair he found a silver flame, with a pointed tip, rising from the center of the seat. If he had been out the night before he might have skewered himself and lost his manhood. He froze and stared down at the thing and saw a piece of paper stuck on the tip of the flame, signed Jim. He looked up and over at

Jim's office and Jim was staring at him with a melancholy grin. Jake reached down and lifted the silver flame emitting from a black granite stand with a small plaque on it that read "Jake Bowen Founders' Group USOIL." He lifted off the note with Jim's handwriting and it said: "They stuck you pal…sorry, the drinks are on me." He looked up again and over at Jim and saw him nodding his head in agreement with what Jake was thinking.

That same day Jake bought five thousand shares of Telefonos de Mexico, at twenty-five cents a share for most of his clients. It also yielded twenty percent in dividends and had every year since inception. He called them one after another and told them to just let it sit as a sleeper and collect the dividends. It was small enough that he knew they wouldn't touch it and as the only telephone company in Mexico they would eventually make money. At least someone won that melancholy day as sometime in the future that stock would go up to forty-five dollars a share and split two for one and go up from there. Jake never bought any for himself as he had been warned by the old man in the green visor with the cigar to never 'invest in what you invest your clients in as it will get too emotional and you will make mistakes.'

That same week Jake would call his gambling clients with Marathon Oil. Jake was excellent at calculating future oil reserve values and he had calculated Marathon Oil as the primary take-over in the oil take over madness that was in the air. He tried to get them to buy straight Call options on the stock. He had forgotten to smile as Jody had told him and no one took the options. He was halfhearted about it which was not serving his clients well as the next week Mobil came after Marathon and the options went through the ceiling. Two clients actually called him upset that he hadn't forced them to buy. He hadn't smiled but he laughed at the irony. He had told one that he had forgotten to smile which left the client confused as Jake hung up the phone. The USOIL failure did bother him.

He later had his 'mob guy' calling him on Resorts International and things were starting to get back to normal as he developed more clients and got referrals from his high-net-worth clients for tax-sheltering. He became the tax-shelter specialist of the office and number one in the firm for shelters. Downtown was starting to look at this twenty something to come down and join the tax-shelter group, with an average age of forty-five, but that would happen later. He was spending many evenings with his crowd of the four of them, as they ran around New York together. Lisa's husband, Jack, would come on occasion but he would let his wife have her mad broker friends for the most part. Jack and Lisa were devoted to each other but gave each other room. Jake admired them.

CHAPTER 8

STUDIO 54, ON THE TOWN AND THE TOURNAMENT

Studio 54 had reopened and they had connections that allowed them to pay the fifty-five-dollar cover charge to get in on the few occasions that they went. Jake met a Swiss model at Studio 54 who was older than he, who would cook him dinner once a week for several months to follow. He would go to her condo, overlooking Central Park from the south, every Friday evening. It had an amazingly beautiful view of the entire park and the city north, and dinner was always an amazing experience.

Her name was Margaux and she was the daughter of a wealthy Swiss banker. She wanted Jake to give up everything and move to Switzerland with her where he would have no financial worries. He wasn't tempted. In a way it started to push him away from this woman who had taught him how to enjoy a long slow meal with a woman and stop being in such a hurry about everything. She taught him other things as well and he respected her for that.

Studio 54 had been an experience and Jake saw things that he never would have imagined. The bartenders wore the collar of a tuxedo shirt, with a partial pleated bib attached, along with the tie of a tuxedo but that was all, besides the black trousers, and the women loved it. He actually saw a beautiful woman, in her early thirties dressed in pink chiffon, dance barefoot on top of the bar with a bottle of vodka in her hand making more than suggestive movements. Other things were happening in the theater seats above and overlooking the floor and when the place started to get fired up the bar would mechanically move to the side and open up to a dance floor, announced by falling balloons and colored confetti. He found it interesting the first few times that he had gone, and on occasion with different people other than the three, then he quickly lost interest.

When the quartet was together, they made the rounds in either a limo for the night or, better yet, Steve's Jeep with the canvas top. The four of them could fit neatly into the Jeep and Jake particularly liked it.

One night they wound up in a place called the Underground. It was filled with beautiful young women and very few men. They found out that only gay men came to the place and that the women liked not getting hit on all the time, so they came as well. The owners had spent a great deal of money on the interior. The women's bathroom had a wall length and ceiling high waterfall coming down the left wall as you walked in. Jake knew this as he had walked in by mistake, captivated by the waterfall. They had tunnels made of large fish tanks connected end to end traversing the center of the club and sitting on a chest high platform. It was art but Jake couldn't resist the second time that they went there and he found himself happily crawling through the connected fish tanks, looking for a way out with the other three laughing on the outside. It was one of those mad nights and when a CBS television crew entered, as Jake meandered through the fish tanks, Lisa knew it was time to go. They wanted to interview the guy in the tanks and got to him before Lisa as he was crawling out of the tank with an opening near the entrance to the bar.

Holding a small mike up to Jake, as he exited, the interviewer simply asked, "Why were you crawling through those tanks?"

"For the same reason George Mallory wanted to climb that damned mountain," he said as he pulled himself completely out of the tank, as Lisa grabbed his arm and they then fled to the Jeep at the side of the building.

In March, of his second year with the firm, Jake's production had topped the entire office and he was invited, with four additional tickets, to the Tournament of Champions at Forest Hills over a month away. His firm had a tent at the tournament and an open bar, and Lumpy was nervous. Jake would always remind him of himself when he was much younger and a hard playing Naval Aviator.

It was early May and it was raining, off and on, the first day of the tournament as Jake showed up for the event with the other three members of the quartet and an old friend from college. Jake had a long trench coat on and wore green aviator Ray-Bans in the half light of an overcast day. As he walked into the open bar area, outside on the Forest Hills grounds, with water drops running down his dark glasses, Lumpy muttered to himself a form of 'uh-oh'. It was afternoon and they were coming from an Irish pub, where they had waited out some of the rain.

Jake walked into the outside enclosure surrounded by a waist high white lattice fence meant to keep non ticket holders out and, thought Jim watching them enter led by Jake, people who just came from a pub. As Jim watched them, he had to smile, remembering his twenties, but he was a bit nervous as Jake noticed him and held his hand high, fingers spread unusually wide, to say hello. He knew they had started their day earlier and he did not move towards them. Let them raise their own mischief without him as part of the scene, he thought. They did, however, give him a certain joy as he watched them.

"You see Lumpy over there," said Jake as he bumped Lisa's shoulder, "he's avoiding us."

Lisa looked over just in time to catch Jim before he turned his attention elsewhere. She smiled with an oversized grin and Jim smiled back trying not to engage them.

"He's easy you know. We could really get him noticeably nervous," she said as she still kept her stare with Jim, and then smiled at him again and looked at Jake.

"Is his lump turning red? I don't want to look and scare him that I might come over. It's also a little dark behind these sunglasses."

"A little crimson and it's not much brighter out here."

"Hey, it's clearing a little and it looks like they're going to continue this match with Lendl," said Steve coming over from the entrance after talking to an official.

"I thought Lendl was allergic to grass!" said Jake.

"Geez Jake, this place hasn't been grass for a few years now," corrected Steve.

"Oh, well the guy plays golf and that's grass so I don't get it."

"Jake, it's clay here now," said Steve.

"Where's Dennis?"

"Where do you think," said Steve.

"At the bar of course," confirmed Lisa as Jake turned to look at the open bar and Dennis turning to look at them with a happy grin, and a tray of drinks in front of him.

"Geez, Marc's there with him; only trouble," laughed Jake about his college buddy who had come along with them. Marc could drink half a fifth of scotch and you wouldn't know it. It was frightening. He also had a habit of taking people to the edge in a conversation and then walking away, leaving the person happy and confused. Jake had always thought it was a marvelous gift but it always made him nervous when Marc did it.

"Hey, you mad bastard," yelled Jake to Marc still at the bar as Dennis walked towards them with a tray of martinis. "You giving the bartender trouble?" It was all too loud, accented by the word bastard and everyone looked at him and then at Marc at the bar responding with a grin and his glass held high. 'Oh, crap' thought Jim.

"Let's go see Lendl, the guy's allergic to grass," yelled Jake again.

"I keep telling you it's clay," said Steve as Dennis came up with the martinis.

"Ah, it's more fun if it's grass," responded Jake.

"You're not going to let Lendl know he's allergic to grass, are you?" asked Steve somewhat in fear as Lisa looked on smiling.

"Never," said Jake and then turning back to the bar and yelling out to Marc again, "Hey numb duds are you coming?"

"Oh, Christ," muttered Jim to himself before taking a big sip of his scotch.

Jake then turned and grabbed one of the martinis in a plastic glass as the other three waited with theirs in their hands.

"To the USOIL king," said Lisa as she raised her glass while Marc started to walk over.

"Great, thanks for reminding me," said Jake as he raised his plastic glass with two olives in it. Then he noticed the olives. "Two olives. Geez Dennis, how'd you do that? Miracle worker!" And he thought of Sheila and her two-olive martini for one brief moment.

"I had a good priest," Dennis smiled, raising his glass.

"Idiots," said Lisa with a laugh.

Steve was lost.

Marc came up, beaming with a slight glow on his face and a scotch in a plastic glass in his right hand. "Tennis, anyone," he said as he raised his glass with the sun coming out from behind a cloud, just that second, to light up his scotch with the twinkle of a star as it came through the light amber of the liquid.

"Yeah, Lendl'll be on the court soon," noted Steve.

"Isn't he allergic to grass?" asked Marc before taking a sip of the golden amber in plastic.

"I told you," said Jake.

"This place hasn't had grass for years, what are you guys talking about?" said Steve with some frustration which Dennis quickly picked up on.

"Geez, how's he gonna do that? He'll be sneezing and hacking and drooling all over the place," added Dennis.

"It's clay for chrissakes," said Steve forgetting he was holding a plastic martini and spilling part of it with his enthusiasm.

"Whaddaya mean clay?" threw in Lisa.

"Christ!" said Steve as he turned and headed for the court area entrance and the arena.

"He's easy too," said Lisa.

"We'd better keep him company or he's liable to get lost, you know these Nutmeggers," said Jake.

"Ya, a nut," said Dennis.

"What the hell's a Nutmegger?" asked Marc.

"Someone from the state of Connecticut," smiled Lisa.

"'Qui transtulit sustinet," muttered Jake.

"What the hell is that?" asked Marc before taking another sip of his scotch.

"'He who transplanted still sustains', the guy's state motto and he's always trying to prove it," said Jake as he raised his martini in the direction of Steve as he started to disappear towards the arena, "Let's follow the man."

"Where do you come up with all of this crap?" asked Dennis.

"I just read a lot of stupid stuff and way too much history; shall we follow the man," said Jake with a grin as he gestured everyone to go ahead of him with his martini loaded left arm extended towards the exit.

Jim watched them leave while in a conversation with one of the firm's executives and he watched with a bit of obvious relief, enough so to get the person he was speaking with to turn and watch the four people leaving, with a guy in a wet trench coat taking up the end of the parade.

"Yours Jim?"

"Only when they're writing tickets Max," smiled Jim as the man returned his attention to Jim who was glad Dennis was not using the umbrella illustrated with bulls fornicating with bears and given to him by a friend from the Bond Club. Small mercies he thought.

As soon as they got to Steve in the stands and sat, Ken Rosewall came out on the court. Jake couldn't believe his luck. Jake played tennis and Rosewall was one of the players that he liked to watch for the chances he took and his mastery over the ball. He watched as Rosewall made a couple of returns and shots that just weren't in the book and the crowd responded with oohs and aahs, and then it started to rain again.

"Jesus Steve, it's raining again," said Dennis.

"Well, I didn't make it rain."

"What about Lendl?" asked Marc with disappointed joy in his voice.

"I don't know, it's raining again," said Steve as they started to cover the clay.

"Hey, I thought that was that all weather clay, why are they covering it?" asked Jake to no one in particular, but it was obviously for Steve.

"Hell, if I know. I thought you thought it was grass," responded Steve.

"I didn't say it was grass."

"Oh hell."

Lisa got up, "Well, I don't know about you boys but what's left of my martini is getting diluted sitting out here," and she turned to head out of the arena, and then they followed.

They collected themselves at the back of the arena under the underside of the concrete structure, all partially dripping.

"I guess it's time to head back to the bar," said Marc as he drained all but a few drops of what was left in his glass, figuring he'd let himself feel as though he had something in his glass until they got to the bar.

"No, no, no, that's still outside in the rain, let me reconnoiter," said Jake, "I'll be back in a couple of minutes, come on Marc," and with that he was gone with Marc following. He had decided that he was going to walk around the exterior of the arena and check out the portion that was surrounded by street, outside the fence, and what restaurants there might be on the other side of the fence, as he was starting to feel hungry.

They had only reached the far right side of the arena and were almost set to turn around and check out the other side when they heard the voices of a crowd coming from under the stands. They walked a bit further and turned the corner to find an entrance, under the stands, with a man in a tuxedo standing under the overhang behind what looked to be a portable lectern.

"Let's just walk by; and don't say anything," said Jake as they headed towards the entrance and then passed it, looking in as they went and trying not to attract the 'maître d's' attention.

Stopping a ways past the entrance Jake turned, looked in the direction of the entrance and said, "Looks like a good party, let's get the others and I'll do the talking."

All five of them were back near the corner of the arena in a matter of minutes and the drizzle was abating again. They were just around the corner from the maître d'.

"Listen, just follow me by ten feet and let me do the talking, and when I nod at you walk in behind me like you own the place," Jake instructed.

"Okay," said Lisa and the others smiled, and Marc toasted with his last few drops of scotch.

Jake walked up to the lectern, and the maître d' behind it, with a grin, the type one shows when seeing an old friend, and proceeded to talk with the man.

The others were watching as Jake spoke with the maître d', who was focused on Jake's words, and then the maître d' cracked a smile and nodded. Jake turned and smiled at the group and, without nodding at them, they started to walk up to him as he said something else to the maître d' and then walked inside out of the rain. The maître d' nodded at all of them in turn, as they walked in behind Jake, and in particular Lisa.

Everyone inside was dressed for a cocktail party, the men in tuxedos and the women in evening gown. Jake led his rabble past every table as though he owned the place, still wearing his Ray Bans, and pulled out a seat on the far side of a large round twelve-person table with no one sitting at it. He smiled at Lisa and nodded down at the chair he was holding, and she gave him a smirk like 'what the hell'.

She sat first and Jake pushed the chair in, and then he sat next to her facing all the others in the room under the stands.

"Why'd you hold the chair and what did you say to the guy outside?" asked Lisa.

"Gotta play the part. I told him you were Caroline Kennedy and friends and I am your Secret Service security.

"Geez."

"Hey that was good," said Marc as he took a seat on one side of Jake. He didn't bother asking Jake how he talked his way in. He had seen it before. He remembered when they were at the Cannes Jazz Festival. They had been bumming around Europe and just bumped into the festival; and Jake had talked his way in, getting a press packet and everything that went with it along with food and drink.

"How'd you do that?" asked Steve.

"You're a friend of Caroline Kennedy."

"Who?"

Jake nodded towards Lisa, "Caroline Kennedy."

"He didn't notice him as a Nutmegger?" asked Dennis.

"Geez Dennis, give me a break."

"Why? You are so proud of being from Connecticut," he said as he turned his head up with his nose in the air in an exaggerated manner and touched its tip. Hey, what happened to Lendl anyway?"

"It rained genius. Hey, ya wanna cut him off."

Just then Jake saw a waiter, in a white waist coat, looking at him and he put his finger up and smiled at the guy, who came over immediately.

"Four vodka martinis dry, two olives each if you have 'em and a scotch; the best scotch you have, please."

"We only have Dewar's."

Jake looked at Marc who thought for a moment and then said, "Hell, why not."

"Okay," said Jake, "Thanks."

As he watched the waiter leave Jake noticed a tall blonde sitting a table away, at a full table. He could tell she was tall and at six feet two inches himself there was something very alluring about tall women. "I'll be right back," he said to the table not taking his eyes off of the blonde, who looked at him as he headed in her direction removing his Ray Bans as he headed towards her.

"What's he up to?" asked Lisa watching him and then seeing him put his arm on the blonde woman's shoulder when he reached her and then bending down to whisper something into her ear just before she smiled up at him. Then she saw him whisper something else and saw the woman say something with a smile before he headed back.

As Jake took his seat, the waiter was already returning with the drinks and the guy sitting next to the tall blonde, whom he'd just had his arm around, was staring hard at him. Jake's whole table had been watching and now they were watching the guy stare at Jake, who wasn't paying attention.

"Geez, that's Cheryl Tiegs," said Steve.

"No it's not," said Jake, looking at her again and staring to see if he could see the famous model in this woman he had just spoken with.

"Yes, it is," said Marc.

"What did you say to her?" asked Lisa.

"She looked bored so I asked her to dance."

"There's no music," said Dennis.

"I told her I would make it happen if she decided she needed a break."

"Geez, that guy she's with doesn't look too happy," said Steve.

Jake continued to look over at the woman, trying to see what they all saw, and then shook his head and took a sip of his new martini.

Before he finished the sip the woman, and the man who appeared upset, seemed to get into an argument.

"This is interesting," said Jake.

"Ah, what did you start?" asked Lisa with humor in her voice.

Then he saw the woman call the waiter over and say something to him.

The waiter immediately started to head towards Jake.

He came up and smiled, "Miss Tiegs would like to buy your table a round. Same thing?"

"Sure," said Jake.

He looked back at her catching her attention and raised his glass with a smile and her face warmed up as she smiled back; then the man next to her said something that changed her expression. She seemed bored to Jake and he smiled again in her direction, shook his head slightly, and then returned his attention to his table.

The tournament rained out that day; they had Chinese across the street and then headed back into the city.

CHAPTER 9

LEAVING THE FOUR AND THE INTERVENING YEARS

Jake became the number one tax-shelter producer in his office. He became so good with them that accountants started calling him. One client wanted three aircraft leasing deals at one hundred and fifty thousand dollars per unit and he had to argue with the accountant that three was just too much for the income and projected income that they had given Jake. He tried to control the client from hurting himself and had the accountant write a letter to him that he had advised them both against three units. He was becoming acquainted with aspects of SEC regulations that most brokers had no idea about and he found he enjoyed the law behind it. It was all so logical to him and he noticed the need to not only protect the clients from some of the brokers he had experienced, but from themselves as well.

In the following year Jim left his position as manager for another firm and the dynamics of the office changed. The new manager was not nearly the same type of manager and Jake found that he did not like the man's ethics. His days in that office would be numbered.

The home office, off of Wall Street, had an opening for an oil and gas tax-shelter expert and they came to Jake with an offer. He could sell his book of business as well as get paid off of it, for a limited time, while working downtown with the head of tax-shelters. It was not only a handsome salary but Jake was, as well, starting to gravitate more towards development and education with regard to these complex investments.

He had accepted their offer with the next step being the approval of his manager. The manager made a percentage of Jake's commission revenue so he had to approve his move, as it would impact his income. The new manager, in the end, denied Jake of his needed approval as he did not want to lose Jakes's production. Jake had a backup just in case. A headhunter had contacted him about wholesaling for a tax-shelter developer, where he would present the product to brokers, clients and accountants. This would suit him as he remembered the oil wholesaler he had met when he had first started. He knew that he now knew more than that man knew and that man had made just over a million dollars a year, although it wasn't just the money that interested Jake. He left the brokerage firm and started wholesaling.

Before leaving, the four friends had managed to live a lifetime of memories and experiences together in such a short time. He would remember the four of them going to the movies straight from the office on occasion, each carrying an open can of beer into the theater. He smiled at the fact that no one stopped them about the beer. They were all well-dressed so maybe it confused the staff at the theaters. He remembered one movie in particular. They had arrived late and sat in the back against the wall with the walkway, leading to the two main aisles, directly behind it, and the movie was Arthur. They had been working hard and the beer was starting to loosen them up when Dudley Moore had his first drunk scene and all was quiet until Lisa let out a chortle which was a unique, caught off guard, laugh that only Lisa could make. This was followed by Jake's guffaw, which reached a volume and wouldn't stop, fueled by Lisa, and that did it; the whole theater started laughing at their laughing. Simple enjoyments. They were noticed wherever they went. He would also miss the due diligence meetings that they'd attend for new issues of penny stock. They could never remember the so-called companies but they usually had beer and shrimp at these extravaganzas, and there always seemed to be a couple of them every week. The due diligence meetings would start the night on most occasions. He would miss them and miss it all, but he was off to something exciting in the business.

————

He enjoyed being the expert for all of the stockbrokers and accountants that he worked with, until the 1986 Tax Act would change the dynamics of the investments he was engaged with. He worked hard and played hard, as they say. The president of the company that he worked for, who developed complicated high-end equipment tax-shelters, lived in Vail and Jake was a skier. It was the blue jeans and military surplus cargo pants days at Vail, where all the hard-core skiers went to avoid the glitz and Hollywood of Aspen. Jake remembered the time when a buddy had rented a Lincoln Continental at Stapleton Airport and showed up at the hotel where several of the wholesalers were staying. Their jaws dropped when they saw the car and they just started laughing. There were three of them going up the mountain that day.

"Howard, why the hell did you rent that boat, we're going up into the mountains?" Jake had asked.

"I got a deal."

"Jesus," said Bob, another wholesaler, "the company pays for it and you make enough."

"Yeah, but a deal's a deal."

The three of them climbed aboard and loaded their skies on the rack, and Howard admitted that the guys at Hertz had laughed at him when he asked for racks.

"Why do you think they laughed Howard?" asked Jake punctuated by a laugh of his own while he loaded his skies on top.

He had just shrugged.

"We'll never make it," added Bob shaking his head.

They had just started the climb when the car started to overheat.

"Roll down the windows and turn up the heat," yelled Jake and the car started to cool again.

They made it as far as the exit to the Do Drop Inn when the 'check engine' light came on at the same time as the 'get to station' light came on, accompanied by a burning rubber smell and smoke.

They cruised into the Do Drop Inn and a party eventually ensued. Cat, the owner's older daughter, cheered them on with her cat calls as they played pool and lost on purpose so they could buy rounds for the bar. They finally made it to Vail early the next morning, all crammed into the cab of a pick-up. Cat's father had taken them from bar to bar, all the way to Vail Village, in his 1952 Ford F-2 pick-up with shark's tooth seat covers in the cab and a dressed-out deer behind them, in the bed of the truck. He introduced them to all his friends on the way up and let them off with a tearful good-bye in the end, after a run down the backside of the mountain from Eisenhower Tunnel.

Jake started spending his off time in Vail, skiing and visiting with Leslie, who worked on the Eagle Ranch and had a condo in Redstone, across Route 6 from the village. They would meet in the Holiday Inn for a quiet drink and a quiet time, and then go to the Red Lion where everyone knew them. He got to know everyone who worked at the Red Lion and they invited him to a party given by Clint Eastwood and Jack Nicholson one night and he did not go because he was too tired from skiing all day. It was the only time that he remembered Hollywood touching Vail, and those two were different anyway. He was sorry he missed it but he was just beat. One night he couldn't easily get into the village, from Route 6, where he had to meet some friends and he was running late, so he took his rental car up the embankment, off 6, and drove it across the walkway of the pedestrian crossover and down the stairs on the other side, and into the village parking lot. No one had been around and it was the easiest way to do it. It was a time of hard work and travel, and enjoying everyone around him, and it was a time of being a little crazy like the moonlit night that he and Jessica climbed up Hunter Mountain in New York, after the mountain was closed down for the night. They had climbed some distance up the mountain, with their skis, and put their clothing in their packs when they reached a point near the top, and skied down naked. He was young and alive and his direction would once again change, as it was meant to do, because time would always force change no matter what.

The Vail connections would end and tax-shelters would disappear but Jake was still sought after and taken by an insurance company. The company was entering the world of financial planning and he started managing five regional financial planning managers and flying the country tirelessly. He did this for several years until he started to get worn down and needed a break. He knew this after waking up one morning in a Hyatt room with that same bright colored 1970's painting of a woman highlighted in orange and yellow in a wide brimmed straw sunhat that seemed to be in every Hyatt room he stayed in. He had awoken to see that picture first and didn't know what town he was in and he had not been drinking the night before. That was it. Using four "buckets of allocation" was his claim to fame, at the company, and that was all he walked away with, along with a great deal of air miles and Hyatt rewards points. He was tired.

The break came in the form of a British bank. He had helped their top executive in the United States with his complex tax and investment situation so much to the man's satisfaction that he recommended Jake for the bank's project to build a cash management account similar to that of Merrill Lynch's CMA account. The hurtle lay in the fact that they had no margin in England nor did they have money markets which were both, together, the foundation of Merrill's account.

Jake spent two years in England living in a three-hundred-year-old cottage, forty-one miles south of London, with his German fiancé. During this time, he built an ingenious money market for the bank using England's trust laws to cobble one together. He then built the bank the first margin account in the United Kingdom, based on the American Regulation T, to allow the English the same market leverage and account borrowing power available in the States. The account was registered with the bank of England and before he submitted the explanation letter on his bank's letterhead, he put some of America in it. The cash value available in the account was named MCM (Market Cash Multiple) for Mickey Charles Mantle. He then returned home, his knowledge of investment law and compliance, both in England and the in the United States, beyond that of most people involved with retail banking and brokerage.

He would come home and eventually have his team of eight, but not before spending three years cleaning up the compliance problems of a small investment company, acquired by a foreign entity, and writing their compliance manual.

He had his team and then lost them that day at the Hyatt, a place that, for him, was deja vu all over again without the rewards points.

He then joined a large brokerage firm, for more than several years, as an in-house compliance consultant. But he eventually, over the ensuing years, found that he missed the action in direct involvement with compliance management and the running of a team. He started reminiscing about it. With the years having fallen off, without him realizing it, he looked to take another position where he might once again enjoy overseeing a team and applying his knowledge of the financial business, along with the compliance regulations that governed it. He had also enjoyed, and now missed, working with financial representatives, or at least most of them, as a productive compliance officer.

He looked broadly for a firm and a position which would fulfill his need to manage compliance actively and one that might nicely cap his career for him. He found it one day in the form of a small insurance and financial office on Park Avenue in Manhattan, with the home office of the firm located in Latham, New York.

CHAPTER 10

A 'BRAVE NEW WORLD'

"An evil soul producing holy witness is like a villain with a smiling cheek, a goodly apple rotten at the heart. O, what a goodly outside falsehood hath!"

— Antonio, The Merchant of Venice
William Shakespeare/Christopher Marlowe?

"Well, this is the last job I'm taking," he said to no one in particular as he sat alone in his new office.

Jake had come a long way since 1980. 'My God, thirty-five years' he thought. He still missed the staff he had built at the last firm, years before, where he had been in a leadership role. He did, however, feel good that he had left them with pride in themselves and an integrity in their group that no one could, or would, dare to tamper with. Now that he was once again in a similar role, he thought of them.

He was sitting in his new office on Park Avenue in New York as a result of word-of-mouth, without a headhunter or an internet posting pulling him in. The new firm was a boutique insurance and financial planning firm, and they were getting nervous about money laundering. Russian money was moving into New York and they had a fear that it might attempt to enter through their planners. They hadn't let him know of their concerns. It was, 'We may have a problem but keep the compliance guy in the dark and see if he bumps into it'. Their thinking was that: 'If he bumps into it and we close some holes and protect the firm great, and if he bumps into it and it blows up the wrong way and upsets the "financial planners" that will fall on him.' He was expendable after all. The Director of the office he was in was happy about Jake for other reasons. He was happy to have an older guy who he thought was hungry for the job, being old and White, because that helped him to get Jake cheaply with no need for a raise down the road, he thought. Afterall, Jake's salary was coming out of his pocket, which seemed to be a conflict of interest to Jake.

Jake knew the firm had a problem, or knew that they thought they did, when they interviewed him at their headquarters in Latham, New York. He had been around too long not to be able to read the tea leaves. They were excited, and nervous and curt, and he felt they were not interviewing him from a position of strength. He had a bad feeling but he qualified the resources he would have and determined the layers of protection he could rely on and decided that he'd take it on. He would take it on as his last stop in this business he had not really intended to step into those many years ago now. He'd take it on and put his principal's license on the line. He had nothing to lose at this point. He now needed the intrigue. What he really wanted to do was push the envelope and shake something up, the way he should have shaken that mobster up when he first started instead of being the man's conduit for Resorts International manipulation.

The song Layla popped into his head and it took him back to Polihale Beach on Kauai with Charlotte. He had been listening to Layla and looking at the cliffs that had a sacredness to the Hawaiians when he felt Charlotte's hand rest softly on his neck and he pulled off the headphones of the Walkman. That was a few years ago now and he was far from there both in time and in space. He was back in New York City and Charlotte was in Germany. He then snapped back to the present and put aside the memory of the only woman he ever wanted to marry. He was older and he was expendable, he smiled with humor and not with sadness; things had been good, no complaints. Now he would take the last 'main drop' of his roller coaster ride after the 'trick hill' he had just been through in his last position. As a kid, there was nothing like that big drop of the Cyclone at Palisades Amusement Park and the cost of admission was only fifty cents, this would be different and might cost far more.

The man he would be working with was a mix of juvenile exuberance and calm maturity, both in conflict with each other. He might be mature in demeanor at times but he was not true to the honest character this demeanor portrayed.

He knew it could be difficult to work with a Director like this. He knew that the man would jump from place to place in his thinking. It would be difficult to get a good read on him in order to be more efficient as a team leader. Jake also felt that the man was wearing a façade and hiding a ruthless individual who would let anyone fall under the bus just so the bus kept running straight ahead. He had also caught the man eyeballing his girlfriend when she visited the office briefly, before returning to Germany, and doing it in less than a covert manner which told Jake something more about the man. Josh Pearlman, who was short and somewhat plump, also carried an air of social superiority which would reveal itself at the most inopportune moments. He could deal with it. He would have to contradict this man subtly in a public setting when he went sideways or he knew he, himself, would be ineffective. If he was going to do it, he was going to do it right. One last factor, the man did not have a high degree of respect for his staff nor did he believe in compensating them properly. Jake had seen this before. The man believed that his staff were nonproducers and therefore an unfortunate waste of money and, anyway, Josh paid closer than normal attention to what Jake liked to call his 'expense ratio'. The expense ratio was a cost ratio used in mutual funds but Jake liked to use it in reference to the cost of an office to procure one dollar of net profit, an inside joke to himself. Jake had to keep this in mind in order to keep strong the team that they were giving him. They would need each other and Jake would need to establish, quickly, that he was there for them.

Jake was given a team of two for compliance oversight. It had been three but they had fired one of the team members for causing disruption among the other team members when she realized that she was not going to get the position they were bringing Jake in to take. When they looked closely, she had not been doing her share of work as evidenced by her lack of sign-off where it should have been. The sign-offs were being done by the other two team members. It was also determined that she was a bit tyrannical with the clerical support so it had been time for her to leave. Evaluating the team, he was fine with two. The third one's damaging effect had been removed, which counted more than an additional person as her debris and roadblocks would now not get in their way.

The team looked good on paper as though it would complement his strengths, which all together would make a dynamic team. Jake also knew he was good at establishing corporate contacts and quickly putting together a good corporate network to help his compliance management and investigations, which in turn would fortify this team. He also knew Securities law better than most, which would be noted by the corporate attorneys, in the near future, when he corrected detrimental errors on the corporate internal website. Errors which, left unchecked, would create problems for the firm and for his flagship office.

Helen, the first member of the team, had been with the firm the longest, having come on fourteen years earlier as a fresh hire. She had been hired by the first compliance officer that they had running the flagship. He had actually run all of the state of New York for this New York firm, which had previously only sold insurance. The first compliance officer knew what he had in Helen and rolled the dice, putting her through all of her licensing requirements short of the principal's 24 license. Jake would find that her evaluations were accurate, that she knew the securities regulations and was excellent at both math and understanding the markets. She was, as well, completely competent with the insurance side of the business. Helen also knew all the financial planners and they all respected her, and she was a ball of energy to top it off. Furthermore, he would find that she had a good 'sniff factor' and was very direct and self-confident. If something bad was starting to brew Helen would smell the bad fish before it became apparent. She would become invaluable.

June was altogether different and had a background that included having been both a financial advisor and a trading assistant early in her career. She was timid and questioned her knowledge of Securities law although Jake would come to see that she knew the law and its regulations thoroughly. June would be their catch basin. She was thorough to the point of overstressing herself, which Jake would need to keep an eye on. She might overstress herself but the thoroughness that came with it would catch any of the minutia that might get by him, or Helen, as they dealt with the bigger picture. She crossed every T and dotted every I, she was priceless and any good team was not without someone like June. Jake would also come to see, very quickly, that they worked well together and understood each other. Jake would label June 'Radar', as in the character Radar O'Reilly from the story MASH. She was that good and many times knew what he was going to say before he said it and would say it before he said it or along with him.

Within the first month Jake had a basic contact list for the home office, a list that contained individuals that he knew he could trust for the right information, or those who could get him what he needed. That list would evolve over time but he was happy to have the master within the first month. Although he worked for this boutique firm in Manhattan its headquarters was located north of the city in upstate New York and as such the headquarters people tended to be less tolerant of New York City people. New York City people seemed to be curt and rude as far as they were concerned. Jake changed this opinion with respect to the city's flagship office. Within the first week he ran into a roadblock at the home office with regard to licensing data that he needed for a basic investigative review. He could hear a delay in the voice of the head of the department and before he would let it go further, only to get a delayed report at the end of the day, he said, "Us New York City folks can really be a pain in the backside, can't we?" and he laughed just at the right moment. The woman on the other end laughed and before she knew what she was saying she said, "Yes." "That's okay," he said in return, "I agree with you." She had never heard this before and had never received a gift from one of the few offices they had, let along one from the number one location. So she was caught off-guard, a few days later, when she opened a box with a dartboard in it, until she read the note: LOUISE, WE APPRECIATE THE HARD WORK THAT YOUR DEPARTMENT DOES DAY IN AND DAY OUT AND WE ALSO REALIZE HOW DEMANDING WE IN THE FIELD CAN BE. WHEN YOU FEEL YOU ARE ABOUT TO EXPLODE PULL OUT A DART, OR TWO, AND LET THEM FLY AGAINST YOUR STRATEGICALLY PLACED DARTBOARD WITH THE MAJOR OFFENDER IN MIND.

Louise had laughed and she loved it as did the whole department and word spread quickly within the small headquarters, in Latham, New York, about how friendly the flagship office had now become. This would establish a positive mark in Jake's relationship with the people in the home office and he never would find that he ran into roadblocks as more and more people came to know him.

He was still getting to know the financial planners in the flagship when June came past the smoked glass of the outside wall of his office and quickly moved across the threshold of his open door. In one fluid motion she had moved to the glass wall next to the door with her back up tight against it cringing as though being chased, with her eyes darted from side to side.

"What the hell's wrong?"

"He, he...yelled at me."

"Who yelled at you?"

"Wayne!"

Already aware that Wayne was known to have a short fuse Jake pursued, "Why?"

"I told him he needed to clear this with us," she said as she flapped a piece of paper up and down making a rustling sound.

"Is that that idiotic marketing piece?"

"Yes."

"Okay, sit down, I'll take care of this," he said as he grabbed the paper and headed out the door to the private office of Wayne Warner.

This was the same advisor that he had seen the Director cower in front of. The man produced good revenue and the Director was intimidated by him so he did not bump heads with the man. His first experience with this was his third day as head of compliance when the Director took him to Wayne's office, as Wayne was complaining about what he thought was a discrepancy in his commission on one recent product sale of another company's product. It was a product that was only approved for this one client of Wayne's for a one-time sale. The commission was reduced from what the outside provider was paying out as the home office, in Latham, was taking two percent of it to cover compliance maintenance and oversight. Josh was dragging Jake along to explain this to the irate Wayne. As they entered Wayne's office Josh slid on his knees past Jake and came to a stop in front of Wayne with his hands in prayer thinking he was being funny. While being slightly embarrassed by this, Jake looked at Wayne, who was equally miffed, and simply said, "What's the problem?" as the Director came to one knee in genuflection.

That first meeting with Wayne had been well over a month earlier and Jake had calmed things down, giving in just a little to Wayne to calm him before he finally figured him out and how to deal with him.

He knew who he was dealing with this time as he entered Wayne's front office. He entered with some steam under the collar as one of his team had just been yelled at for trying to 'help and protect this idiot,' he thought.

"Is Wayne in Clare?" he stated more than asked one of Wayne's two assistants in the work area before his inner office door.

She knew what it was about and saw Jake's face in a way she had never seen before, on anyone of authority in the office let alone Jake. She was nervous but also curious. 'This ought to be interesting', she thought as she announced Jake over the phone to Wayne.

"You can go in," she said with a warm smile of anticipation.

As Jake entered, paper in hand, Wayne was waiting for him with a scowl on his face.

Holding the paper up, "Wayne, why in hell did you yell at June over this piece of marketing?"

"Because there is no reason that it should not have gone out already."

"Yes there are reasons," said Jake as he proceeded to pull the mass marketing letter apart in front of Wayne, explaining what each concern was and what the concerning items could cause the client in confusion and he, Wayne, in regulatory reprimand. He also explained the red flagging that the piece would give him for the regulatory investigators of FINRA. FINRA was made up of overzealous neophytes and with electronic monitoring these days they would go after a lot more than their predecessor, the NASD, did in the days of paper files. FINRA was a jumping off place, or initial training ground, for young securities lawyers and principals who had their eyes on the private sector financial corporations themselves. They had no long-term intention of staying with the self- regulatory body of the investment houses or the Financial Industry Regulatory Authority better known as FINRA. They used it as a self-proving ground. As FINRA was paid by the financial firms they tended to be more aggressive than the SEC in order to prove their value, until the brokerage/financial houses pushed back in mass, temporarily altering FINRA's tack, or course, until the next cycle of push-back.

"There is no reason to hold this up," said Wayne after all the explanation.

"Well, you're going to have to change it and don't you ever scream at one of my people again."

"I'll scream at whoever I want to scream at," screamed Wayne as his voice started to escalate feeling that he had the upper hand with Jake, as he always did with anyone in authority.

Jake came back with an even louder voice, "You will not, do you hear me, you will not raise your voice at my people ever again."

"I'll do what the hell I want to do," yelled Wayne in an even louder voice.

"If you do you will have to deal with me, and frankly I don't give a shit who you go crying to," said Jake loud enough to be heard in the hallway and certainly in the fore office where Clare and Karen, the other assistant, could hear him.

This shocked Wayne, he had never had anyone escalate with him before and he started to calm down.

By the time Jake left, things had quieted down completely and Wayne had agreed to let Jake tell him what he needed to do to fix the piece. Wayne was engaged in trying to market a high-end tax shelter scheme that was too complicated without the proper corporate disclaimer. It involved trusts and security-based life insurance product and when Jake first saw it, he just muttered, 'crap' to himself. He knew word would get around on it, that it would be misrepresented to clients, and he would have to clean it up around the office. It would be like cleaning up after a herd of tomcats marking their territory, it would never really go away. The stink would last.

When Jake left, Clare gave him a sparkling smile and he assumed Karen was smiling too but he could not see her behind the column she sat by.

After this episode, Wayne went out of his way to say hello to Jake. He would call Jake before doing anything 'stupid' and genuinely liked Jake better than anyone else in the office and never again yelled at June or anyone else other than Josh.

By the third month Jake knew the financial planners he was dealing with and they knew him as they gained respect for his knowledge and his ability to help them as opposed to hindering them.

He knew who he should be worried about and who was not a high priority concern, but he also knew, from past experience, that this would change. Financial Planners were good at hiding their true selves, for a while at least; after all, they were salesmen at the end of the day and, for the most part, just plugged in pre-packaged product unlike his days as a broker.

In some ways they reminded him of good ol' Sheila O'Brien who put all of her clients in Ginnie Mae funds. He had only touched one mutual fund when he was a stockbroker and that was a utility fund, of all funds. He had jumped on the band wagon with it as it popped out a good level of yield and he liked the manager. He had heard her speak and liked the fact that she was using options to bolster the yield and growth of the fund. He had also liked that she was using some sort of new gizmo, at the time, that would allow her to see the options while on a beach, as she said. It had been intriguing and he had taken down a large number of shares for his clients as a lay away and 'forget about it' investment, or what he had called a sleeper. This had been similar to what he had done with Telofonos de Mexico where he bought 5,000 shares of the stock at twenty-five cents a share for every one of his clients, as a sleeper.

The new days were different, institutional buyers made up most of the market without the heavy percentage of retail buyers that made up the market in the early days. Mutual funds made up ninety-five percent of the client's portfolio whereas you could barely find them in a portfolio when he was a broker. It was the inverse of his world as a stockbroker. In many ways it took the management away from the financial representative, which could be safer for the client. But it made the average representative less knowledgeable on investments and the markets while giving them the time to bring on many more clients than a broker could handle in his day. He remembered the days of managing portfolios and getting creative with Margin Accounts, and the Market Minder he had on his screen. The Market Minder tagged every stock he had for clients and an alarm would go off when they hit a particular high or low, to warn him. He also used options to hedge his accounts against adverse market activity. It was like flying a plane and juggling at the same time. At least then you had to know how to fly the plane, now they had autopilot with very little clue as to how to really fly. They had become asset gathers.

There were only two option accounts in the entire office of just under one hundred planners and less than a handful of Type 2 Margin Accounts. Most everyone in his book, as a broker, had a Margin Account. Times were different and the individuals holding a newly minted securities license, for the most part, lacked the basic knowledge to actively manage a securities account. They did, however, know how to gather funds and they had the time to do it. This was dangerous for the office in the long run as it would be easier for someone to pass funds through this type of environment for the purpose of Laundering than it had been thirty-five years earlier.

He smiled to himself, thinking of the difference in the times knowing that at some point there would be no human planners. A future he hoped he would not be around to see, but it was coming. He smiled, too, because he knew he was sitting in an environment ripe for money laundering and he also knew that the Russians were big players in this particular market. He had already had a taste of money laundering coming out of the Azerbaijan offshore and onshore oil fields before sitting in his current office.

Interfering with the layering in and integration of oil money into the system, which had been absconded with by the family of a former Azerbaijan government official, had given him a black mark from the New York Director of Sales for that previous firm. It is a strange experience for doing one's job well. The FBI had stepped in on that one as he tried to follow it. Once they stepped in, the channel of information back to him was shut down. All he had known was that a member of an important family in Azerbaijan had been given protection by the United States in the US and was not supposed to leave the country.

They discovered that she had left the United States and had tried to cover her tracks back to Azerbaijan by traveling through Europe and down through Italy as her last true European stop. Oil funds had been moved and that is where his channel of information was cut. He had laughed at the time that no one would have paid attention to her prohibited movement if he hadn't detected and reported the cash 'drop-ins'. Since Watergate the CIA and the FBI no longer talked, 'while she walked' he had thought; absolutely brilliant.

He knew he was now dealing with a lot more than just oil money. There had recently been a Russian immigrant couple who had been busted trying to move large sums from Russia through Citibank. It was a desperate move by this couple that they tried moving too much too quickly and 'Citi' had quickly picked up on it in their Forest Hills location. But this was only the tip of the iceberg and it was a very clumsy and thoughtless attempt at moving large sums of cash into the US. They were caught on two hundred and fifty thousand dollars of movement in an attempt to eventually move ten million dollars into the United States. The humorous side of this event was that the money was thought to be from aid monies that the US had given Russia to help with the safe storage of bomb grade uranium.

Through the diversity of the Russian economy, with the advent of Glasnost, the Soviet Union started its move towards the future Russia and Jake would be backstopping dirty funds from multiple types of sources. Former KGB members were now in the United States with the aid of a New Jersey senator by the name of Frank Lautenberg. Jake had briefly dated a woman who had been with the State Department and had been working in an upper tier position at the US embassy in Moscow in the late 80's early 90's when Mr. Lautenberg's Amendment, which they called 'Magic Carpet' (In satirical reference to the operation to bring American troops home at the end of WWII.), was pushed through. She had shaken her head. The idea was fine but the execution was flawed due to Mr. Lautenberg's aggressive and threatening push to have it put in place with great immediacy in order to satisfy his political needs. The plan was to get Russian Jews out of Russia and to the US but it was an open portal for the Jewish mob in Russia. The US embassy wanted better vetting and a more stringent process with tight protocols. The Senator would not hear of it and in the end, they executed the plan which left the door wide open into the United States. "Instead of giving us the time to erect a proper screen door Lautenberg used his weight to open the door without a filter and the flies came in. We warned the man that the Jewish mob in Russia, along with former KGB associates, would be able to walk right in. He did not care; so, huzzah, look what we have; c'est la vie," she had said with exasperation and humor mixed. Such is politics he had thought, leaving the rest of us to clean it up. Years later the director of the FBI, Louis Freeh, would say that the Russian-Jewish mafia posed the greatest threat to American security.

Jake envisioned himself as the guy at the tail end of the parade, just behind the elephant, with the shovel and the bucket. It was actually a humorous thought and he would smile whenever it came to mind, and it always did when he was cleaning up a compliance mess.

He knew he would be dealing with everything from drug money to human trafficking money as Russia was considered a Tier 3 nation, or a nation not doing the minimum to eliminate human trafficking, and this became more dangerous than oil money. What a different world, this new world of 'finance'. When he was a stockbroker he never really thought of the markets as a way to launder money. It wasn't prevalent. Investment fraud, stock manipulation or insider trading were the only problems that he had heard of at the time. Those were the days before the current day mentality of 'asset gathering' where large cash movements became somewhat lost in the mix, even with the additional bite of the Patriot Act. Today's financial advisors simply wanted to gather as many assets as possible, under management, because they really did not have to manage it as they did thirty years before. Jake remembered when you would need a minimum of five million dollars in manageable assets in order to have it managed for you by your firm. Then Dean Witter came out with a management program which needed a minimum of just five hundred thousand dollars. Now, with the aid of mutual funds, firms could offer a type of managed program for as little as fifty thousand dollars to start. Employment of mutual funds not only made it affordable to manage a large number of small accounts using a skeleton crew, it was a goldmine in profitability. The world had changed. When he was a broker the 'house' made money on the rate on Margin Accounts and now they were making it on mutual fund management, which seemed to him to be an absurd redundancy. It was somewhat similar to the ultra-safe 'fund of funds' concept that he had put together in England to entice the country's 'savers' from their bank accounts into the markets.

Jake knew his world history and this did not help his calm when it came to the Russians. The twenty million Russians killed in the purges, as a rough guestimate, was something that stuck in his mind with a frightening image of Stalin. As a child he had had nightmares, for some reason, about the murder of the Romanoff's in that small basement room with bullets bouncing off of the jewels that the girls had hidden in the lining of their clothing before they were finally gunned down. He knew of the horrors committed in Poland by the Russians, such as the Katyn Massacres in 1940, as allies to the Nazis through the Non-Aggression Pact with Hitler until Hitler turned and invaded Russia. He knew of the Nazi razing of Warsaw while the Soviets, now adversaries of the Nazis, stood by and watched, wanting it to happen. He knew of American flyers and servicemen killed by the Russians during WWII while they were supposed to be an Ally of the United States, and while receiving American aid. He knew that during the war they would unwittingly try to undermine US military efforts that would actually help them as an ally because they were paranoid and did not trust the United States, simply because they knew themselves to be untrustworthy. They had promised to attack Japan to relieve some of the pressure on US forces and never did. But they did finally declare war on Japan after the bombing of Hiroshima and then invaded Japanese held Manchuria on the day of the Nagasaki bombing, knowing that the Japanese would soon surrender and they could grab what they could.

He knew of the historical ruthlessness and untrustworthiness of the Russians and this had him on edge, as a compliance officer, as the Russian community started to grow in Brooklyn, and elsewhere, with the 'Magic Carpet' infiltrators in their midst. There was a great deal of money now in Russia looking for a way out and he would be in the middle of it with former KGB and Russian mob members now on this side of the Atlantic and Pacific.

He as yet did not have any Russian advisors in the firm, at least that he knew of, but they did have Russian clients and that number was rising, and he knew that was why he was brought into the firm.

As the months passed, and he settled in, he knew he would have to set up an in-house system for reviewing all Russian accounts. He would have to review them with an eye towards abnormal money movements and, in particular, those movements of cash that were under the ten-thousand-dollar reportable amount. He remembered it was multiples just under ten thousand dollars that had led him to the oil money years before. Sometimes the obvious was not so obvious.

He would review these clients along with the general community of clients within the firm so a light would not shine on what he was doing. He would also have to set up an email review system that would include random reviews of email to and from particular clients, besides review of the general population of email, which he was required to do. He would have to request specific batches of email and each request would require a good reason along with his Director's sign-off, so he might have to get creative. He laughed to himself knowing that the firm wanted him to do this and, to a certain point, would not give him pushback. If it became noticeable, they might give him pushback to distance themselves from what he was doing although they wanted him to do it. He also knew that if he turned up something, he would have to position it so that the firm looked clean and not invasive of expected client privacy. But, in the end, he would set it up so that they would have to handle the handling of any dangerous mess. He would, above all, protect his team.

Jake would also need to set up liaison through the headquarters that could work with the legal department and have random names of concern run past the FBI for comment, if need be, or just one list of names run, that he had in mind soon after his arrival on the job. That particular list was all ready for review. As an investment firm they could do this and it would not necessarily look out of the ordinary to the FBI. He would submit the list of names for review that he did have, as soon as he possibly could without alarm. Such a review would let Jake know what he might be dealing with, if anything. However, he did have his concerns about the FBI and how they might or might not react even though he would need them to review names for his team and the firm. He thought of Richard Jewell and how the FBI had rewarded him for his alertness and his saving of people in the Centennial Olympic Park bombing in 1996. Their ineptness and political structure had led them to falsely accuse the actual savior of the day and ruin his life. He thought of John O'Neil who was a special agent at the FBI and their leading expert on al-Qaeda and Osama bin Laden. Jake had almost lost his girlfriend under Tower Two on September 11 and Mr. O'Neil may have stopped that attack if it were not for the US ambassador to Yemen, and her vanity, along with the FBI. He may have stopped it if it were not for the politics of the FBI. Jake had heard from a friend, working with the FBI at the time, that John O'Neil had been on top of bin Laden but the FBI, behind the scenes, was quietly saying that he had 'sharp elbows.' He was doing his job too well and making the politicians in the FBI look bad. John O'Neil was a tireless worker when it came to stopping bin Laden and it was known that he would take classified papers home to continue working through the night and during weekends. The FBI had set him up at a conference where they knew he had some classified documents, for work, in his briefcase. The 'disappearance' of the briefcase led him to leave the FBI. He had been the agent who tried to connect the FBI with the CIA with regard to the terrorists learning to fly. The communication back to O'Neil and the FBI had been blocked. John O'Neil would die with the collapse of the towers on September 11, 2001, where he was head of security. He would die as he lived, trying to save people from the result of terrorism as he would not leave the building that day while he tried to get people out. Jake thought of all of this which left him cautious about the FBI but he would never bother his team with his concerns, those particular concerns he kept behind the curtain. Compliance was not cut-and-dried; it could be paved with landmines and politics. In the end, maybe he thought too much about the dark side of even the FBI, but years in the financial industry and a long relationship with compliance had him look hard at the downside of things. He had anything but blind trust in those bureaucracies and organizations that were supposed to support his effort.

Now that he was at least comfortable with the flagship office and his staff he would need to sit with both Helen and June and let them know: first, of the concerns of the firm and then second, his concerns with the office, along with his approach. He knew that as soon as he had a final list of clients that were of concern, if any, after the FBI review of his original list, he would have that meeting in the privacy of a public place, such as Bryant Park behind the New York Public Library. He hated this covert approach to such matters but it was better to look ridiculous to Helen and June and be safe, and he would as well explain this to the two of them as being a matter of habit. He did not want his team to exist in a state of nervousness so he would downplay certain aspects of his concerns with levity and use some purposeful goading to create momentary anxiety and then relieve it. But yet, through it all, they would maintain secrecy, which compliance people were automatically dialed into.

It was mid-August, near the end of the summer, with fall almost in the air, when he received word back on the list of Russian clients that he had finally submitted to home office for FBI review. The clients of concern, and there were three of them, had primary residences in Florida but yet they were doing business through the New York office of his firm. They might have contacts in New York, they might think that they might not stand out in a boutique firm in New York City or they may know something about his firm that he did not yet know. The clients were spread between two financial advisors and were three names among over a dozen naturalized former Russian citizens in the books. There were five more who were in Florida but did not pop on the FBI list as primary concerns, but he was warned to keep an eye on them due to their close proximity, in Florida, to other known Russian mob members.

It was time to take Helen and June to lunch in the park. It was a beautiful late summer day and he grabbed them a table in front of the William Dodge bust to give them some privacy and then took their sandwich orders and let them talk between themselves while he went to the sandwich kiosk.

They were both relaxed with each other by the time he came back with the sandwiches, which is exactly what he wanted. The office environment was so energized and hectic that the two women never really had a chance to sit down and just talk with each other and even though he screamed at them not to, they still took lunch in front of their computers not really giving themselves a break. He loved them for it but he as well knew he needed to force them to give themselves breaks before one of them broke.

"Well, we couldn't have asked for a better day than this," he said as he put the sandwiches on the table in a cardboard carry tray with three water bottles and then pulled out his green painted chair with an accompanying, quick, screeching scrape on the slate of the park's terrace, which was dotted with small round green tables and green folding chairs.

"What's the occasion?" asked Helen, getting right to the point, "it's not that 'it was about time you got us out.'"

June was fully occupied with the unwrapping of her sandwich as Helen started to unwrap hers and wait for Jake's answer.

"I needed to get you both out of the reach of prying ears."

June now looked up, having taken the first bite of her sandwich.

"We're checking on the Russians," said Helen as she took a bite of her sandwich and June all of a sudden froze with traces of panic on her face.

"I'll tell you Helen, you have a better sniff factor than I do. I've been known to fall sucker for people because I trust them too much but you can smell a problem before it starts," and he smiled and took a bite of his sandwich, knowing that the three of them together were a perfect compliance team. Alone, they would not be as efficient.

"Russians?" asked June before taking another, yet tentative, bite from her sandwich.

"Yeah, whaddaya think?" said Helen looking at her.

"Well, we do have some Russian clients and with the recent concern about Russian money laundering I'm taking a closer look. I have to tell you that three of those clients are on the Russian mob watch list that the FBI maintains. Of course, this does not go past this table and I will go over each one of these clients with you individually at a later date, once I get some additional information, if it comes."

Swallowing her last bite hard and still looking like a deer caught in the headlights June asked, "What do we do?" as simple as that.

"We watch, that's it. We watch quietly and when I say quietly, we don't let anyone in our office or home office know we are viewing any one of these clients by tipping our hand with a request or query coming from us directly; at least initially. Home office does know we have a list but how far we look into that list is our concern to start. When it comes to these clients any concerns you may develop has to come to me first and I'll decide if it's important enough to make an inquiry or put a light on it, no matter how dull that light. We'll also use Josh where we need to and where we don't need to, as best we can, avoid him to keep the light off of us," he said knowing that he would have to bring Josh in early, at least for emails; which he felt would be a primary focus. They all knew that home office would probably get an idea as to what they were looking at sooner rather than later but he wanted them to try to be quiet to begin with. It was just a good practice to do so.

"Just under ten thousand dollars, and multiple times?" asked Helen.

Jake smiled, "You've got it all down Helen; I know that. It may be as simple as that. Let's keep a closer eye on life insurance as boring as that may be because that is the easiest place to layer money in. They think no one looks there because it isn't as high visibility as securities or because it's 'boring', until it is used to move money. Everything from drop-ins to overfunding policy funding accounts. Activities like this would give us the first tip-off and no doubt they would have multiple accounts with other firms if we notice a pattern here."

"Helen knows life insurance better than I do; you know my background is heavy securities without life insurance experience like hers."

"I know June, and don't worry about this, every firm in the City is doing what we're going to do. You are also the most meticulous of us and I prefer you look at securities transactions anyway."

June took another bite of her roast beef on rye and looked at the table in thought with some nervousness in her eyes that Jake knew he was going to have to allay.

"Email is key," piped in Helen.

"I can't agree more," confirmed Jake. She was talking right on que about what he wanted to go over. 'Thank God,' he thought, 'did I ever get lucky with this team.' But he still wanted to keep it low key even though they may need to go after emails not readily available to them without request.

"We are getting some emails that have Russian in them," commented Helen, "they are usually a thread through 'reply all' with our rep added, and the note to the rep in English of course. It's obvious they are dialing in a Russian or two with their correspondence to our guy."

"We're going to have to get a translation on some of this."

"Our system is picking it up but not highlighting it as the 'foreign language' is not the active part of the email."

"If it's centered around the two reps with the Russian clients, we'll just have to look at all of their mail to and from specific Russians if our system isn't picking them up. And we may have to request old email." Now he realized that he would have to request it. "We can use some outside software for translation in order to keep it private and protected. I can quietly get approval on that. I've been thinking about it," he said as he glanced over at June concentrating on what was left of her sandwich and in her own world. Jake knew that she was getting more nervous and he needed to play it down.

"That would be excellent," said Helen as she lifted her sandwich calmly.

"I'm not too concerned about what the Russian will translate out to," he said for June's benefit, "and don't forget, we get more than a sniff of money laundering the cat is out of the bag and it jumps from our pan to corporate investigation and we are out of it at that point," he added to further calm June.

"What about Josh?" asked Helen.

June looked up at Jake with concern because Josh was where her paycheck came from.

"I'll dial him in on anything that gets threatening to the firm and to his office," he said, emphasizing 'his office', "and in the meantime use him where I think we can but we'll need him for requested emails if we go that way, which it appears we will with the Russians," he finished.

"I don't know, I have a bad feeling with him, he could put the kibosh on something we want to pass on to home office," said Helen. "He's nothing like Roger Hillary," she added, referencing the man who had managed the office for twenty years before retiring the previous year, a man she had started with and the only other manager or Director she had ever worked with.

"Yeah, I heard about Roger; he would have been my type of guy but we are dealing with what we have, …not the same level of integrity."

June looked at them both, hearing these thoughts for the first time.

Helen noticing June's concern, "Don't worry June, but don't let him fool you either," she said.

"Whaddaya mean?" asked June, now really concerned as Helen smiled.

"Listen June, there is nothing to worry about. He's like any manager, just a bit more money driven is all. He has me convinced that he is behind us a hundred percent but that's mostly because I want to believe that. There is something that doesn't quite settle with me," answered Jake.

"Yeah, he's cheap where it counts," said Helen.

"What, I was going to say is that he's just different from the types of managers I've known in the past and at some point, I'll figure it out and get comfortable with it. All that you need to know is that you are my responsibility. Anything that you do that goes sideways or makes you uncomfortable comes from my desk."

"Uncomfortable?" asked June with more concern.

"If you need to send out a letter of advisement on a securities situation and you feel uncomfortable sending it, say to Wayne for example."

She shuttered and Helen laughed.

"Well, in any situation like that use my desk. Let them know it is coming from me. I back anything that you do and I expect you to make mistakes like we all do."

"Rarely does that happen," piped in Helen.

"Listen June, you know securities regulations inside and out, you understand trading and options and equities better than most of these so-called advisors we are overseeing, so I trust you to go with your gut and that may generate a mistake once in a while, which I'll take responsibility for."

"I can't make a mistake," she said with her eyes in a panic.

"You've gotta loosen up," said Helen.

"Just know that I expect you to make a mistake not that I want you to, but you will, I certainly have. That's why they put the damned eraser on the end of a pencil."

"I write in pen," said Helen with a grin.

"You're not helping," said Jake and Helen laughed.

"You'll be okay," said Helen looking at June.

"At the end of the day you two are my first responsibility and you will just have to have trust in that."

June nodded, with her eyes calming a bit.

"Okay, let's approach this not from the viewpoint that we have money laundering going on but just from the viewpoint that our reps or advisors, or whatever you want to call them, are innocent and need protecting."

June nodded and calmed down. That was what she needed to hear and Jake and Helen looked at each other in mutual confirmation of this.

"Okay, it's straight forward, any questions?" asked Jake as he finally picked up his sandwich again after only one bite.

"Yeah, you need to eat your lunch," said June with friendly concern for the man she felt comfortable and safe working for. She knew he would watch her back even though she would always stay a bit nervous.

"Yeah, well I'd better catch up. Anyone want a coffee?" he asked as he took a bite noticing that June was finished and Helen was getting there."

Finishing more of her sandwich and nodding her head and raising her hand yes as she tried to swallow the bite she had just taken, "Yes, me. I'll always take a coffee," said Helen.

"I'll get them," volunteered June.

Jake pulled his wallet out of this coat pocket and handed her a ten-dollar bill, "Black. Thanks June."

"Cream and sugar," said Helen.

As June neared the kiosk Jake looked at Helen with a grin, "She'll be all right, but we need to keep an eye on her and if we see her fraying at the corners, we'll need to calm her down. Do me a favor would you."

"Sure, what?"

"As ridiculous as it sounds reinforce the fact that it's okay to make a mistake. I can't have her holding back because she's afraid of making one."

"But that's what she does well, she catches mistakes. She's more meticulous than my aging grandmother back in Ireland and that is meticulous."

"No, I appreciate that and we need a meticulous personality in the team but there is just too much going on here for her to hold back and question her knowledge because she's afraid of making a mistake. One more thing, she is going to get a larger workload like we all will as we start to employ a more microscopic overview and it's going to stress her. She can take twice as long as you and I on a review because it is part of her meticulous nature. And no matter how much we work on her to accept a mistake she won't completely change and, like over-feeding a gold fish, she will eat the work that is thrown at her, without pushback, until she explodes."

Helen started laughing, "I like that analogy,... an explosive goldfish."

"Seriously, we need to keep an eye on her, you know this could happen."

"No, I know."

"I also need to talk with her and let her know that if she starts to get stressed, she has to tell me because I know, in the short time that I've been here, she will try to suck it up and not say anything."

"You are right about that."

"To change subjects, what's your thinking about the two guys who have the Russian clients?"

"Randy Phelps and Chris Jenkins?"

"Yup."

"They've both been in the business just over five years. They are friends because they were in the same entry class that came in here, I think it was spring, five years ago. I remember because Randy was always trying to be funny at Chris's expense and then they became close friends."

"Funny how that works sometimes, isn't it."

"It was. I remember it pretty well because Chris wasn't happy about it and was pretty quiet until one day, while I was helping teach one of their classes, he blew up at Randy. It was pretty good. He didn't just blow up but put Randy in his place with some pretty smart humor. Randy had no come back and after that they were almost inseparable."

"As I say, funny how that works. Any reason why they would share over a dozen Russian clients among themselves? They are the only ones to have Russians."

"Well, some of those would be referrals from the original Russian clients."

"Granted and that is my concern."

"Whaddaya mean?"

"There is something that the original client, or clients, like about these two guys that had them bring their friends and acquaintances in."

"Well, that's true."

"I think you and I have to look at it like Randy and Chris have a weakness and what is it. I'm not saying that they do and the Russians found it and figured out a way to use it but if you and I look at it that way we will find it if it exists. And we can't tell June about our secondary concerns of a Russian connection because she'll see Boris and Natasha under ever rock. But we will need to tell her we are looking for potential money handling weaknesses with these two as we look for weaknesses."

"Boris and Natasha?"

"Bullwinkle Moose and Rocky, used to watch it as a kid."

"I'll have to YouTube that one," laughed Helen.

"If we don't tell her that we are working this way she may stumble upon it through her thoroughness and get overly disturbed before she needs to."

"Got it, she'll be real nervous if she finds something nonetheless."

"I know but it'll be like a canary in a mine not fully realizing it could have a deep Russian connection."

"Yeah, except I hope the canary doesn't die."

Jake laughed, "She'll be okay if we catch her before she hits the bottom of the cage or bumps into a live Russian. Between the three of us we'll be able to find and stop anything before it gets too dangerous."

"This'll be fun."

Jake just grinned as June started coming back from the Kiosk.

June placed the cardboard carry-all, with the coffee, in the center of the table.

"Helen, I didn't know how much cream you wanted. I thought about it but wasn't sure so I got this cup with some cream," and looking at Jake, "you're easy, black no sugar."

"Oh, but I wanted sugar mixed in while it was being poured."

"What, what? You didn't say that! I heard you. Just black. You didn't say sugar."

Helen started to laugh.

"I'm only kidding June, black no sugar it is. Just rattling your cage a bit. Just to let you know, Helen and I might start rattling you like this so you learn not to let the little things phase you. Please, sit down."

As she sat he continued, "Listen, I will say it again, you are an integral part of this team and you complete the team with your meticulous nature but we will keep an eye on you. If you bite off more than you can chew, we will let you know and pull you back but you also have to let us know if you are getting buried. Is that a promise?"

"I will."

"We'll see," said Helen.

"No, I will."

"Ok," said Jake with a smile as he took his coffee knowing that it was a work in progress to keep June on the rails.

"Oh, here's your change."

"Thanks. This is a beautiful park isn't it."

"My favorite," commented June before taking a sip of her coffee.

"I don't know if you two know, but this used to be a shooting gallery."

"A what?" asked June

Helen laughed.

"In the seventies you couldn't come within two blocks of this place because it was loaded with bums shooting up. The City was a frightening place back then."

"I really didn't come in, I was just a little kid," said June.

"Thanks," said Jake with a smile.

"I heard Time Square was loaded with prostitutes," commented Helen.

"Yeah, and porno shops and shows, you just couldn't walk through it. I remember in high school walking across Time Square and getting propositioned twice before I made it across. Bad days."

"I can't imagine," said June.

"It got so bad, nonstop, that people were getting used to it and dealing with it until Koch and Giuliani teamed up to reduce the organized crime behind some of it. Then there was a stumble in crime reduction when Dinkins got in for one term, then Giuliani became mayor and the renaissance was completed."

"That simple!?" exclaimed Helen

"Not really, it was a lot of work and politics but in the end the hard work was realized by everyone in the city and politics took a seat on the sidelines for a while. I was amazed, they actually got Disney to take over the old New Amsterdam Theatre off Time Square, and incredibly they were able to move the pornography which really disappeared, thankfully. It was mob controlled and I saw that when I was a stockbroker."

"Mob?" asked June.

"Yeah, one of the brokers I worked with had a guy in the Mafia who owned one of those peep shows and he dragged me down to the guy's office one day because he was nervous and we saw a room with barrels full of quarters. Funny, if you think of it, two conservatively dressed guys in their twenties, one in a three-piece suit, standing in the back of a dreary back room to a peep show, staring down at barrels of quarters; a little unnerving actually. He dumped the client."

"Quarters?" asked June.

Helen started to laugh, "Peep shows, they put quarters in to see."

"I don't get it," said June and Helen laughed again.

"You don't have to. I doubted that they could clean it up but they did and we got this beautiful city. They just analyzed the problems and then systematically removed them or countered them. That's what we do. There is no problem too big that can't be handled calmly and effectively, and safely," said Jake to June as he glanced at Helen with a wink.

"That makes sense; systematically."

"Yeah, but now look what's happening with this guy DeBlasio," said Helen changing the subject back.

"Whaddaya mean?" asked June.

"I remember when Giuliani stopped squeegee guys, one of the small details but they all added up to a safe city," Jake jumped in, "They also made it illegal to give money to panhandlers in the subway after someone was killed. The little things that made it better. Now we have bums in the street and they can get mean and pushy, that's what she means."

Jake laughed to himself and continued, "God, I had forgotten about those squeegee guys. There were actually fights over that. They'd come up to your car at a long light and start cleaning your window, even when you said no, and then they'd get aggressive to get paid for it," he laughed, "I remember one of these idiots tried that on me coming off the Henry Hudson at 54th Street and when the light turned, I took off with his damned squeegee stuck between my windshield and windshield wiper," and he shook his head.

Helen laughed, "Did he chase you?"

"Yeah, he tried," and then Jake and Helen laughed.

"I didn't know any of that," said June

"Yeah, well it's long gone but this new mayor is laying the groundwork to have it start again after thirty years of hard work to get rid of it. People forget. They take safety for granted until something blows up and that's why we are here. June," looking right at her, "if we keep our eyes open and get on top of something before it really starts, we have the tools to quietly fix it without most people knowing it. If we do it right, people should just see business as usually even though we hit a bump. We're the shock absorbers or, I guess today, the struts."

"Now I do know what those are," laughed June.

"Okay, we're glad you know," he said looking right at June as she grinned in agreement.

"And the guy from Boston, not even a New Yorker," said Helen out of nowhere.

"Who?" asked June.

"DeBlasio, he's from Boston, not New York so what the hell is he doing messing up our city?"

"Good question," said Jake, "we can only do our bit where we work," and he lifted his coffee cup up in a toast, and they all joined.

"Gee, it's like the Three Musketeers," said Helen and she laughed.

"Good analogy yourself," said Jake, "cheers."

"God, we have the best police force in the world and it's going to be torn down," Helen said to no one in particular, almost muttering to herself.

"Yeah, well hopefully that won't happen."

"Well, it won't happen to us," said June with pride and Jake and Helen looked at her dumbfounded, then at each other with a grin.

Jake felt June was not secure. He and Helen would just need to give her the proper backup when they felt she needed it.

Then a whiff of marijuana floated across beautiful Bryant Park on a sunny day with tourists from across the US and the world. Jake, for one brief moment, was yanked back to the horrible 70's and a city under extreme stress, and he just shook his head as he briefly thought of his recent conversations with two of New York City's Finest. They didn't want to be cops in the city anymore. They wanted to retire early and no one wanted to replace them, this was a problem and the city was in trouble again.

"What was that for?" asked Helen with a laugh in her voice.

"Oh, I don't know. I guess June just let us know that no matter what happens in the world around us we will always be a solid team." This put a smile on June's face.

They headed back to the office when they finished their coffee. They walked past the north side of the New York Public Library. Jake glanced over at Patience and Fortitude, the two lions guarding knowledge. Their sinew and strength were made of good Tennessee pink marble and a great mayor, years before, had named them. They would get past this present mayor, he hoped, as his team would get past any problems they may encounter, and reinforce the integrity of the office they were in charge of.

They crossed Fifth Avenue and then cut through Grand Central Station on their way to Park Avenue on the other side of the Helmsley Building, through one of the two pedestrian tunnels.

They walked up Park Avenue, past St. Bartholomew's and the Waldorf Astoria. They finally came to their building, entered and then passed through security to the elevators, took the middle elevator, and then walked into their 10th Floor office together twenty seconds later. They were noticed as none of them ever took lunch, let alone together; something Jake would change.

Josh caught them as they entered, "What's this, my compliance out on the town together?"

"Yeah, team time. Needed to get them away from their computer terminals for an hour."

"Sounds good, you weren't plotting a takeover?" asked Josh with a laugh trying to be funny.

"No, we'll let you know before we do that," said Jake as both a joke and a test.

He saw Josh's face change just ever so much and briefly, and Helen caught it too. June didn't notice it, thankfully.

"I better build up my defenses. You have a receipt for your lunch? I'll treat you."

"No; I paid in cash, no receipt."

"Next time," said Josh like it was a big deal.

"Next time then."

"You all have everything you need?"

"Well, we could use a new scanner."

"Talk to Doris about that."

"I have Josh, several times, and I keep getting push back on a two-hundred-and-fifty-dollar item that is essential."

"Okay, I'll mention it to her."

"That would be appreciated," said Jake as June and Helen took it all in knowing it was like pulling teeth to get anything out of their cheap chief financial officer. She was cheap to the point of hurting compliance and Jake knew that Josh bought in to her tight reins on every little item although, on the outside, he made it seem that he was overly generous with money.

Jake was on the verge of buying his own scanner while his Director had a box at Yankee Stadium. Jake was the financial responsibility of the Director along with his team and he knew he was being underpaid. He also knew that this was due to the fact that he was an OWG and the Director thought he had him by the short hairs. He was in the Old White Guy category. Susan Lockner covered the easier Long Island office for the company, with the same number of reps, and she was making half again what he was being compensated, but that was another matter he would deal with at a later date.

The following week he received a scanner. It was actually a scanning bar. It was the first generation of scanners and the CFO had found it in the back of a closet someplace. When he attempted to program it, it came up with a date seven years earlier. It was old and useless and he bought a good scanner for his team out of his own pocket, even though he calculated that the Director was pulling down well over a million dollars a year and closer to two. This was an indication of what he was dealing with.

He was beginning to see what Helen had told him about Josh

since day one. The man had a subtle condescending attitude while he tried to patronize certain groups. Jake was sure that he ridiculed the staff in private, with his wife, when he was home in his Greenwich, Connecticut mini-estate. He needed to be careful about what was behind him while he viewed what was in front of him and, most importantly, he needed to protect his team and insulate them as best as he could. He felt that Josh would drop a dime on the team behind their backs, if he felt his income stream might be put in jeopardy.

Two weeks after their Bryant Park lunch, Jake had to take the plunge with Josh. There had been no additional information to come from the home office or the FBI. He needed to view certain batches of emails and he had to have the Director's sign off to obtain them. This would be a test in more ways than one. He would have the team with him to make it a public discussion and prevent any politics between himself and Josh, at least that's what he hoped for.

Instead of Josh's office they met in a small conference room. Jake had wondered why, and then of course Helen came up with the answer. She knew that the conference rooms were extra sound proof, with two that were completely sound poof, and that Josh's office wasn't. It had always been a joke with the previous Director.

They were sitting in the small conference room for close to twenty minutes past the scheduled time when Josh finally showed up and entered in a rush, as though he was partly out of breath.

He grinned a Cheshire Cat grin as he entered, knowing he was very late, "Sorry, my bad, had a really good candidate that we really want, didn't want to take the chance of losing her. She's a good one and we get to add to our Diversity and Inclusion pool, which you will all agree is a priority," he concluded looking directly at Helen and then June in turn. It was obvious and Jake felt a bit embarrassed as it demeaned two of the best people in the business. Helen got it too and he could tell she did not like it.

"So, we need to talk about emails?" he asked as he took a seat at the end of the short table.

"Yes, pretty simple really," said Jake.

"How do you mean?"

"We get current emails flagged by our system and we'd like to go back in time to correspondence that is to and from some of the reps who received or sent the flagged email."

"It's advisors!"

"Excuse me."

"Call them advisors, not reps!" he commanded with a grin of superiority.

"Fine, advisors it is," said Jake and he could feel Helen's steam rising a bit, he knew her by now.

"So, why do you need old email?"

"Trends and relationship!" said Jake, "We want to see how the flagged email may have developed and to look at any patterns of repetition with concerning dialogue."

"I don't see why you need that."

Jake could feel Helen moving in her chair not happy with what she was hearing and he glanced at June quickly, just to check, and her eyes were starting to get that deer in the headlights look.

"We need it so that we can be in front of anything that might happen before it happens, we've all been in the business long enough to know how to interpret trends."

"What can happen? And if word gets out that we are reading all this email the advisors won't be happy."

"Josh," and this got his attention, "we're in the securities business. I appreciate that you come from insurance but you are sitting with three people that have a total of just under sixty years of combined experience in securities. They will not know we are reading the email unless we find something that we deem dangerous and, anyway, they know that all email in this business is overseen. If we find something like that, that's dangerous, you will be the first to know and we will outline our concerns and then discuss it with you. We are required by FINRA to review everything that pertains to the selling and buying of securities and we, of course, are bound to maintain privacy. What we see is only discussed between us, for proper oversight and review," concluded Jake making no mention of a potential concern with regard to Russian money-laundering.

"My concern is overstepping and tramping on rights."

"All three of us are good students of the Constitution and respect rights," said Jake somewhat with tongue in cheek.

"The Constitution was written by White men," said Josh with a slightly sheepish smile.

Everything went quiet as June fidgeted in her chair and looked down at her pad, and Helen gave Jake a side glance like, 'what the hell?'

Jake looked at him for five embarrassingly quiet seconds. "I couldn't care if they were Martians, it is the most brilliant document in Western democracy and the basis for Western democracy with the Magna Carte at its heart," said Jake with authority before he realized what he had said.

June started looking worse like the car was right up on her as she stood stock still in the middle of the road while Helen grinned slightly.

"Well, we live in a diverse society and they were all White."

"They knew the world and society would evolve, that document was written for the millennia. They also knew that slavery should not and could not exist and that eventually all members of society, no matter their sex, religion, or color of skin, would finally be on an equal plane as 'We hold these truths to be self-evident, that all men are created equal...'. Lincoln reaffirmed these words and finally put them in context almost one hundred years later when he said in the Gettysburg Address: '... our fathers brought forth...a new nation, conceived in Liberty, and dedicated to the proposition that all men are created equal.' He went on to sum up: '...that government of the people, by the people, for the people shall not perish from the earth.' That war was the tempering of the steel that became America and that address was the hand extended to bring the North and the South together as one; to bring this nation together as one. He was White too. Have you ever read The Federalist Papers?"

Somewhat stunned, "Why no, I heard of them. And how do you know the Gettysburg Address?"

"We all memorized the address in grade school way back when, when education was thorough; and I guess you haven't read   de Tocqueville then," followed Jake not realizing completely what he was saying until just that moment. He then checked June and Helen to make sure they were okay. June was in a frozen stare and Helen was looking down at her pad smiling.

Then he heard Josh's voice, "No, who is he?" he just couldn't help himself and Jake could hear Helen holding back a laugh so subtle that only he could hear and understand it. He briefly thought of the way this new generation was rewriting history because they weren't being taught history and wondering where they learned the nonsense that they espoused. Just part of 'moon suit lies' he smiled to himself. They could be anything one wanted them to be.

"It doesn't matter really. If you like, I'll buy you his first volume," said Jake trying to be somewhat conciliatory by offering to buy Josh the book, which just made it all worse.

"No, that's okay," finished Josh.

"Getting back to email, can we get your sign off?"

"No, I'd rather not; not just yet."

"Then when? As you know our job is three-fold: to protect the client; to protect the rep, or advisor and to protect the firm and office as one."

"I know that. If you have correspondence that makes you nervous bring it to me, if you feel you need more, and we'll decide."

"That does limit us and narrows our view. Some of this flagged email will be misleading positives."

"What does that mean?"

"The mail may be flagged for a menial item when in reality there is something potentially more threatening behind it than that item. We have been around long enough to get that feeling that tells us to look at other emails remotely related to the one that concerns us. It begs the question, what are we missing as the important issues are not being picked up by our system."

"Well, if it's not right in the email you'd be fishing."

"The firm and you hired us for our experience and expertise in an investment environment which is broader than it was years ago and is increasing in its complexity and speed of transactions. When I say complexity, it is not just the old days of checks and financial wires and paper transactions. The world is becoming a smaller place as a result."

"What's your main concern?"

"Movement of funds."

"Movement of funds?"

"More precisely, illicit funds or potential money laundering."

"That would never happen here."

June broke her stare and looked at Jake while Helen doodled, making a dollar sign and retracing it over and over again until it started to make a hole in the paper and then she too looked over at Jake with a fatalistic smile.

For some reason the image of Frank Zappa's brilliant smile and Sinclair Lewis's emotionally devoid gaze came to Jake's mind together and he almost laughed and said, "But it can happen here."

"I'm sure it can happen anyplace, but not here."

"And why do you say that?"

"We're the flagship office of a boutique firm. Why would anyone do that here?"

"You are right. We are a small boutique firm and this is the firm's main office in the heart of Manhattan, and that is precisely why someone might want to launder money here."

"It doesn't make any sense, what you are saying."

"Let me put it this way," continued Jake feeling the unease of his team, "would you be more readily noticed fishing on a large lake with other people fishing around you, say like New York City, or a small pond, say like Greenwich, Connecticut; and while fishing on that big lake you decide to fish in an inlet to the boat landing, which is small and mostly unnoticed."

"I don't fish."

"Bad analogy maybe, but we are in the center of finance here in New York City. International funds flow in and out daily. This is a perfect place to be to move funds around and then it might make sense to move funds into the system through a small, almost unnoticed, firm that the regulators rarely look at."

"If you find an email that indicates that, then let me know and we will look at it."

Jake could feel the exasperation coming from Helen to his immediate right. He could hear the groan although she didn't make a sound, she didn't have to. They were swimming upstream here and he knew that this was an indicator of things to come.

"Okay, then we will go that way," said Jake giving up the pursuit, "but if we find an email that is a misleading positive, as I had mentioned, and we can explain the logic behind our need to see more mail will you back us up then?" he asked just trying to get a final feel for the situation.

"We'll see. Are we done here, or do you have more to say, because I have another candidate coming in in about fifteen minutes and I need to make a couple of calls before that?"

"No, we're done. Good luck with the candidate," said Jake with subtle sarcasm that his team could hear but went right past Josh concentrating on his candidate.

"Should be a good one; just graduated from Fairleigh Dickinson," he concluded as he stood up to leave.

As he closed the door behind him and headed down the hall Jake turned to look at his team.

"Is he kidding!" said Helen.

"I'm afraid not," confirmed Jake.

"How are we going to know what's going on?" added June, her eyes still a bit panic stricken as she looked at her team.

"We're going to learn how to fly blind," answered Jake to a team member who was scared to death to fly blind.

"'...written by White men', what the hell did that mean?" asked Helen with disdain.

Jake chuckled and bent his head downward looking at is pad, "We are in the throes of the offspring of Political Correctness. I am an unacceptable species."

"What, I don't understand," said June as Helen laughed.

"I'm an OWG since this generation seems to be completely enamored by acronyms, even unpronounceable acronyms."

Helen got it and laughed more, "God, I can get any boss and I get an Old Guy," and she laughed more.

"Funny! You forgot White."

"Old White Guy," said June now getting it, "that's pretty stupid."

"It's the world we live in now," said Helen looking at June, "you need to get used to it."

"I'm surprised they hired me, actually," said Jake with a smile.

"They just couldn't help themselves. The firm wanted the experience in here and Josh, I know, figured he could lowball you and get you cheaply because you are that endangered species," qualified Helen

"I still don't get it," said June.

"Well, I don't fit their 'minority quota' and if you hire someone over fifty there is fear that you could get a lawsuit if you need to 'let them go.'"

"It doesn't make sense," said June.

Jake laughed, "It shouldn't in a way June. You have an analytical mind and this stuff doesn't fit in like a nice easy puzzle piece."

"Does this mean that the three of us may not be together long-term?" asked June with a nervous voice.

"No, don't worry about it. I'm not going anywhere soon, and neither are you two unless you decide to. And if for some reason I went to another firm I'd try to take the two of you, which simply means that we have a great team and I'm not going to let anything happen to it, if I can help it."

June started to look a little relieved, but Jake and Helen knew she'd be nervous the rest of the day.

"June, you just need to do what you do best and leave it to me to protect the team. Nothing is going to happen while I'm here and I'm not going anywhere right now," he said just trying to add some more relief for her by repeating himself.

"June, Josh knows squat about securities. I'm here to tell you that he does know that he has the best team in the firm and because he's so cheap he will try to keep us off-balance," added Helen.

"Why would he want to do that?"

"As I said, he's cheap. He thinks if he keeps us off-balance we won't gripe about a raise, that we'll be too nervous about our jobs. So don't be nervous,"

"Helen's right June, it's just a game. He needs us more than we need him and he knows it so let Helen and me stand up front and deal with his nonsense."

She nodded her head tentatively, "Okay."

"Okay, that's settled. We are now restricted in our scope of view, which just makes things more interesting."

"Yeah, let's hope we don't miss something major and lose our licenses for 'failure to supervise'," said Helen with a laugh, then realizing that June was taking this in, "I'm joking June."

"That could happen couldn't it? We get fined and banned from the business for failure to supervise."

"No. You're too meticulous June. We will push right up against Josh and document everything. We can't push the door open on him but we can sure bang on it loud enough and let the regulatory bodies know we did our job as far as we could push it and we will dial in Latham if need be," assured Jake.

"If you let headquarters in Latham know something then he will know too," said June with concern.

"Yup and that is part of the point of the exercise. And as I said, that is all me so don't worry about it."

"This is going to be fun," said Helen half to herself.

Jake smiled at June, "You are the best at what you do so just do it. This is all part of the job and I know none of us are politicians, so we play it with the tools that we work best with and that is securities and insurance law, and rules and regulations. If we need something badly enough and we get road blocked we simple tighten the screws on basic regulations that we can normally give leeway on until he caves and gives us what we need, and we can do this without being overt. We will act innocent when we do that, he'll really not fully know why we are tightening the screws on something minor, but he will react if we get to him and control it. As I said, it's all a game."

"Sounds like politics to me," said Helen with a gleam in her eye.

"Our politics," said Jake as he looked at June for effect and could see that she was a bit more relaxed.

"Okay, I wanna start looking at some of those Russians, on that list I mentioned, with what we have. I'll meet with both of you individually in your offices starting in a half hour and go over the names on the list and what your portion of review may look like."

June looked at him questioningly.

"I don't want to have a general discussion with the two of you together, I want you both to target your piece of the market and focus on those names with the approach we decide on individually. I don't want to corrupt that individual focus with what each of you are doing."

"Makes sense," said Helen as June nodded her head in agreement.

"To some degree we are going to be very methodical which will fall perfectly in your basket June."

She nodded her head again with more relief, which was obvious to both Jake and Helen.

"Okay, any questions?"

"Nope," said Helen as June shook her head.

"Okay, Helen, I'll see you in a half hour and June probably in two hours, let's say," as he looked at his watch. "Oh, hell, I forgot about lunch. Let's make it one o'clock June."

"I can eat lunch while we talk," offered June.

"No, you're taking a break for your lunch," said Jake as he stood and started to collect his papers.

A half hour later Jake was sitting in Helen's office on the opposite side of her desk.

"Okay, June's a bit nervous."

"You think?" laughed Helen.

"Listen, I want you to back her on stepping out and making decisions. I don't care if she makes mistakes. We all do. I need her to be confident in her knowledge and ability, so we don't miss anything."

"I'll work on it."

"And redirect her when she goes off onto an unnecessary tangent."

"I've found that the word 'stop' works," Helen laughed.

"Whatever works. I need you to look at these clients and their insurance business," said Jake as he slid a list of names across the desk and watched Helen raise her brow, "I know, I know, we're limited in what we can see here but you know these systems better than June and me so do the best you can. You know; stuff like repeated addresses and overloaded funding accounts and any multiple policies that don't seem to make sense, things that we may have not been looking at closely in the past. Then we can pay attention to what related emails we can see at this point."

"You're not bad for an old White guy," said Helen looking up from the list.

"You like that."

"You've got to admit it's funny. Ben Franklin was an old White guy too and he's on the hundred."

Jake just grinned, "Okay so he's on a different page than us. He's playing the 'inclusion and diversity and entitlement' game a bit over the top. That should tell you that he would goose step down the halls if that were the new social criteria."

Helen giggled, "Yeah, well as far as I'm concerned that makes him unstable and unpredictable."

"Maybe it makes him predictable. Once we figure the guy out, we'll know better how to work; he has one weakness."

"What's that?"

"He's condescending with a subtle air of social superiority and thinks he knows everyone but knows no one. God only knows why. He hasn't walked in my moccasins but yet he thinks he knows what my life experiences have been, as he does with everyone."

"Yeah, I've noticed that, and no one would ever know your life experiences, I imagine," she grinned. "Want a coffee?" she then asked as she turned partly in her swivel chair and quickly threw a cartridge into her Keurig coffee maker before turning back again to face him.

"No, I'm good and my life experiences are secret," he smiled and then added, "Don't you think you're moving fast enough? You move twice as fast as June or me without coffee."

"Habit," she said grinning as the cup started to fill under the spout of the coffee maker on the shelf behind her.

"Look at that list. The three highlighted in yellow are our boys, pay attention to them."

"Why isn't the FBI more engaged?"

"These guys are just on a watch list but now that the FBI knows we know, because they told us, they may watch us."

"Don't let June know," and they both started laughing.

"Geez, we'd never see her again," said Jake.

Helen, looking down at the list, "One of these guys in yellow's been repetitive in those mixed language emails which include other Russians."

"I'll need to get that translation software. I'll pay for it myself. We'd never see it if we had to have Doris get it for us. I have never worked in a place as cheap as this. Spend a dollar to save a dime."

Helen laughed, looking up, "It's just a game."

"Yeah, great; who said that? Thank God toilet paper comes with the rent."

"Do I detect sarcasm?"

"You do. Listen, I want you to take care of all the email review. We don't need June bumping into what she might perceive to be Attila the Hun and seeing Visigoths around every corner."

"Visigoths?" asked Helen as she turned and retrieved her coffee from the coffee machine.

"They sacked the Roman Empire; barbarians."

"Ah," laughed Helen, "She would see them," she said as she added milk to her coffee from a one shot container and then a packet of sugar on top of it, and then started stirring it all together as she looked up.

"She's also too methodical and analytical with numbers; she'd miss the undertones in a revealing email that you'd pick up immediately. You have a better feel than anyone I know so you have to be the one to review all email."

She grinned and took a sip of her coffee.

"I know, it's burdensome but it's important and the only place where we can find an indicator of a problem before it becomes one, and a direction of where to look."

"No, I can't argue that one."

"I'll order the translation software today. We simply cannot use Google translator for security reasons."

"Got it."

"Because we don't have systems for review of money transfers in and out of insurance accounts, we are going to have to request them when we stumble upon a concerning account."

"What about Josh?"

"He shouldn't be too concerned if he finds out about any of these types of requests."

"Finds out?"

"Yeah, well I won't tell him until we run into a bomb ready to go off. We don't need him to sign off, like with the emails, and he won't be informed of our requests. I'll also try to shape them as random by checking a range of other accounts, we'll just look very industrious."

"You just can't trust you OWG's," and she laughed.

"Smart!" he said with a smile, "Us old White guys do have a different way of handling things, we handle them pragmatically. Helen, I don't give a damn about being politically correct or curtailing our freedom of speech due to prevailing winds. We will do what we need to do to protect this office and its clients. I'll be the megaphone. Hell, as you've pointed out I'm the old White guy so I'm already toast, might as well just add to the pile and they would expect that from someone from my generation. It's convenient in a way. Anything that you feel needs airing or put out there in one form or another that may shake the boat give it to me and I'll take the heat. They would expect that, as I say, and not look broadly at our team."

"You got it."

"Geez, I hope you've got it. It's not like you're not known for speaking your mind, but we don't need them tiptoeing around you."

"No, I know what you mean and we'll run it your way, makes sense."

———

Jake walked into June's open office, knocking on the door as he did so. She was still eating her lunch while she worked on the computer.

"How many times have I told you to get out of here or shut the computer down while you have lunch! Anyway, I thought I gave you enough time to have your lunch."

"I don't have the time and it got away from me so I'm eating now."

"Well, I don't want to come in here and pick you up off the floor one of these days because a gear finally broke from your non-stop work."

"I'm okay."

"Okay, enough said about that. Helen is squared away on the review of insurance product with regard to a small group of clients," he said as he slipped a copy of the list of names onto her desk. It was the same list he had just given Helen.

"Are these the clients?"

"Yup" and he waited for what he knew was coming as she looked at the list, focused and became stock still.

"They're Russian names!"

"Yup, as I had mentioned. The list I first brought up in the park and why we are meeting," and he waited again. She had known the list was coming two weeks before but now it was real and he waited for her to digest the reality of it.

"Umm, ah," her eyes stared at the paper, "what do we look for?"

"Layering and integration of dirty money, you know what that is. Stupid money in, stupid money out. Investing that doesn't make sense for the investor or something that looks like a day trade but isn't. June, you know this stuff, you've seen it before."

"I know, but they're Russian."

"The new boys in town; different day, different mob."

"They don't play by rules."

Jake was surprised, "You're right there but in a way that makes them easier to be caught, they lose methodology and take too many risks not supported by well thought out movement. Only you and Helen see this list and if you see something that really bothers you come to my office or see Helen. Don't do anything with these people. Having said that, I do want you to make decisions and take actions that you feel necessary outside of this group and their reps. Got it?"

"Yeah," she said, her eyes still focused on the list of names, "What about the FBI?"

"The highlighted names are only on their watch list. Believe me, we find something we will move it through channels and then corporate law to the FBI if need be. We are only watching, not fighting."

June's face went pale.

"Bad choice of words, not fighting, not getting involved other than reporting to the powers that be."

"What about him," she said glancing sideways towards Josh's office.

"We don't need to engage him unless we stumble onto something really bad,… I mean important, which will have to go up the chain. Don't worry about him, he will not get in your way or give you trouble.

If you feel that he is doing something to get in your way, whatever that is, you let me know."

"Okay," she said with some hesitation.

"Okay, what?" he asked knowing what was on her mind.

"But what if he finds out and doesn't like it?"

"Finds out what?" he asked, knowing it was better to let her explain it to herself out loud.

"You know; looking at investments and not telling him about it."

"And that's what we do day in and day out. What is the difference now?"

"The Russians."

"As I said, nothing has changed, we will be watching and analyzing as we always do and if something starts to develop and it looks concerning, we will call a meeting with Josh. If for some reason he questions what you are doing act dumb and send him to my office."

"Okay."

"We okay? I'm depending on your skills remaining unimpeded. You know that as your boss you and Helen are my responsibility and come first before anything else. I'm here to take the flak if any, and there won't be any."

"Okay."

"Now that we have that settled, I want your focus on these people but not to the exclusion of other accounts. Some of these guys in here are beginning to think they are real market gurus with trading expertise simply because you can do no wrong in this extended Bull Market. We really need to rein them in when they step too far out so they don't kill themselves and take their clients along with them. If anything, and I mean anything, looks odd to you as a former trading assistant and advisor, I want to know about it. I never find you to be wrong and I don't really care if you are on occasion, you have great market sense and know the mechanics."

"I will," she said with her eyes intense again like a deer caught in the headlights and nervous, but focused.

"Good."

Before leaving her office, he turned at the door, "Have faith in your ability and knowledge because I do; you are good at what you do," and before he turned again to leave, "door open or closed."

"Closed please."

"Talk with you later," and he left closing the door behind him.

As he passed Helen's office, he heard a laugh and, "You have to see this."

Jake stopped, "Uh-oh, already?"

"No, it's someone else," she said as he walked in and closed the door behind him while Helen's printer was printing.

"Okay, what's so funny?"

She turned to the printer under her desk to her left and retrieved a small pile of printed pages, turned back, and slapped them down in front of Jake, "It's not the Russians, it's the new Chinese girl who we can barely understand. Check out her recent emails."

"Oh-no, what?" he asked as he picked up the pile of paper looking at Helen with a grin on her face.

Adjusting his glasses, he started to read the emails.

"Are you kidding," he said as he lowered the pages when he finished. "They're cookie cutters."

"She's making the same mutual fund recommendations to all three of these people and I saw four more, the same thing. And guess what?"

"Oh-no."

"She's only insurance licensed."

"Great, this place is a bit of a horror show. This is what happens when you have insurance people getting into the securities industry, even if it's only mutual funds. What's the attachment I see in these emails?"

"It gets better," and Helen threw a clipped, half inch thick stack of paper on the desk in front of Jake.

"What's this?"

"I don't know, it's in Chinese."

"Well, that's just wonderful," said Jake picking up the attached pile of paper and then looking at it quietly.

"I don't know anyone in house who can translate that."

"Oh Christ," muttered Jake still flipping the pages. "I think I'm holding a Reg D real estate private placement. Shit."

"Oh, that's good."

"Yeah, and it appears to be offering an EB-5 visa, at least I can read EB-5," said Jake as he quickly started skipping through the rest of the pages and then stopped to read again before looking up at Helen, "and past all the Chinese is this little disclaimer page in English for a Reg D, Jeezus."

"What's an EB-5?" asked Helen as Jake handed the printed memorandum back to her before she started to look at it again.

"It's a way to get green cards for foreign investors. They invest so much and generate so many jobs and they get a green card from Uncle Sam."

"Sweet," she said as she turned the pages looking for the disclaimer in English.

"Yeah, and it looks like these are ten-thousand-dollar units and an EB-5 takes a minimum investment of five hundred thousand, as I recall."

"Can it get any better, sort of a type of bait and switch," she said as she looked back at Jake and dropped the document on the desk.

"Sorta; bait and fish more like it. Call her desk, let's get her in here now."

Jake waited while Helen called the extension and then shook her head and hung up, "Voicemail but not set up yet, just a generic greeting."

"Oh, good. Well what would we expect. Try the receptionist."

Helen dialed, "Have you seen Lin Loo today?" then waited for the answer. "When's the last time you saw her? … Okay, thanks."

"Well?"

"She saw her yesterday late and that was the last."

"She's new, she should be in in the mornings making cold calls," said Jake as Helen picked up the memorandum and started to glance at it again. "Hell, let me know when you find her," he said as he stood to leave.

Just as he opened the door to leave Helen laughed behind him and said, "I think I know where she is."

"Where?" he asked as he turned back around.

"Today's the last day for subscription to the deal as far as I can tell from these signature pages," she said as she laughed again and turned the memorandum around with her thumb under the date so Jake could see it."

"Oh great, you can't make this stuff up."

"I love this job," smiled Helen.

"I'm glad you're happy. Keep trying to track her down and when you do send her to my office. Better give me all the emails and that memorandum."

Two weeks later, after Lin Loo had given her guarantee that she did not sell any of the real estate units, Jake was able to get her a letter of reprimand with heightened supervision. This was after several discussions with the home office legal group. Not yet being security licensed she fell under the protection of 'ignorance'. She was given a second chance and Jake sat with her and educated her as to her mistakes and missteps and she was to report to him once a week. He received approval from Josh to review all of her email once he reassured Josh that they would be able to keep her. Josh was more concerned about his diversity number and did not want to lose a woman, and in particular an Asian woman.

"Helen, pull up what you can of Loo's incoming emails starting two weeks ago, just for grins. We're going to have to make this a regular process if they look bad," said Jake over the phone to Helen.

An hour later Helen was back on the phone to Jake, "I think you better come in here."

"Oh, Christ, what now? Be right over."

As soon as Jake walked into Helen's office, she reached up with a paper in her hand, it was a printed email, "You'll love this one."

Jake took the paper and started scanning it, "Oh, crap."

"I told you you'd love it."

"A thank you note for the ten-thousand-dollar real estate investment, in English too; nice."

"Yeah, and he wants a receipt too," added Helen with a grin.

"Jeezus, a receipt for a Reg D deal; that's even wrong. She's done now," looking up at Helen from the email, "see what other emails you have to add to this but don't kill yourself doing it. I'll get Josh now. She has to go today to preempt any 'failure to supervise' concerns."

"Figured. Okay," answered Helen as Jake turned to leave with the electronic missive in his hand.

"Made in China 2025," Jake said to himself just as he crossed the threshold of her door, but Helen heard it.

"What is that?"

"Oh, the Chinese have an official plan to be top economic dog by 2025, by hook or by crook," he said after stopping and turning towards Helen again.

"I guess they're headed that way."

"Yeah, I was just laughing to myself that this might be an early taste of the future of Mao's Century Plan in its different machinations. They are trying to shortcut Mao's target of 2049. God knows what they will do to make that happen besides bankrupting small countries and putting them in debt to the Chinese government; and on top of that, cornering the market on strategic materials. They may use any weapon at their disposal, including nuclear and biological, according to Unrestricted Warfare, which they published in 1999. Scary stuff. That book was a marker for a move towards extremism."

"What?"

"Don't mind me, I'm just a crazy old White guy with ramblings, who's been thinking about too much lately."

"I know that," she laughed.

"Okay, let me get to this and I'll talk with you later," he said as he turned and headed up the hall.

Lin Loo was in and Josh was scared enough that he dropped everything, including an interview, and had the young woman in his office within the hour. When she walked out, she was terminated through a mutual agreement and not 'for cause'. This concerned Jake but he knew that the home office would put the cause on her U5 paperwork for the governing body FINRA. He needed to make sure that the office and his team was protected from any following fallout as well as protecting the public from such a person. She had lied to a compliance officer besides selling something she had no business getting involved with.

Jake would find out a month later that Lin Loo had moved her show to Boston and was hired by a firm there, another insurance-advisory company. Unfortunately, she had only been registered with FINRA and had not yet taken a securities exam so a U5 documentation of bad behavior became somewhat of a moot point, as her previous transgressions would be left for debate and therefore not considered. Jake did not like the new business model, for the general public, that he saw in the investment world.

Caution, practicality and standards were falling to the wayside in the name of volume and preference. Volume was the method of hiring anyone they could convince to come into the firm and start life making cold calls with the unofficial title of advisor. Jake would say, 'put a mirror under their nose and if it fogs up you got yourself an advisor.' He wasn't excited about the reality of that statement which was close to the truth with the exception that most would have to test at a certain level in a test designed to determine not only a basic ability for math but, more importantly, a drive for sales. If they had enough people going through the system, they'd wind up with someone who would stick and get sales along the way as they would get all new people to sell to their family members and friends. Preference was what concerned Jake even more. Josh, with the firm's emphasis on it, was targeting Black candidates to the point of taking any Black applicant that walked through the door even if their test results determined that they would fail in sales. The job was built for somewhat pushy people who could call on people all day long and come back each day for more and only a single digit percentage of candidates fell into that category. Josh would keep Black hires well past the point where they failed and would have, and should have, been coached out of the business. The average White male who failed would be talked with in an attempt to help them find an alternative career to sales. They would be saved the agony of lingering in a position that did not suit them, whereas a Black or female rep would be kept lingering as they struggled on the road to failure. But they were kept on the books as a minority, or 'diversity and inclusion' number, as long as it would last. Jake tried to help them when he could because he knew what was going on. He found it not only sad that people were being used in this way, but it angered him; the first time he had been angry about anything in years.

He had let a couple of people in Latham know about his concerns, those people who would listen. There were only a couple and they saw the injustice in what was happening as well. It was more commiserating than gaining an effective solution that would respect these young people. Although people were told to speak their minds they did not for fear of reprisal. One confidant in home office was incensed as much as Jake and she would try to bring the subject up as subtly as she could when she attended one of her monthly meetings with the legal department. That was that. He could only try to help them and voice his concern if the opportunity arose, as the controlling management might then label him as a racist, if he spoke too loudly, making him less effective or, worse yet, interpret it that he was calling them racist, which would create destructive animosity. In either of these situations he would be rendered useless in any attempt to create an atmosphere of honest respect and not one of self-aggrandizing through destructively patronizing behavior. He had been there before, when he stood his ground years before on gaining raises for his entire team when they had earned it and he was told to lower their high evaluations and he wouldn't. That had been different but with similar effect, it had blacklisted him as well as uncovering the Azerbaijan oil money had blacklisted him. But now he was dealing with political correctness and 'diversity and inclusion' gone wild to the point of hurting the same people it had been trying to protect and advance in life. It was a difficult issue but he was getting older, near the end of his career, and there was just so much he could, and would, take as he watched young people being used. At the end of the day, what could they do, fire him? They couldn't line him up against a wall and shoot him, or could they, he laughed to himself sarcastically.

CHAPTER 11

ALFRED E. NEUMAN

"It's not the Russians but I have a few accounts that are creating a bad pattern," said June from the other end of the line after Jake answered his phone.

"Who is it?"

"Alfred E. Neuman," said June buying into the team humor.

"Oh Christ, Walter."

"You got it."

"Be right there," Jake said as he shook his head and hung up the phone. Walter's face, looking very much like Mad Magazine's Alfred E. Neuman with a little Howdy Doody thrown in, crossed his mind's eye for a brief moment. Walter was a walking disaster, but he was persistent and tenacious, and Josh liked that, even though he trampled clients on the way to jeopardizing the office.

"Okay, what do we have?" asked Jake as he stepped through June's open door and closed it behind him.

"I started checking out these new UIT sales. There was a lot in a short time all coming from Walter so I thought I should take a closer look."

"And?... And where the hell did he learn about them?"

"He's dumped the same equity UIT's in maybe thirty IRA accounts as far back as I've gone so far. These aren't the old bond Unit Investment Trusts we used to use for older clients."

"Yeah, I know them. They make no sense and have a high commission."

"Well, not only has he made a lot of buys for IRA's over the past month but going back even further into other IRA's he has dropped the same ones or similar in every IRA account for the past year, with different maturity dates and short maturities."

"Oh no. I hate these things. They make no sense outside of the self-liquidating bond baskets of years past for retirees. I don't want to hear that we have cash positions sitting in IRA's of young people."

June just nodded her head up and down tight lipped.

"Oh, Christ."

Walter had seeded IRA's with short maturity equity UIT's over the previous two years, it would turn out, and not just one, and as they self-liquidated they left un-invested cash behind in retirement accounts with long time horizons, and in a hot market. Walter did not know what he was doing. He was a ball of energy, as if he were on amphetamines, who opened account after account, and in this case IRA's, with the same investments in each no matter the risk tolerance of the client. He looked for the highest commission payouts and he found it in UIT's. He dropped them into accounts, collected the commission and then moved on to the next potential client. Most of the IRA's were made up of these UIT's only. These particular IRA's would eventually wind up as all cash and not one client had complained, which did not make sense.

"I'll get you a list of the accounts for the last year."

"Good for a start. Man, I hate having him work with these people after this screw-up but he's going to have to go back to each one and explain the cash situation."

"You think he can do that?"

"No, but we have to give it a go and if he fails early and generates a complaint, I'm placing them all with someone with more competence."

"Josh won't like that."

Jake looked at her, "Good, you said that calmly and you seem to be relaxed."

"Helen's been working on me."

"Anything to be concerned about with the Russians?"

"Not on the security side that I can see."

"Okay, get me a list of all accounts sitting with cash from these damned things for the past year and I'll see if I can get this idiot started."

"If you can catch him. He's like a blur, he moves so fast."

"Ah, good. Humor. I told you this job can be fun. Okay, get them to me as soon as you can and I'll see if I can track him down," concluded Jake as he turned to head for the office's Bullpen in the off chance that Walter was in his cubicle. It was a Bullpen like any other and similar to the one he had started in and Walter spent most of his time there on the phone, nonstop.

"Got it," he heard June behind him as he opened the door, stepped out and turned left down the hall, leaving June's door open.

As Walter Crouchticker looked like a strange cross between Alfred E. Neuman and Howdy Doody he could set off laughter at first sight, so when he all of a sudden appeared in Jake's doorway with a big Howdy Doody smile on his face Jake was hard-pressed to restrain his laughter.

"You wanna see me bossman?"

"Not really, but I have to," said Jake appealing to Walter's sense of humor, knowing that was the best way to get him to listen.

"Can I grab a seat? I won't take it anywhere."

"Be my guest. I'm curious; you have any idea why I've asked you to my office."

"I don't know, you like my company."

"Not that much," said Jake as he dropped a stack of papers in front of Walter while he was taking his seat directly across the desk from Jake.

"You giving me accounts Captain?"

"Now it's captain."

"Oh Captain, My Captain," he said fidgeting as though he had someplace else to be.

"Can you sit still and keep your mind in one spot for a few minutes here, we can talk about Walt Whitman another time."

"Very good professor."

"Jesus Walter, how do you manage to get clients?"

"They can't resist my charm."

"Evidently. Look at those accounts in front of you. Any names at a glance look familiar?" Jake asked, having started the pile with the oldest accounts and blacking out the rep's name.

"No, why?"

"They're your accounts Mr. Whitman."

Walter looked again lifting the first account up close to his face, short of having a magnifying glass in his hand. Then putting it down he did the same with the next account, put it down and grinned, "I guess they're mine on close examination."

"Jesus Walter, pay attention. They are all IRA's with the same equity UIT's in every one of them. Or should I say, had the same equity UIT's. The one's you are looking at on top are all in cash now."

"So, what's wrong?"

"They're IRA's for Pete's sake."

"Who's Pete?"

"Oh Christ Walter, do you get it?"

"No, there's nothing wrong."

"These people are sitting in cash in a retirement deferred account that they won't touch for maybe the next thirty years on average, and in a hot market."

"Yeah, well that's okay. Not like I'm gambling with their money or anything."

"The problem is that you are. You're smarter than this, or at least I hope you are."

"I don't get what you mean, I gotta go soon."

"Okay, these people are at risk right now. You are forfeiting the time value of money."

"What?"

"Ever hear of inflation. Nasty little mouse that eats the cheese."

"I like that, 'eats the cheese.'"

"Listen, you are in a hot market with clients sitting in cash and they don't seem to know it as we haven't had a complaint. These people are losing growth."

Walter shrugged.

"What the hell's that for?"

"I don't know, I can't keep track of everything."

"The problem is that you are supposed to."

"Supposed to what?"

"Ah geez Walter, you have to slow down and deal with the clients that you now have before adding more. You are going to have to talk with the clients that are now in cash and invest that cash."

"I don't have time and I have something better than UIT's."

"Let's put it this way. Contact the first twenty people in this pile within the next week and let me know what you did. If I don't hear from you, I will have someone else take over the accounts... What do you have 'better than UIT's'? I'm afraid to ask."

"Life insurance."

"Well, people need life insurance but that doesn't satisfy investment needs."

"I have this great piece about life insurance being like a Swiss Army knife. It does everything and is better than an IRA."

"No, no, you are not going there. Life insurance is not an asset and don't get into this non-correlating asset nonsense that I'm seeing."

"What's that?"

"That insurance is a better investment than securities and does not get affected by the markets."

"But it doesn't."

"You cannot position it as an investment. It is life insurance with the primary purpose of giving the client a death benefit."

"Well other companies are selling it that way."

"We are not other companies, don't do it. You'll wind up in a world of hurt if a complaint gets filed from a client who thought you were selling them a retirement account and not life insurance. I wanna hear back on those clients," Jake nodded towards the pile in front of Walter, "by the end of next week or I'll give the accounts to someone else."

"You can't do that."

"Oh, I can."

"Well, I have more clients."

"Geez Walter, you have a brain, get it straight. You need to understand how these things work."

"What?"

"Investments that you are selling people. You are grabbing one product with a high commission and putting everyone in that product no matter what their needs are or what risk tolerance they have."

"I just don't have time."

"You had better find it."

"I gotta go."

"All right, let me know where these clients stand."

"Ok," he said, his mind someplace else as he got up and started to leave.

"Walter."

"What?"

"It might help if you take this stack of accounts so you know who to call."

"Oh," he said as he snatched the pile and headed for the door turning briefly as he was exiting and grinning like Howdy Doody.

"Christ," muttered Jake.

Two weeks later Jake hadn't heard from Walter and started repositioning the accounts with two other reps, without telling Josh. He was going to let Josh find out on his own, if he could, and come to him about it.

Walter did not say a word about his IRA accounts being given to other reps because he wasn't paying attention to what was behind him, and he probably wouldn't care in the end.

Josh found out a week later when a complaint came in from a client who was concerned that his account was sitting in cash when the stock market was going up, and he couldn't get ahold of his rep, Walter Crouchticker. Jake had to fill Josh in at this point. At least there was no problem with the Russian accounts and the Lin Loo affair had been tied up with a neat bow and closed with the legal department, to remain only as a bad memory.

"What's this complaint for?" asked Josh just after Jake entered his office. This time Josh was standing on the other side of the conference table in his office near the window on Park.

"They can't get ahold of Walter and they are concerned because they are sitting in cash in their IRA in an up market."

"Where is he?"

"Out getting new clients I suppose. We have over two dozen of these clients sitting in cash. He bought short maturing UIT's in every IRA he opened over the past two years. I met with him about it two weeks ago."

"What are UIT's?"

"Equity Unit Investment Trusts. Stocks held short term in a fixed portfolio basket that self-liquidates short term on a given date; in a matter of months in Walter's case," said Jake as he felt like shaking his head.

"Why would someone buy that?"

"Because Walter told them to. Listen, when I met with him, I told him to call these clients sitting in cash and he wouldn't, so I moved them to two other reps."

"Why did you do that?"

"To take care of the clients properly and avoid a complaint."

"But we got a complaint anyway."

"Yeah, from one of the clients not yet contacted; we're probably stopping more complaints. I don't mean to add further to this little mess, but I just had a senior partner in a law firm call me complaining about Walter."

Josh, having turned to start walking towards his large glass window, ten stories up, stopped and turned, "About what?"

"Walter bothering the partners and the other attorneys."

"What's their concern?"

"They don't want him calling them. They have asked him to cease and desist and he won't."

Josh looked satisfied, "Well that's what he's supposed to do."

"We're not selling vacuums," snapped Jake.

"What's that supposed to mean?" asked Josh now facing Jake.

"He should be showing a degree of professionalism and not hounding people to the point that his compliance officer gets a call about it. I have assured her that he will stop. I have also left him a voicemail to that effect and want him in my office."

At that moment Walter was in the front lobby of the law firm seconds away from confronting the partner who had called Jake, but that partner did not know Walter by appearance or voice.

He was talking with the receptionist and making her laugh when the partner came up and asked if she could help him.

"Yes, I need to see Paul Brubaker."

"Is he expecting you?"

"No, but you can tell him Walter is here," he said as he pulled out one of his cards and handed it to her.

"You! You're Walter Crotchlite!"

"Crouchtiker, it's Walter Crouchtiker."

She looked at the card again holding it up at eye level with a slight bit of rage in her eyes and read off his name, "Well Mr. Couchlicker, I'm a senior partner in this firm and I have to ask you to leave right now."

"Jeesus, it's Crouchtiker and I guess you won't need that then!" he said as he snatched his card back out of her hand, and left her standing there staring at his back as he pushed his way through the double glass doors of the office and headed towards the elevator banks.

Jake had a voicemail waiting for him after he left Josh's office.

'Mr. Bowen, this is Sarah Haskill. That salesman of yours was here again. I thought that was going to be dealt with. Can you please stop him from harassing this office! If not, your firm will receive a letter from ours. Good day,' and the phone clicked off on the voicemail.

"Oh, crap."

Jake pulled up Walter's cell phone number and dialed it immediately.

"Who's this," he answered seeing the firm's name pop up on his display.

"Who in hell do you think it is?"

"Captain?"

"Captain of the Valkyries and I've come to send you to Valhalla you idiot."

"Is this Odin?"

"It could be; very good Walter."

"Yeah, well, mythology is one of my hobbies."

"Well, you need to get your head out of the clouds or out of something else because that law firm just called me again."

"I left."

"Yeah, but not until lighting a fire under them again. This one I have to write up as a warning and put it in your file, which protects everyone; if and when the complaint comes in."

"Why?"

"Because you don't listen Walter. Stay away from that damned office. If you have any accounts there work them remotely or meet them outside of that office. Got it?"

"Got it Captain."

"Oh, God. I'll have the warning letter in your mailbox for you to countersign by the end of the day. I also want to see you in my office; listen to your voicemail."

"Okay, gotta go," and he hung up.

CHAPTER 12

THE PHANTOM UKRAINIAN

"Mr. Bowen, can I talk with you?"

Jake looked up at the quiet voice of Jim Parker who was standing in the doorway to his office. Jim had been so quiet it had startled Jake.

"Come in Jim, what's up? Shut the door behind you and grab a seat."

Jim sat and looked across the desk at Jake as though waiting for the word to start talking.

"What's on your mind?"

"I have a death claim."

"Not fun. I guess it's your first."

"Yes, but…"

Jake knew to just wait and not say anything.

"Well, he died in the Ukraine and he's still there. His wife notified me."

"Oh, crap," muttered Jake partly under his breath. Jim was a young kid, part of Josh's minority number. Jake had tried to help him get through his Series 6 but he had failed twice with a 35% which told Jake he hadn't studied. The kid, as Jake looked at him, had been put under undo pressure to succeed which robbed him of time to study.

He was one of Josh's keep at all costs reps even if it cost the kid. As Jake knew, if he were White he would have been helped or coached out of the business so he could go on to what suited him best. Financial sales was only for a small group of people who in today's age were consummate salesmen. Jim, he felt, was more thoughtful and somewhat reserved and might be better, ironically, in human resources at some advertising firm but he was being carelessly dragged along by Josh. Now it seemed that he had become an easy target for a potential scam because he was young, and desperate to achieve what he was being driven to achieve.

"How much was he insured for?"

"One and a half million."

"Then he's an American."

"Not exactly. He has dual citizenship."

"Ya gotta love dual citizenship," said Jake shaking his head which just seemed to make Jim more nervous.

"Maybe I should have hesitated, it was the easiest sale I ever had, and he called me. I don't even know how he got my name. I was so excited by the case I didn't even ask. This is not good, this is not good," said Jim shaking his head and looking down.

"That's what I'm here for Jim. Our business has always been a target and always will be; and who knows, this may be legitimate. "

"There's another thing," said Jim looking up and at Jake.

'Here it comes. We probably do have a problem,' thought Jake.

"He and Nadia, his wife, opened up several service accounts dropping in just under ten thousand dollars on a somewhat regular basis, and then moving it out again," said Jim as he moved a piece of paper across the desk to Jake with the account information of one of the accounts on it. Just what Jake had been worried about with the Russian accounts.

Geez, why didn't we catch that thought Jake. Our lousy systems. "When did you notice this?" asked Jake as he took the paper, pulled it up and looked briefly at it.

"Just after getting the death notification and claim request from his wife late yesterday."

"Our wonderful systems Jim," said Jake as he lay the account paper on his desk and gave Jim his full attention. "We can't see everything home office sees unless we order it up and we get jammed by this inefficiency. Okay, we probably have a problem, but as I say, that's what I'm here for and I don't want you to worry about it."

"Yeah, but I opened the case and wrote the policy with a strange feeling; it was pretty big."

"Jim, they targeted you because you are new and hungry for business. It is usually new reps who are the targets. Your gut was probably right about the policy, in that you felt strange about it, but you did not do anything wrong."

"What about the claim?"

"We'll file it together. I want them to know that you had a concern and came to see me. It'll be in my notes too. I'll as well make a call. They'll have an international investigator verify the legitimacy of the claim."

"How?"

"They'll probably need to see the body and of course the death certificate. Fill out a death claim and come back. In the meantime, we'll look into the service accounts and try to put together a profile of what we see." Jake stayed away from the phrase money laundering as the kid was nervous enough and didn't need to hear the confirming words.

Jim started to leave as Jake picked up the phone but stopped and turned, and Jake froze with the phone in his hand, "Mr. Bowen, will this ruin my chances to be a financial planner?"

"No Jim, and maybe we need to go out to lunch and look at what you want to do with your career."

"Thanks Mr. Bowen," said Jim with a noticeable degree of relief on his face. He hesitated, then turned and left.

Jake looked at where Jim had just stood, for a second, and shook his head, 'goddamned Josh,' he thought before punching the auto dial for Helen.

"We may have a problem, pull everything you can on Nadia and Ignat Oblonsky. O-B-L-O-N-S-K-Y,….Yeah, Ignat… Yeah, I know… Okay, I didn't give the man his name… Okay, pull everything up you can and I'll be over in about ten minutes."

Ten minutes later Jake appeared at Helen's door and she looked up with a grin, "I've got a little dossier on 'Ignat' and company."

"You like that, huh," he said as he closed the door behind him.

"It's different and he and Nadia have been busy," she said as she dropped the small pile of paper on her desk in front of Jake as he sat down.

As he read, Helen spoke briefly, "As you'll see, they may have been using their funding accounts as a bank, at least the ones we can see right now. I can't see the transfer of funds in and out but the amounts in the accounts are too large," and then she let Jake continue silently through the papers.

He finally dropped them back on the desk and looked up at her, "Christ, don't you love the warning systems we don't have. We should have been able to recognize this before it got started. We're probably going to have to file an S.A.R."

"Suspicious Activity Report, if I remember correctly. I've never had to file one of those."

"Well, welcome to the club. Get a request to home office for the actual money movement in and out of those accounts so we have it, but it looks obvious."

"If I'm finally going to get introduced to an investigation it might as well be an Ignat," and she grinned again, "Josh'll love this."

"Yeah, well Parker's a little nervous about something else, and I didn't fill you in on that one yet."

"Oh, this'll be good."

"Right up your alley; Ignat bit the dust."

"What?"

"Yeah, he is reportedly muerto, finito, kaputt for good, shuffled off this mortal coil or whatever meets your fancy."

"Geez, where did this happen?"

"The Ukraine."

"You're kidding, right."

"Nope and the kid is working on a death claim as we speak."

"Josh'll really love this. How much?"

"One point five."

"It only gets better."

"Yeah, well this one smells."

"You think ol' Ignat is still running around someplace."

"I'll lay odds on it. I'll query some people at home office when I let them know about the claim and that the 'body' is still in the Ukraine."

"Oh, they'll love you too."

"Yeah, well, I've gotta deal with Josh on this and I'm going to hit him square between the eyes with dragging these kids past common sense just so he can hold onto his 'diversity and inclusion' number. Parker doesn't know how to get off the horse because no one is helping him. I'm going to take him to lunch and try to get him on a better path, to hell with Josh's crap"

"Oh, that'll be good too."

"You wanna join me in the meeting?" asked Jake more as a joke than a reality.

"I think I'll skip that one although it's about time someone says something."

"Yeah, well, I've seen enough and what are they gonna do to me, fire me? Hell, I'm just an old White guy anyway as you keep reminding me. Funny thing is he might be frightened to fire me because of 'age discrimination,' but maybe I'll give him an out. He also doesn't like how close I am to his 'advisors.' I kept telling him to walk around and get to know them. Things are really an upside-down mess these days, and not only here."

"Yeah, well I'm glad I don't have kids."

"Helen, any child of yours would be able to weather any storm this society threw at him, assuming he's a boy," and he grinned.

"I'd hate to subject him to this stupidity."

"Hell, he'd find the humor in it the way you do and he wouldn't be an everybody gets a trophy kid," he said as he started to push himself up out of the chair and briefly thought about his first cross-country race as an eight-year-old, when he didn't win a ribbon. Only first, second and third won ribbons so he had worked hard, with the help of his father, and won the race the following year and became a competitive runner after that; and he smiled to himself without anyone noticing, as he stood.

"Well, I guess we audda see if we can find the Ignat first," she laughed.

"Yeah, time to pull young Parker's butt outta the fire. Can you dig up a Sar and start it, I'm gonna see how he's doing with that claim and then call home office," he said as he opened the door to walk out.

"Will do boss."

"Funny." Jake said over his shoulder as he left Helen's office.

———

After meeting with Jim and talking with the home office to let them know that they would be receiving a death claim, with the body in the Ukraine and still waiting on the death certificate, Jake knocked on Josh's door. He knew he was in and his assistant Marsha had stepped away for lunch.

"Can you come back, I'm tied up," came from the other side of the door.

"This can't wait Josh. We have what might be a problem."

"Okay, if you have to. Come in."

Josh was standing at his standing desk reading his email so Jake waited, taking a seat facing Josh's stand-up desk, at the small conference table in the office. After a minute Josh stopped and turned, "So what's so important."

"Mr. Parker has a death claim."

"Good experience for him."

"Well, not really a good experience and particularly not in this case. I think it may be a fraud."

"How can that happen?"

"An out of country death in a place that is not easily accessible. Saw one once out of South America, fake body and all and they almost got away with it. This one's in the Ukraine."

"So, what!"

"Well, it's not the most stable place in the world right now and the body is still there and apparently not going anyplace including the US. I've let home office know that I am concerned that it may be fraudulent."

"Why'd you do that?"

"Because it's my job and young Mr. Parker is hanging by his fingertips. It appears that the deceased and his wife may have been laundering funds before he decided to take a dirt nap."

"Is that supposed to be funny?"

"Not really but this situation has an absurdity to it that is in plain view. This is how it will work. Home office will hire a firm which specializes in foreign investigations to determine a legitimate death as this is not new to the world of forensics. I am sure they will find a problem with the legitimacy here as the shape of this case, topped by what appears to be an extended period of money laundering, is leading towards criminal behavior. My job is not only to help in the facilitation of this investigation but more importantly to protect Mr. Parker from being culpable, which he is not."

"How do you know that?"

"What?"

"That he's not culpable."

Jake held his breath for a second with his blood rising before he responded, "He admits he felt initially uneasy about such a large case just dropping into his lap but he moved forward anyway to make his numbers. He had too much pressure put on him to write business that he skipped over the first trip wire and I cannot completely blame him for that. He did not facilitate this fraud."

"Well, who's going to take the blame if this turns out to be fraud?"

"The client."

"But what about here? Shouldn't Parker take the blame so it doesn't fall on this office."

"You're kidding me, right?"

"Whaddaya mean?"

"The only thing Mr. Parker is guilty of is staying on this job too long but then no one gave him the right direction."

"I don't follow."

"Jim Parker is part of your 'diversity and inclusion' number, like a couple of other people here who are dragged way past the point where they should be coached out of the business."

"That's nonsense."

"Oh, is it? Why do we push our Black reps, new to the business, past the time and requirements put on White males? We coach the White males out of the business when they reach the failing threshold. We help them with an alternative to something we know they will probably never survive in."

"Well…they deserve more of a chance…"

"Well, that statement is bias and by doing this you take their chances away of moving to a profession more fitting for their skill set and temperament. Not everyone makes a salesman. On top of this, if that individual continues to fail and get more pressure put on him he may perceive it as racism, which to a degree it is, and sue you."

"That's nonsense, and whaddaya mean salesman?"

"This is a salesman's job Josh. You can put all the lipstick you want on it at this level but a pig is still a pig and these kids deserve better."

"A pig?"

"Call it what you will. Mr. Parker has scored thirty-five, give or take, on two Series 6 exams because he's being pushed to sell so many life policies in a given time. This is pure sales and we know the ones who usually make it through this period can sell pig shit to a hog farmer. Does that make it clear?"

Josh just looked at Jake dumbfounded.

"I suggest we support Mr. Parker through this and then help him to determine an alternative career because this one does not suit him," continued Jake.

"How do you know! I intend to make Mr. Parker work if he is not involved in this."

"Christ," muttered Jake. "Okay, I'm making you aware of the situation. We are collecting additional data on the potential money laundering involved with this case and filing a Sar in the meantime."

"What's that?"

"What's what?" Jake wanted to hear him ask for the definition of S.A.R. which Jake pronounced simply Sar, as a word.

"What's a sare?"

"It's S-A-R, for Suspicious Activity Report, which we are required to file when we become aware of potential money laundering."

"But I didn't say you could."

"It has to be filed at an indication of a money laundering scheme even if in the end it turns out to be harmless. Under the Patriot Act, if we do not act when presented with what we feel is money laundering we can be held culpable."

"So you can just file this thing whenever you want!?"

"No, there are red flags that pop up that tell us that there is more than strong indication that money laundering is going on, and in this case we have strong indication. This is the first Sar that this team will have filed."

"Well, I hope it's the last."

"I certainly hope so too."

"What does that mean!?"

"Just what I said, that I hope this is the first and last Sar we submit. I'll keep you informed about the investigation into the client's reported death," said Jake in preparation to leave Josh's office. Enough had been said.

"What's the name of the client?"

"Ignat Oblonsky," said Jake as he stood and gathered the few papers he had spread out, with information which Josh did not bother to ask about.

"Geez, Ignat; isn't that a cartoon character?"

"Wouldn't know but he's our bogey until it can be sorted out, and it's for one and a half million, by-the-way."

"Well, that's a lot. How's Jim Parker?"

Jake was glad he finally asked, "Unduly worried, I'm going to take him out to lunch next week and get him away from this."

"Why?"

"To allay his fears," Jake didn't bother to tell him that he was also going to try to help the young man and coach him to a better career.

"Okay, let me know what happens," said Josh as he went back to his emails.

"Will do," and Jake left the office closing the door behind him.

CHAPTER 13

A NEW CAREER

A week later Helen had the first S.A.R. filed and Jake took Jim out to lunch on Lexington Avenue, where he was able to get Jim at ease with the knowledge that the compliance team was behind him working for him in helping to clean up the Oblonsky case. He was relieved. Jake also spoke with him about the financial business. Jake, having started life as a stockbroker, albeit in a different time, was able to relate to cold-calling and the need to generate business. It was a bit different now as the volume of clients per rep was higher and it centered more around sales pitches. It was less about getting to know your client, as it had been when Jake was a broker, and formulating an approach to building an investment portfolio and managing it, sometimes actively aggressive depending on the clients' engagement with the financial markets. It was now more about bringing the client in, selling him life insurance and moving on to the next one, and then circling back and selling packaged investments to those same clients once the rep had his securities license.

Jim felt comfortable with Jake and stopped hiding his, somewhat, dislike for what he was doing. He wasn't trying to hide it from a sales manager now. He was talking with the compliance officer who seemed to know what he was going through and, as Jake had done by giving him study guidance for his securities exam, was trying to help. Receiving Jake's real concern again, Jim felt guilty about failing his securities exam twice and admitted so.

"Sorry Mr. Bowen," said Jim, coming from left field while they were discussing the long hours of cold-calling.

"Sorry about what Jim?"

"Failing the Series 6, twice."

"You didn't study."

Jim liked this man. He didn't mince words and he spoke the truth, and he cared.

"I know. I tried, but I just couldn't get the time."

"Listen, I understand and quite frankly I have a problem with the whole process and how they go about it. They are trying to create financial reps on the cheap without a stipend. Back in 1980 I was paid a thirty-five-thousand-dollar salary as a guarantee. It was also forgivable, so I just needed to concentrate on getting my securities and commodities licenses and building a book of clients; and we didn't sell life insurance, we teamed with an insurance guy for that. It's different here."

"You can say that again Mr. Bowen."

Jake thought of telling him to call him Jake and stopped. The young man attributed a guiding strength to Jake by addressing him by his surname, so Jake left it that way. He needed to get this kid, as he saw him, on the right path and financial sales was not it.

"Jim, let me ask you this, because I'm curious. What do you dream of doing when you're daydreaming? We all daydream."

He looked at Jake as though he had been waiting a long time for someone to ask and he had been barely able to hold it back for all that time.

"I think a lot about flying an airplane, you know, an F-16 like the Blue Angels fly or even a large airliner, just so I'm in the air."

Jake felt a rush of adrenaline and a knowing grin came to his face.

"Let me ask you this: why didn't you ever pursue it, you have a college degree?"

"I don't know, I guess I was afraid of failing."

"Well, you're failing here."

"I know."

"That's the first step, to admit it. Do you know why?"

"I don't like it."

"For starters yes and I can see that. Your heart is just not in it and your heart is just not in it because you are not a salesman. I would imagine that besides getting stressed over money you are bored repeating the same ol' sales pitch over and over."

"Yeah."

"You think flying would bore you."

Jim's face lit up, "No!"

"What the hell are you waiting for then? You can fly for any branch of the service but if you keep dreaming of the F-16 you need to talk to the Air Force recruiter in Time Square."

Jim hesitated in his response but before he could say anything Jake spoke again.

"Listen, we all fail but hesitation and delay for fear of failure is worse than failing. I've never told anyone in this office this but I'm going to tell you. When I was twenty-six and a stockbroker I was still dreaming of flying," this got Jim's concentrated attention, "Yeah, me. Another broker knew about my love of flying and I was in the process of getting my private pilot's license."

"I didn't know you fly."

"Not now, for many reasons, but at the time I dreamed of flying jets and in particular the A-6 Intruder off of a carrier. I had always wanted to go to Annapolis, since I was seven, and was always on the honor roll in high school with the academy in mind but with Vietnam and other things, that I won't get into, it all went sideways quickly at the end of my junior year."

"Sorry Mr. Bowen."

"Nothing to be sorry for Jim. It was my own fault but this other broker I mention had heard a radio ad for Naval Aviation and that they had upped the age to twenty-six and he let me know."

Jake could see that Jim was now in another world along with him; he could see it in his eyes. He would drag the kid down to the Air Force recruiter if he didn't go on his own.

"To make a long story short, after talking with my father and my manager I decided to go down to Wall Street and see the Navy recruiter. It turned out that my manager had been a carrier pilot, which I knew, but what I didn't know is that he thought I would make a great Naval Aviator when he first interviewed me but never told me. As a result, he bit the bullet and got behind me one hundred percent"

"What happened?"

"Delay happened. I walked into the recruiter in a three-piece suit and the lieutenant behind the desk looked up at me and just said one word, 'jets' and I nodded my head. They had me watch a video of a lot of jet crashes on and off carriers and then asked me, 'do you still want to fly jets?' and 'absolutely' came out of my mouth. I took the test and they had me wait. The lieutenant finally came out somewhat hung-head and said, 'we have a problem'. I would be one week into my twenty-seventh year when I hit primary flight after boot camp. They looked at it every which way and couldn't get around it. My manager even jumped in and called a Marine Corps general buddy of his and no dice, I was done. So, you see; hesitation, for whatever reason, is the final nail in the coffin. You cannot be afraid of failing Jim. You have to go at it one hundred percent with the attitude that you will succeed and 'what if' is not part of your lexicon."

Jim sat there for a second and he was someplace else, and it wasn't sitting in a restaurant on Lexington Avenue. Then he looked at Jake with an intensity Jake had never seen in him before, "I'm going to go to the recruiter, I'm going to fly…"

"Don't worry about what's going on here, we're taking care of that for you. You don't need to tell anyone until you have signed up and are ready to go. Let me know if you need anything from me," Jake hesitated and looked Jim straight in the eyes, "I don't mean to be a selfish bastard but you are taking a little piece of me along with you and I appreciate it. I wanna know how you're doing along the way."

Jake knew that this put extra pressure on the kid but just enough to know he had someone betting on him to get into the cockpit of an F-16.

With a show of growing confidence and resolve Jim agreed that he would stay in touch with his compliance officer as he progressed towards his goal. Mr. Bowen was now more than a compliance officer to him. He had been more right from the start with his help on the securities exam, but now it was way more.

When they returned from lunch Jim headed towards his cube in the Bullpen and Jake headed towards Helen's office.

Helen's door was open, and she looked up as he stood on the threshold of the doorway, "How was lunch with Parker?"

"It was good," he said as he walked in shutting the door behind him and then taking the seat in front of Helen's desk as she looked on quietly for a second.

"Something's up."

Jake grinned, "Mr. Parker has been coached out of the business."

"Geez, how'd you do that?"

"It was simple, he's always known what he really wanted to do; no one ever helped him with it."

"And what's that?"

"The Air Force."

Helen laughed, "Oh, Josh will love that one too."

"He won't know till Parker's already signed up and ready to walk out so it stays with just you and me. I won't let June know either and she'd agree with that. She lets things slip once and awhile without thinking about it."

"Got it. I also have something else for you," she said as she picked up a FedEx envelope from her side of the desk and handed it over. "It's from the international investigation group you mentioned."

"That fast!?"

Jake opened the envelope and read the letter then glanced over an attached report and the papers along with it. With a broad grin and shake of his head he looked up at Helen when he finished skimming the report, "Our boy Ignat is still with us. The idiot used his US passport to cross the Russian border after he was dead."

Helen laughed, "Nice trick."

"Yeah, well it gets better," Jake said as he tossed the report to Helen, "the body that the local investigator viewed turned out to be a John Doe who had gone missing a year ago."

"Cold storage?"

"Oh, that's cold."

"What next?"

"They'll set up an interview with Mr. Parker now and try to interview Nadia as well, unless she's in the wind; they notified her of the corpus delicti."

"What?'

"They have proof of potential fraud and they let Nadia know that the body in Kharkiv is not Ignat's," he said pointing and looking at the papers now in Helen's hands.

"Oh swell, so she'll be gone."

"Unless she's just plain greedy and thinks she can explain this one away. I really don't think they thought of international investigators being engaged."

"How can she explain a ghost crossing into Russia with a passport?"

"That would be interesting and there's a chance she might stay and try to explain, as I say. One point five million would go a long way in the Ukraine. They'd live like kings."

"King Ignat," grinned Helen.

"Funny. Now I've gotta brief Josh on this and set Mr. Parker up for handling the interview without getting nervous," he said as he pushed himself up out of the chair. "I'll need that report too, you can go through it later."

Next Jake found himself standing in front of Marsha trying to get time with Josh.

After looking at her computer calendar for a matter of seconds, she looked up and said, "I don't see anything until tomorrow."

"Just tell him, 'Ukraine', and that he needs to see me," he told her, and then thanked her and headed back to see Jim Parker.

Jake pulled Parker out of the Bullpen and into a small conference room and locked the door.

"Okay Jim, the investigators are back to us already with their initial report on the Oblonskys. Ignat Oblonsky's body was not found and they found activity on his passport after the declared death," said Jake while he remained standing after Jim took a chair.

Looking a bit nervous Jim hesitated, "What happens next?"

"They are going to set up an interview with you to get the facts behind the case. Just answer their questions simply; short and direct. Do not elaborate and give them more than they ask for. How did you feel when you were presented with a case right off the street for a million five?"

"Excited."

"That is your answer only. Did you think it strange that you would get such a large case like that without ever having spoken with the client other than their call to you?" Jake asked in a tone other than his own.

"Yes, I never experienced anything like that before."

"Good answer, keep it simple. Do not get into a discussion about possibly having reported this. You are too new to the business. 'You never experienced anything like that before' is the answer. Any reevaluation after the fact is conjecture, don't go there. You did what you were supposed to do. As far as the potential money laundering, you wouldn't necessarily see that as we didn't and they won't know to ask about that anyway. They'll only ask you about the policy purchase and information around it. I'm going to see if I can sit with you during the interview but if I can't you'll be fine."

"Glad you think so."

"Don't worry about it, you are not the criminal here; Ignat and Nadia are the criminals, remember that."

"I will."

"On another note, when are you seeing the recruiter?"

"Tomorrow."

"Okay, good. We'll take care of this and then look forward to getting you headed towards airplanes."

Jim beamed with this and all of the angst and concern that Jake had seen on his face, when he grabbed him from the Bullpen, was gone.

"I envy you in a good way. You are young, healthy, educated and bright; and you want it and I know you will be competitive once you are in the right atmosphere. You are perfect for pilot training. Don't worry about having not studied for the securities exam when you start on your new path. You were not focused here. You were just trying to survive financially in a salesman's position; your heart wasn't in it. You will be focused when you get into training with the Air Force. You will find reserves and concentration that you never thought you had because that is what you want. You are lucky you found it when you did."

"With your help."

"Nah, you knew it all along, you just needed someone to remind you and tell you to reach for the ring and take the chance."

"How can I thank you Mr. Bowen?"

"Ah, you will. I get to ride along from afar and watch you become a pilot. Just send me a postcard every once and awhile and let me know how you're doing." Jake also knew that if he was part of Jim's conscious and Jim 'reported' to him, as he worked through the pilot training program, Jim would hang tougher, even if just a little bit more, with him in the background. He also knew that Jim knew that he could contact Jake if he needed moral support as they thought similarly about flying.

"Will do."

"Okay, let's get out of here before the Bullpen hens think you are in trouble and the gossip mill starts up."

Jim nodded with renewed energy and a self-assured attitude as he got up and followed Jake out of the small conference room.

Back in his office Jake saw a shadow move quickly against the frosted glass wall that represented the front of his office, just in time to be able to look right at Josh when he appeared at his door as though he were in a hurry. The man would do this whenever he was upset with him, he had discovered.

"What's Ukraine? I need to know before you do anything."

Jake looked up with a grin and did not say a word for a good five seconds then, "The Ukraine is where our dead client seems to have resurrected himself and I don't understand what you mean by doing anything before you know. Know what? You may want to close the door and take a look at this," he said as he picked up the contents of the FedEx envelope and handed it to Josh.

Josh closed the door behind him and remained standing, he would never sit in Jake's office. As he looked down at the papers Jake handed him, with some confusion on his face, Jake gave him the quick Cliff Notes version.

Looking up stunned, after skimming the report and the attached papers, "What do we do now?"

"Nothing, they'll want to interview Mr. Parker next."

"Am I in trouble?"

Jake, hesitating again, hearing this man reveal his true character, replied, "No one is in trouble and Mr. Parker will handle the interview just fine."

"How do you know that? I've never been involved in anything like this."

"How do I know what? That no one is in trouble or that Mr. Parker will handle his investigative interview?" Jake threw the word 'investigative' into the sentence just for Josh. He found he was baiting him and didn't realize it for a second. Then he clarified the situation as Josh remained frozen, "No one did anything wrong except the Oblonskys.

We did everything right and Mr. Parker did everything right. Your office is solid so don't worry about it."

"I don't need things like this."

"Well, that's why you have me and my team, to protect you from things like this because they will happen in the New York market and you want to be in the New York market," said Jake, giving him a pill of comfort.

"Okay, but I don't like this," said Josh as he handed the papers back.

"No one does."

"When does Parker take his securities exam again?"

"He has thirty days cooling off before we can open another exam window."

"Can you help him with that exam again, we need to keep him."

Automatically baiting him again, "Why do we need to keep him? If he fails again it will be a hundred and eighty day cooling off period. He will be well past the company cut-off to meet licensing requirements before the next test window, even without that hundred and eighty days if he fails again. You may want to consider coaching him out."

"We need him for our Diversity and Inclusion number and home office will let us keep him past the deadline. They need that number as much as we do."

"Why do they need that number? We're talking about dragging a young man along on possibly the wrong path."

"Whaddaya mean wrong path? And we need him here because it is the thing to do. What's your problem!"

"I guess I'm just an old White guy."

"What does that mean?"

"I don't know, I'm taking your lead on that one. 'The Constitution was written by White men', whatever that means."

Josh froze for a moment, "Well, they weren't minorities, they didn't understand. Like the Aryan types at my country club."

Jake's ears felt like falling off, for a bright man Josh Pearlman was really not an educated man, he thought; and God help us, this generation and those following seemed to have less and less exposure to history, basic civics and reality.

"These guys walk around my country club in groups like they own the place," continued Josh in the vacuum of Jake's thoughtful silence.

"What are Aryans?"

"You know, Nazis."

"You have Nazis at your country club?"

"Yeah, well, you know what I mean."

"Not really, I thought we finished the Nazi's off in '45."

"What?"

"The end of the war, you know WW two."

"Oh, that."

"Yeah, it was sort of a big deal for my parents and their friends. We got rid of those book burners."

"Well, they're conservative."

"Oh, then they must be rednecks if not Nazis," Jake couldn't help himself.

"Sort of."

"So why are you a member?"

"Because it's the best club in the state."

"Oh, okay. They must have a nice pool."

"I never use the pool."

"Well, that's a waste, don't you think."

"Where are you going with this?"

"Just want to know why you'd expose yourself and your family to a bunch of Nazis."

Josh had an air of superiority that followed him around and the man seemed not to know it. He had no answer and Jake decided to back off. It wasn't worth it. He had already approached Josh with the notion that it might be a nice gift to give his employees one day at his club's pool as the previous manager had done with the staff, inviting them to an office day at his club. That was the highlight every year for the staff with the previous Director but Josh would never let them amongst the Aryans, that was reserved just for him.

"Not to get off this tantalizing subject but we as well have what appears to be a money laundering scheme along with this false death claim, as I told you the first time that we discussed this."

"Yeah, yeah, a 'sare' or something like that."

"Very good, yes. We filed the Sar and home office is investigating as well, and upon further review, from our end, there is no deniability."

"What do you mean deniability?"

"It's money laundering. I would also like access to a broader spectrum of emails in this office as I'd mentioned before."

"No, I don't even want this to get out, let alone have you start meddling with our clients' email."

"Josh, they will not know we are reading the email unless something pops up in them that is harmful to this office. The filters don't pick up everything."

"No!"

"Suit yourself but home office may recommend it once they conclude their investigation."

"I don't see why."

Jake knew there was nothing more to say, he would also save Mr. Parker's enlistment news for another time.

"Let me know what happens with the Ukraine," said Josh as he turned, opened the door and simply left.

"God," whispered Jake as the shadow passed his window in the direction from which it had come.

CHAPTER 14

THE RUSSIANS

He picked up the phone and dialed a four-digit extension and waited two rings before it picked up on the other end, "June, we have news on Parker's case from the Ukraine, I'll be right over and fill you in," he said and then hung up as soon as she acknowledged it.

Stepping into her doorway, with the FedEx documents back in the FedEx envelope, Jake saw June's head lift up as she looked over her computer screen at him. She looked worried.

"Nothing to worry about," he said while lifting the FedEx envelope above his head and closing the door behind him as he entered.

He took a seat in the chair next to her desk, looked at her and grinned, "The man still breathes."

"Uh-oh."

"No uh-oh, he appears to be alive and well."

She still didn't say a word after a few seconds.

"It's okay June. Mr. Parker did everything right he just got picked for his inexperience and didn't realize it; you can read this," he said as he handed June the envelope.

She took it gingerly, as though it were a bowl of water ready to spill, while Jake went into a brief synopsis of the events contained in the brief, and as soon as he said, "... and the guy crossed the Russian border with his U.S. passport after he was dead," June's eyes bugged out.

"Russians!?"

"Russia; don't worry, it's not the mob," assured Jake almost tempted to get a little more out of June's paranoia with regard to the Russian mob by purposely rattling her cage productively.

"Oh. What about the, ...body?"

"Oh; in the morgue, the missing guy?" he couldn't resist just a little more for development's sake, "Turns out he was a guy who went missing a year earlier and they figured the mob got him. A little do-re-mi and he becomes I. Oblonsky." He could see June getting nervous, "This isn't the workings of the mob but one single guy and his wife who wanted to have a moat and an Olympic pool in the Ukraine. One point five million would've taken them a long way."

"What happens next?"

"They'll interview Mr. Parker and all will be well. Don't worry about this. I just want you to concentrate on what you're doing and watch for strange investment movement."

"What about their money laundering?" asked June.

Jake knew where she was headed with the question. "Not our problem, it was clumsy and Mr. Oblonsky may be in trouble with other people other than us. Sometimes problems take care of themselves," alluding to Ignat's disappearance, "and the Sar Helen filed will put it in corporate's lap," and he saw June's face change again as she put it together.

"Anything we may find with regard to Russian money laundering falls right into Latham's lap as well. We put the pieces together and deliver it to them. June, these guys are not going to mess with us, it isn't like the movies," he said trying to stop her from fixating on the Russian mob although he had partially instigated it.

She looked at him and nodded and then added, "I found a peculiarity in one of the Russian accounts."

'Oh great,' he thought but waited for June to continue on. He now knew that this was part of the reason for her nervousness.

"They're day trading utilities."

"Are you serious?"

"Look at this," she said as she slid a page from the daily trading blotter across the desk to Jake, "I was just going to call you on it. This isn't the only one, but I wanted to see more than just one day before I spoke to you."

"Crap, Integration" said Jake looking down at the trade blotter where she had highlighted both a buy and a sell of utility ETF's under the same name, and without looking up he asked, "How many days do you have of this and how many trades?" Then he looked up to get her answer.

"Ten, on and off over the past sixty days. We didn't really notice them as they were split up, but there is a pattern."

"Why didn't we at least pick this up on potential churning of the guy's account?"

"It just got buried behind OTC review and options review."

"The innocuous coupled with bad systems. Okay, let's pull trading on this account and the other Russian clients of these two reps. Well, I guess that would be all of our Russian clients, over a dozen not just those on our watch list. Make sure you get the top three on the list first, then the following five on the list before looking at the remaining Russians. I know it's a lot but let's go back six months and see what we can see."

"Okay, I can pull that all up in an hour," she assured him in a hesitantly nervous voice.

"Don't worry June."

"Yeah, well things seem to be happening all at once."

"It's just your attention to detail and sensitivity to the Russians."

"Yeah, well they're Russians."

"Yup. We'll find what we need, dial in Josh and then let Latham do the dirty work. Go back those six months," he said as he pushed himself up out of the chair next to her desk, grabbing the FedEx envelope in front of her, "and let me know when you have it and we'll take a full look at what we've got."

"Okay."

"Open or closed?" he asked as he started to exit her office.

"Open is okay."

He headed over to Helen's office, still carrying the FedEx envelope with the letter which June did not even get to pull out before she froze.

He stopped at the threshold of the door and looked in as she looked up and held her gaze. He then stepped in, closed the door behind him and took a seat in front of her desk.

"Just told June about 'the body' and the dead guy crossing into Russia," he said as he put the FedEx envelope on Helen's desk.

"I bet that went over well," she said with a grin.

"Yeah, as you would expect. I want you to keep the paper file on this one. Scan the letter and send me a copy."

"Will do."

"Oh, one more thing."

"Uh-oh."

"That's what June said about the body then she dropped some aggressive churning activity on me."

"Oh crap."

"That's what I said."

"Russians, laundering?"

"You bet, but the really good part is that they are doing it with utility ETF's for integration into the system. Pretty clumsy way of starting to launder except it is not trading that would readily catch our eyes."

"Geez, how did June look when she told you this?"

"Much as you'd expect."

"Eyes bugging out like the Russian mob was on her doorstep."

"Yeah, to a degree. And I just couldn't help myself, and she could use a little cage rattling and then a reprieve. I put a little gas on the fire before she told me. I think I calmed her though. I shouldn't do it too much but I think she sees it coming when I do."

Helen laughed, "Ah, it'll toughen her up."

"Yeah, just an old White guy trying to be funny."

"Yeah, and I bet they profile you at the airport."

"Don't laugh, they do. I'm just an OWG target. They need to show off that they are actually trying to protect everyone by patting me down and swiping my hands for explosive residue every time I go through TSA. Last time, as the guy was going through his speech about patting me down in the rear and the groin, I said, 'it's okay I'm an old White guy and I've heard it before', he laughed and said he knew but he had to say the whole thing anyway."

"You're kidding."

"No, I should get award points for every pat down I get. Never saw anyone in TSA around me get the same treatment. Hell, I don't think I look that scary."

"It depends," said Helen with a comical grin.

"Thanks for being on my side."

"I can't help it. I laugh every time I think of that tall young blonde in the piano club that was seated next to you."

"Oh, you liked that."

"It was funny when she said, 'and they have to sit me down next to an old guy', and on top of it you couldn't hear her and had to ask me what she said. Now that was funny."

"It was sort of funny but I had to put her in a cab and get her back to her room at the end of the night after all those martinis."

"Ah, your civic duty to step in and no one would accuse you of sexual harassment."

"Geez thanks, that's setting a low bar these days. I remember help-ing a young woman when I was young and almost got my leg broken," commented Jake looking out the window in a stare back in time.

"How did you do that?" asked Helen, bringing him back to the present as he broke his stare out the window and looked back at her.

"I was young and stupid. I thought I was Sir Galahad. I was a stockbroker at the time and stopped into a bar in Fort Lee, New Jersey one night on my way home from work. I had left my car in Fort Lee to get the bus which I never did. Anyway, I stopped into this place, and I'd never been there before. I was minding my own business at the end of this u-shaped bar, having a Johnnie Walker, near the door when I noticed these three guys my age hassling this young woman, to the point of aggression, at the other end of the bar to the side. The bar was empty except for us and I could hear every word they said. Well, I told them to leave her alone which wasn't so clever," he had Helen's curious attention as she never heard anything like this from her 'boss'. "They told me to shut up and mind my own business. You would think that that would do the trick and I'd shut up but I didn't. I persisted and told them to leave the girl alone. Next thing I knew they had me out in front of the place on the ground. Three young mob guys I would figure out later. Anyway, they had my right leg over the curb as they held me down and they kept smacking it on the edge of the curb trying to break it and they couldn't. I drank a lot of milk when I was a kid," grinned Jake. "So, I do the next brightest thing and start laughing because they can't break my leg."

Helen just stared at him with a wince knowing her 'boss' would have done something like this to help someone but she had never imagined it happened, "My God, what did they do?"

"They finally gave up, called me some names and went back into the bar. Geez, that leg bugged me for a couple of years after that. I think it was the bullying I got in grade school and high school that made me step in."

"How's that?"

"In both cases I was the new kid in town and the one who always raised his hand and had the answers. I answered questions knowing it would get me in trouble but it bothered me that no one else was answering and hell, I knew the answers."

"Uh-oh."

"Yeah, well, I just couldn't help myself on knowing the answers. The first time, in grade school, the older bully and his younger brother Billy, who was my age, called me names and said they'd find me after school. They did the first time and not too far from the school. I remember a circle around us as Billy's older brother taunted his younger brother to hit me. We tussled and that's where I learned to hit. I remember dodging them once after that first time and going home the long way through deep snow. They finally gave up. In high school it was these two tough guys who called me names and threatened to beat me up after school because I was new and knew the answers. They were big guys," Jake continued to speak as Helen listened with rapt attention, "and I was nervous. I even spoke to my father about it. He asked me what I wanted to do and I told him I would have to handle it. He just told me to hit quickly and first if it was coming to blows and that might end it."

"Whad you do?"

"Hit first. They approached me after school. They were what we called greasers with their sleeves rolled up to their armpits and a cigarette pack tucked into one of the rolls and a cigarette behind the ear when they weren't on school grounds. Let's put it this way, they didn't do very well on the SAT's."

"So, what happened?"

"I hit the biggest one of the two as they came towards me. I leaned into it and he went down. The other guy backed away. Within minutes they wanted to be best friends and I never had a problem after that. I had one football player, a big lineman, who would come up to me and ask me if everything was all right on occasion after he'd heard about it; he became my guardian angel the rest of high school. It's all just learning how to fit in, socialize and survive. I would not have traded either of those situations and I am so glad that I experienced them and was left to figure them out on my own. I remember being scared at the time but it made me stronger and made me the guy who stepped in when those guys were giving that woman trouble."

"I never would have imagined that happening to you. I guess I would if I think about it and peal back some years. That's why June trusts you. She can see that guy who almost got his leg broken to protect someone else. Maybe you were a little wild too," and she smiled.

"Now it's getting embarrassing. June just has no choice but to trust both you and me, and I was pretty boring back then," he grinned.

"What about the utilities?"

"These people are actually churning ETF's, and utility ETF's at that. And like I say, our great up-to-date systems did not flag one. It'll flag things like different load mutual funds in the same account or C-share mutual funds in educational accounts where it's a judgment call, all because FINRA has its knickers in a knot over this stuff, instead of filtering for unobvious ways of laundering money."

"Knickers?"

"Yeah, you know, underwear."

"What century was that?"

He just stared at her for a second, "Geez, I guess grand kids would have come in handy to remind me to update my vocabulary and phraseology."

She laughed, "Oh, I like that."

"June's going back six months on this account, along with the other Russian accounts. We should get a pretty good picture. I guess another Sar may be in order."

"I hang around you and June and get to experience the things in this business that I've only heard about. You going to ask Josh to personally file this one?"

"Funny. He'll probably think that we're out to get him this time."

"Why don't you wrap Jim Parker's imminent departure around it and see what happens."

Jake grinned, "Don't give me bad ideas. But they will be announced close to each other. Let's let one settle in before we clobber him with the next. The guy's seeing Nazis."

"What?"

"Not worth the explanation. I'll let Josh know about Parker's trek towards the wild blue yonder after the investigators interview him on the Oblonsky saga."

"You speak in tongue."

"Oh, wild blue yonder, Air Force. It's their song."

"Wanna sing a couple of bars."

He looked at her with a grin, "Maybe I'll conclude my notification to Josh with my rendition of the song, it's very stirring."

"Well, I need to be there."

"I wouldn't leave you out. I just want to get the kid through the interview and off to the Air Force where he belongs."

"One success!?"

"You might say. You know this guy plays with people for his own ends. He wants to be the golden boy for 'diversity and inclusion' in the home office. It gets him things and he knows that he can push the envelope on other issues which have to do with lining his pockets; it's more than just patronizing and feeling good about himself."

"We are cynical aren't we!"

"I just can't help myself," he said with a closed grin. "It reminds me of Malcolm X."

"Who?"

"Malcolm X. He was a civil rights activist and member of the Nation of Islam when I was a kid. He was pretty fiery and aggressive, and professed violence that scared the hell out of me as a kid. There seemed to be too much violence in his talk for a kid my age but he did say, 'the worst enemy that the Negro has is the white man that runs around here drooling at the mouth professing to love Negros and calling himself a liberal. It is following these white liberals that has perpetuated problems that the Negroes have', and he went on to say, 'If the Negro wasn't taken, tricked or deceived by the white liberal, then Negros would get together and solve our own problems.' And he went on from there."

"Negro, wow, he said that with that word? How can you recall all of that?"

Jake laughed, "I just remember speeches and what people say when it strikes me a certain way; and I remember poems and sonnets, don't ask why and sometimes it can be a curse. I read this speech years later as an adult while remembering how he scared me as a kid so every word of the speech stuck. Yeah, and 'Negro' was the word used back then. Even though the man scared me as a kid and professed violence he was right in many ways, as Martin Luther King would agree, and he knew that Welfare was not a help but a yoke."

"What happened to him? I never heard of him."

"He was shot."

Just remembering to bring up something that had been on her mind Helen changed the subject, "You heard about the LGBTQ museum field trip for the 'diversity and inclusion' gang didn't you?"

"No, what's that? L-G, what?"

"The Museum of Gay and Lesbian Art in SoHo. I'd never heard of it either but they found it."

"Who's they, the 'diversity and inclusion' committee?"

"Yes, and leadership."

"I'm part of leadership."

"You're an OWG, they're not going to invite you."

"How do you know this and I don't?"

"I overheard the CFO and the COO talking about LGBTQ, and the museum, when I went into the kitchen; they were pretty shocked by what they saw," she said with a laugh. "Don't you know that compliance is the last to be informed about anything in this office."

"You're starting to like this acronym thing aren't you."

"Yeah, it sorta fits the environment. I don't care about not being told about this but it's the other stuff they don't tell you."

"Ah, we're the cops don't you know. We may be the police but they still don't understand that we protect the masses. They will if the proverbial shit hits the fan on something big that's kept from us. This office is like a mine field sometimes."

"Sure is different from the way it was before Josh got here."

"I would have liked to have worked with that Director, he sounds like my type of guy: pragmatic and real."

"He was, and a lot different from what we have now."

"Well, we need to work with what we have been bequeathed."

"It's not quite a gift."

"But he was under the wing of the last Director then left behind when he retired, or passed into the sunset shall we say," he said as he started to push himself up out of the chair, "Get together with June within the next hour and formulate the information for this new Sar so we can get it started and then we'll let her file it; it'll be a good experience for her. I'll see if I can get an audience with the guiding light."

"You're getting too poetic for me. Just don't start playing Sir Galahad, we need you walking and talking right here."

He grinned, "I'm not going anywhere. Now to try to get in to see him," he said as he stood next to the now empty chair then turned and headed out the door to Josh's office and Marsha the gate keeper."

———

"Marsha, I need to see him."

"He's busy, Jake."

"It's important. We have to do something required by law immediately and he wants to know before we do anything."

She picked up the phone immediately, seeing the feigned desperation on Jake's face. A little theater never hurt he thought as she let Josh know that he was there with something urgent.

The man was standing at his computer again when Jake entered. Jake stood off to Josh's left, by the small conference table, until Josh recognized that he was there.

"What's so important? I'm pretty busy and have an interview in twenty minutes," he said still looking at his computer screen and typing.

"It won't take long. We are in the process of putting together another Sar report and will notify home office before it's filed."

Josh stopped and turned, "I thought we weren't going to do this again."

"Do what again?" Jake couldn't help himself; he liked his version of the Socratic method with Josh.

"File one of these things, this sare."

"Yeah, well that would be nice and I'd like nothing better but we have a Russian client churning utility ETF's and there may be more than just one."

"Russian? Doing what?"

Josh was, all of a sudden, a bit more nervous as Jake got his full attention.

"Churning ETF's."

"What's that?"

"He's buying and selling the same ETF, which is liquid like stock, almost like a day trade as more money comes into the account; just under ten thousand dollars in each case with very little commission."

"That's not a lot of money. And what does that mean anyway?"

"Well, it is a pattern of layering and integrating the money into the system and he may be doing it with other firms besides us. He moves the money in, invests it and it comes out the backside a day or two later as investment return of capital plus gain or loss and minus the small commission. This is a simplified explanation, but it establishes the activities that require a Sar."

"It doesn't sound like a big deal," said Josh giving Jake a questioning look, "and we don't want to upset the Russian clients."

"What do you mean?"

"You know, the Russians, just don't want to upset them too much."

"Do you know something that I don't?"

"No, but they are bringing money into the agency with some nice life policies."

"And that could be another issue. I really would like to be able to have access to more of the warehoused emails coming from chosen clients."

"You mean the Russians."

"Right now, yes, and this brings up another topic. Leadership traveled to a museum in SoHo like it was a class trip and as a member of leadership I was the only one not informed. It's not the museum that I care about but the mindset to pick and choose what you inform me about that the rest of leadership knows."

"That museum was shocking," said Josh trying to change the subject. "My hairdresser is gay and I told him that I visited the museum and how great it was and he made no comment. You would have thought he'd be pleased. I don't understand."

Jake could not believe what he was hearing, both the contradiction and the obvious patronizing, besides Josh trying to change the subject knowing full well that he purposely did not inform him. The guy insulted his hairdresser with his patronizing superiority and did not get it. He didn't get a lot when it dealt with other people outside of his immediate circle.

"Maybe he was just too pleased to say anything but getting back to my point, you need to dial us into everything that leadership is dialed into. Sometimes the innocuous can have hidden dangers."

"I don't want you reading more emails than the ones you can access without authority," he said changing the subject once again.

"I can only tell you that my hands will be tied to a degree."

"Well, we're doing okay without you having carte blanche with our clients' mail."

"Well, it's our mail, we are a securities firm of sorts and we've been lucky so far to stop what we needed to stop. Who knows what else is going on that we can't see."

"What do you mean 'of sorts'? We are actually a financial planning firm and the preeminent firm in New York."

"Preeminent with regard to what?"

"What do you mean?"

"What are we the best at?"

"Financial planning."

"We sell life insurance and mutual funds in different forms. The only filled in fact-finder that I've seen in this office, so far, was filled in with stick figures and little sailboats and other doodles. I take it the client was boring in this particular case."

"We have managed accounts."

"Thank God we don't, at least not by anyone in here anyway. We have managed accounts that are managed by home office plugging in mutual funds at an exorbitant cost to the client."

"Well, that's not right."

"It would appear that it isn't right but on a better note, Mr. Parker is going to have his insurance investigation interview then he is out the door to the United States Air Force." Jake couldn't hold it back and he also wanted to wake Josh up a little.

"What are you talking about?"

"I coached Mr. Parker out of the business."

"You what?"

"He's going to do what he wants to do and that's fly airplanes."

"He can't do that."

"I think he'll make the grade and be damned good at it; it's in his heart."

"I don't care what's in his heart, he belongs here. He's part of my number."

"What number?"

"My diversity number!"

"Do you know anything about the guy?"

"Of course I do, and that's why he'll make a good financial planner."

"He's barely hanging on with the life insurance production demands we make and the lack of supporting pay. Hell, the guy can't even afford to go to the doctor if he needs to, and that's another problem with our lack of proper compensation and this great medical system we have. He wants to fly and the Air Force will take care of all of that for him."

"What do you mean our 'great' medical system? That sounds sarcastic," said Josh changing the subject from compensation.

"It's not sarcasm, it's reality. It's too expensive but everybody needs it."

"We have the best medicine in the world and it will cost for the best. We have sheiks and people from all over the world flying in here for our medicine so what are you talking about?"

"That's just the problem, the average American is not a sheik and can't afford it like you can."

"I'm not a sheik and our staff have insurance."

"You're pulling seven figures out of this office; it is expensive to the rest of us. That monster malpractice along with non-paying patients with no forwarding address have run the price up beyond comprehension. We ran fifty-four billion dollars in unneeded medical tests in this country last year just as an example."

"What do you mean unneeded and where did you get that from?"

"It was in the Wall Street Journal; I try to keep up. Doctors are protecting themselves from any liability by running every test in the book, in some cases when they know it's not needed. They call it Zebra hunting."

"What? Well, I'm sure they were needed."

"When I was a young stockbroker, I could pay my medical out of my own pocket it was so reasonable."

"I doubt that."

"I broke my hand in 1981 and saw three docs in the local ER. The ER doc, an orthopedic and a radiologist. They took some pictures and put on a half cast and I paid the eight-five-dollar bill when I walked out. That translates to about two hundred and sixty dollars today. I don't think I could get out of an ER today on the smallest of injuries for under two or three thousand dollars. God help us if a national health disaster hits us like a pandemic, which we are overdue for. We will feel the punch. Americans have not as a whole exercised their need to engage in preventative and maintenance medicine as other developed counties have which puts our population at higher risk and costs more in the long run. We are just short of having catastrophic coverage only."

"That all can't be right." The man would never get it even though he acted the part of the defender of the lower classes, or anyone below him in the financial stratum.

"I guess not but Mr. Parker will have his covered by the US government shortly and excelling at something he will be good at. He's not a salesman."

"He's a financial planner and he really shouldn't leave."

"I don't know what to tell you but if you keep dragging these kids along towards doom because of the color of their skin it will come back to bite you. This will happen if doing the right thing doesn't start to register with you."

"That's racist and what do you mean come back and bite me?"

"At some point one of these kids will just not fit into the sales environment like most White kids we bring in don't fit into it. Except, unlike the White kids who are not built for this business, they will be kept here and start to feel looked down upon because they are not succeeding. And then you may have a lawsuit stating racial discrimination as the primary accusation. Feel lucky that we just coached one young man in the right direction."

Josh stood stock still and looked at Jake with fire in his eyes, "I disagree," he said in a way that told Jake he should not be speaking his mind.

"Listen Josh, you have preached to the leadership team that you want the truth and you want people to speak up. Well, I'm an old school pragmatist who cannot just stand by and I will speak up for everyone's benefit."

"Maybe you need to watch what you say."

Jake could feel the anger coming from Josh, but, again, what's the worst he could do, fire him. What Jake did not know for sure, but had a suspicion of, was that Josh was nervous about a lawsuit if he let Jake go as Jake was an 'old guy'. Josh was frightened of an age discrimination lawsuit not understanding that Jake was not of that ilk. Jake would never sue. Jake would always remember the time he was run over in fourth grade by a woman speeding in the school parking lot. Jake had walked out from behind a school bus, after he and another student had returned a cooler to his teacher's car, when he was hit by a baby blue 1956 Ford Fairlane Victoria. He was hit so hard that it split his black trousers and left blue on them, knocking him flat to the pavement before running over his legs. The driver was the mother of one of his classmates and she was drunk. He was up and walking in a day although it ached and he had tread marks across the upper part of his legs that all the kids wanted to see. The doctors said his bones were still soft and he was knocked flat by her speed, which made the tires travel quickly over what was more like a pillow than the hard firm legs that an adult would have. The school principal Mr. Van, a WWII Marine Corps combat vet who was someone everyone looked up to, had visited him at home that night. When he went to court with his father and his father's attorney friend the three of them were on the elevator alone in the court building when his father pushed the emergency stop button which did not have a bell in those days. Both his father and the attorney looked at him. His father explained that the woman was so distraught that she was being sedated and Jake knew that they were poor too. His father then asked his fourth grader what he wanted to do with regard to the suit explaining the possibilities. Jake had simply said, 'I just want the hospital paid for.' He remembered that his father and his father's friend had smiled at each other and then his father said, "Good, I knew you would say that." He then pulled out the emergency stop and they went to court not out for blood. Josh was not of the same generation.

"Josh, I will always tell you the truth whether you like it or not. I just can't help myself," and he grinned to himself.

"But you coached Mr. Parker out."

"He was in a bad place with this fraudulent death claim and I hit the relief valve for him and pointed him in the right direction, and out of this firm. Look at is this way, the aura of the fraudulent claim leaves with him," said Jake knowing this would pacify Josh, not that it really made a difference.

"That's right. Okay. How about the investigator's interview before he leaves, will that be okay?"

"He will handle it well and this whole case will go away."

"Good."

"We are still filing that new Sar. And thinking about this again, you may want to reconsider giving us more email access in case the FBI steps in so that they can see we are thorough and not culpable," he said taking a chance on over disturbing Josh.

"What are you saying is going on here?"

"I gave you the report, three of the Florida Russians we have on the books are on the FBI watch list of known or suspected Russian mobsters," Jake loved using the word mobsters, he could see Josh flinch.

"Okay, okay, okay. Let me know the email accounts you want full access too and I'll authorize it. What happens if they find out?"

"If who finds out?" asked Jake knowing full well who he was talking about, he just wanted the man to finally use the words.

"The Russian mob! What if they find out and get mad?"

"Get mad, we aren't dealing with grade schoolers here. They won't know and if for some reason they thought someone was looking at them they would probably leave quietly. If accused of anything they will probably fight which has been my one and only experience in the recent past."

"And what was that?"

"At another firm we received an article from a European periodical that accused this one client of killing people in Estonia with regard to drugs."

"You're kidding," responded Josh nervously.

"Nope, and the guy would not leave. He said we couldn't drop his account."

"What did you do?"

"We dropped his account."

"What happened?"

"The rep complained and the client put one verbal shot across our bow, like a middle finger salute, and then just vanished, probably with the FBI trailing him as long as he stayed in the States. This can be the problem with some of these guys with money. They have a legitimate US address to open an account with and they may have gotten a green card or, in the occasional case, they have dual citizenship which should not exist for a myriad of reasons."

"How do you know all of this?"

"I read compliance reports along with reported FINRA cases and compliance is a small community, we talk with each other."

"Are we okay?" asked Josh showing real concern for once.

"Yeah, we're good. I'll get you the names of the clients we'd like on the email list for your authorization along with the lookback time spans. Also, I have been given authorization to put Russian translating software on the team's computers. We get 'sideways' emails in Russian."

"What's that mean, 'sideways.'"

"One Russian may write our rep in English accompanied with a previous email in Russian and this is copied to several other Russians and in many cases sent blind."

"How can you tell it is going to other Russians?"

"In the cases where it may have originally gone 'blind copy' we've seen a couple of replies in Russian where they mistakenly hit 'Reply All' at some point. We've kept a list of those email addresses."

"This is getting complicated."

"Not really and the software will help. I've looked at a couple of packages and vetted one with home office."

"Let Doris know so she can order it for you."

"We know where that goes. Quite frankly she won't spend the eighty dollars so I'll buy it on my own."

Josh did not say a word as he knew his CFO was stupidly cheap, but he quietly agreed with her. More money in his pocket. Jake just shook his head. The man would spend two thousand dollars on an office lunch like he was a big spender instead of giving bonuses or raises where due. The employees would smirk to each other at these lunches. He didn't get it, even when they left in larger numbers for other jobs, more so than Jake had ever seen at any place he had worked before. It wouldn't change.

Josh just grinned in a manner which appeared as 'whatever,' which was his usual reaction when he was called out on money and then he'd change the subject to his form of compassion for the recipient.

"So, how's the team doing? Do you need anything? Tell them they're doing a good job."

"They know they are but I'll tell them." Jake could not accept this type of patronizing to avoid an issue and could never take it graciously.

Josh got a little bite from the reply and showed it on his face, unable to hide it.

"Anything else?"

"No. I'll fill you in on Mr. Parker's interview once it takes place, along with his date of departure."

"Fine," said Josh as he walked back to his standing desk and computer as Jake turned towards the door, never having taken a seat.

"I'll close the door behind me," was all he said as he headed for the door and then left.

He headed for Helen's office after nodding his thanks to Marsha.

As he walked in, he saw Helen sitting at her desk looking at a neat pile of finely torn up paper in the center of her desk blotter.

Noticing his presence at her door, but still staring at the pile as though mesmerized, she said, "Finely done, don't you think?" and laughed.

"What is it?"

"Henry. He told me that he left that damned Switch Form on my desk for that large mutual fund position he swapped out." She looked up laughing.

"That's it?"

She nodded her head and they both started laughing. They all hated these Switch Forms. They were annoying to both the clients and the reps as they had to be filled out by the rep and signed by the client every time that they sold one fund in one family of funds and bought into another family of funds. FINRA just did not trust compliance to see churning in an account, although the utility ETF's, that were being churned, had initially eluded them. At least that was the message that FINRA was sending, but the self-regulatory body was doing this as part of the self-legitimization of their existence. After all, they were compensated by the profitability of the brokerage firms because the SEC did not have the resources to have their own oversight arm. Jake appreciated the joke as he looked at the net pile in front of Helen.

"It's a work of art; I don't want to touch it," she stammered between laughs.

Henry was their humor. He was their Lewis Black with a dose of Buster Keaton thrown in, and one of the reps who actually knew what he was doing.

"What's Henry have to say these days besides FINRA is full of it?"

"He calls Phelps and Jenkins Mutt and Jeff and says they both like to play the 'ponies' and try to keep it quiet."

"And what does he mean by that? It's legal. Are they overextended? Then we may have a problem."

"I think it's worse than that."

"How so?"

"He made some passing comment that if they didn't watch it, they'd wind up in Siberia."

"Did you ask him what he meant by that?"

"Of course, but you know Henry. He just smiled at me and walked away."

"Oh, crap."

"Haven't we used that word too many times today?" she grinned.

"Yeah, it comes in threes."

"Whadda ya think?"

"I think we may have a problem with Mutt and Jeff and their Russian clients to compound matters beyond the simple use of ETF's to integrate money into the system."

"Just what I was thinking, but you know Henry; he'll always just give you enough and then move on to something else."

"Yeah, well, we'll have to look a little deeper and I'm going to order that translator software today."

"What about June?"

"Oh God, let's hold off until we have something. We don't need her eyes bugging out more than they are over the utility ETF churning. She'll understand by the time we dial her in. She knows we are cushioning things for her, so that works."

Helen started to laugh, "I can just see her behind her computer working on what she knows we have and then dropping more Russian intrigue on her."

"Would not be fun to see. I think the software and access to emails will help."

"Access to email?"

"Yeah, I scared Josh with the FBI card and he's decided to get us all the emails we want."

"Finally. Oh, I need to tell you something."

"Oh, no."

"It's Josh's tendency to imitate people."

"Who, this time?"

"June, speaking of eyes bugging out."

"Oh, no."

"Yeah, he stopped in earlier to ask if I knew anything about when the interview with Mr. Parker might take place. I forgot to tell you."

"The guy just has to creep around. I told him I'd keep him informed."

"I think he is a bit paranoid that you may be manipulating him."

"Geez."

"Well, he imitated June's nervousness over the fraudulent death claim not that he saw her reaction and I think it was partly to cover his nervousness over it."

"What did he do?"

"He bugged his eyes out, hunkered down and moved his head from side-to-side over-exaggerating June when she gets nervous. He got it down pretty well. I wonder how he imitates you and me behind our backs."

"Yeah, well you can't trust someone like that. He did that with an under five rep who is becoming successful along with our plant guy, who may be gay, and I snapped at him, in a way, without thinking. I like both those guys and I really did not like what he did."

"When was that?"

"Oh, at a leadership meeting a couple of weeks ago. After he did that with both of them, I just said, 'But I like those guys'. They all stopped laughing and it got quiet. I later told him he could not do that."

"Well, it didn't work."

"Yeah, well you can't change a skunk even if you paint over his stripes."

Helen just looked at him for a second, then laughed, "Where did you come up with that, isn't it a tiger?"

"Freudian slip, I just hate that sophomoric need to ridicule people," then he briefly thought, 'Pepe Le Pew.'

"Yeah, well this is who we are dealing with. It's embarrassing. It reminds me of high school, which I'd rather forget."

"You didn't like your high school years?"

"Well, they were okay I just wanted to move on by my sophomore year. I had things to do and too much exposure to Josh type humor. It gets old fast."

"I miss the sports."

"You?"

"Yeah, I wasn't always an old guy."

"I can imagine."

"I came in here to talk with you about our new Sar but let's get the ball rolling on this Russian oversight. I'll take over and complete the Sar with June, with the research she now has and not wait for any email review which might expand this. It'll be a good experience for her to file it as I said. Hell, this'll no doubt tie in with the first Sar. Henry's comment has me worried. We may have two reps knowingly engaged in money laundering for specific reasons. Exciting times," he said with a sarcastic frown. "Put a list together of all the email addresses in the group mails we have going to and coming from Phelps and Jenkins from their Russian clients and get them to Josh as our requested email research. Oh, also, order those emails back six months, I know it's a lot but we can set up a system for fast review." He thought for a moment looking off into the distance, then looking back at Helen, "Anything else you can think of right now?"

"Nope, but I'll see if I can get some more out of Henry."

"Okay, let me see June on the Sar then I'll send a backup note to Josh once I see your list to him. I feel a little bit better now that we have the ball rolling."

"Just so it doesn't run down hill on us."

"Funny woman; see you in a bit," and he turned to head for June's office down the hall.

———

June was concentrating on one of her two screens; with a glare as though she were mad at it, her intensity was so complete.

"June,… June," he said as he knocked on the open door.

Her eyes came up and looked at him while still looking elsewhere for a second or two, "The reps may be working with the Russians and I need to keep that in mind while we work on the Sar, which we should get in soon," she blurted out.

"Geez Radar. Well, yes. You are ahead of me but I was initially going to hold off," he started to say as he closed the door before saying anything else, "I was initially going to hold off on the Sar and discussing, with you, any possible connection with reps until we could read more email but I want to get the Sar in now and it seems you agree," he finished just after the door closed completely with a final click of the door latch. He had once again subtly tried to allay her fear by putting off the inevitable. This time, however, she announced the inevitable before he had a chance. It was progress for her.

"You got the email we need!"

"We'll be getting it. Helen's making a list as we speak," he didn't bother asking her how she knew that he finally got the agreement to get the email he wanted, she just did.

"You know Jenkins has a Land Rover?"

"Where did that come from?" he asked, caught off guard.

"The Russians drive those things," she stated.

"May be, no account for bad choice in quality," he said trying to get her off one of her fixations where her imagination became more creative than was healthy, "Hell, I used to work on a ranch out West when I was in college and they would always say, 'Don't take the Land Rover, it's junk. Take the Jeep or the Harvester…,' when you needed to take a four wheel someplace for a chore."

"Well, it means something to the Russians, they mentioned it a couple of times in the emails Helen gave me for this one client trading utility ETF's," she said looking back at her screen still somewhat fixated.

"They're overrated, the first Land Rover was introduced in 1948 and was simply a Land Rover body put on top of an American Willys Jeep chassis and engine. The first Land Rovers were actually American Lend-Lease Jeeps."

"I guess it doesn't matter then," she was getting somewhat out of her fixation. "How do you know that?" she asked looking up from the screen and directly at him.

"I just know stuff that's unimportant; you just do when you've been around long enough," he said softly, knowing she was now completely back; he thought. Discounting things related to her concerns seemed to work with her.

She shook her head and looked back at the screen. It didn't happen too often but when she went off on a tangent like this, for no reason, Jake was experienced enough to know that her imagination was running wild in a quiet way and that he needed to disrupt it and get her thinking back to reality. It was a strange phenomenon but part of a mind that had the ability to jump forward just a little and predict what was going to be said or what might happen: Radar. She would on occasion over talk Jake with his thoughts just like the character in the movie, but it was something Jake came to appreciate.

"Ya know, they're out to get compliance officers."

"Who? What?"

"The Russian mob…they kill compliance officers."

"Geez June, where did you get that?" she was still fixated and off on another tangent.

"The internet."

"You can't believe much of what you read on the internet and especially in so called social media. They see you looking into certain things online and the systems will start feeding you every piece of information on the subject in a controlled manner and a majority of it is conspiracy nonsense or just plain incorrect. Unfortunately, those platforms are also trying, in many ways, to manipulate the US political landscape to their own liking with adverse influence and manipulation. Corporations have tried their own brand of political manipulation over the generations, mostly with the help of lobbies, but the Googles of the world have cornered the market, literally. Don't believe everything you read online June. The Google platform, for example, evaluates what you look at and assigns you a quality score somewhat like the Chinese social credit system and then controls what you see and, for some, what they say. It's a brave new world we live in."

"Well, I think I read it on Wikipedia. They're factual."

"Geez June, Wikipedia?" he said trying to defuse her destructive paranoia, "I've read a lot of books on history, maybe too many actually, and just for grins have pulled up Wikipedia on some of the subjects that I know well to see what they say; you know it's written by the general public."

"And what do they say?" she asked with concern in her eyes.

"I find in particular that Brits like to re-write the history of WWII, similar to how our history is being re-written at home to suit the needs of a particular group." He shook his head and then thought to himself briefly, 'it's easier to build the past that you want than the future that you need, one clouds over the other; and where are people learning this historical nonsense that they espouse these days if not from the internet and a second-rate educational system.' He thought this while June was contemplating what he had said. She was taking him away from the immediate concerns in the office to thoughts of societal concerns while he was trying to steer her to pragmatic calm.

"Whaddaya mean?"

Good, she was swinging away from her fear, "Well, they will downplay American achievements in the war or just plain take credit for it for themselves and they will downplay their failures or blame it on the Americans, or blame us for something totally contrived. They are re-writing history by small degrees by aggressively using that damned Wikipedia, and YouTube, to do so."

"How do you know?"

"The spelling of honor or favor or harbor with a U on American topics in Wikipedia is a dead giveaway; like H-A-R-B-O-U-R. Or they use 'whilst' all the time. I also ran into two of these jerks when I tried to straighten out a couple of gross exaggerations and cover-ups on Wikipedia and they came back at me, and they were both Brits. There are people out there who spend all of their time on these sites and they know how to manipulate them for their own edification." He thought briefly of the time when he lived in England and he had seen an English father stoop down to his five or six-year-old son in an air museum, point to a manikin in a case wearing a moon suit with the American flag removed and a picture of the lunar surface with the American flag in a shadow and tell his child that that was an Englishman on the moon. Jake had thought briefly, at the time, that he was joking but he wasn't. The 'moon suit lie'. It was a lie by those wanting to re-write history. He would later, at the same airfield museum, get into a discussion about the American Lockheed

C-130 Hercules and the Englishman had become irate with Jake for not understanding that the airplane was British designed and built. Experiences like this made him a sceptic early on, before the internet, of anything that came from the general public. And yet to come would be the World Wide Web morphing into the modern internet of social media. Global warming, Al Gore and Nobel together on the internet was also intriguing these days in a show of overbearing and possibly misleading influence as he had learned about the ill effects of Green House gases and the famines to follow, in 7th grade. This was back in 1968 when he was shown a slide of Florida half underwater as projected by 2050 and taught some of the science of it at the time. He had also learned of the potentially large migrations that would be caused by weather change and famine. They, after all, always had the famines of Biafra on the screen. It was not an unknown problem lacking concern but the fact that the internet treated it as such clouded much that had gone before since its discovery in the latter part of the 19th century, when it was first thought to be benevolent. The internet made it fodder for argument and anger, and the science of global warming, which he had learned about in 7th grade, got lost in the mix and became questionable by too many. Ah, social media and the internet, what a mess; the little moon suit liars had a global audience for themselves while many rational people kept quiet for fear of public castigation and exposure to the gauntlet of idiocy, as he saw it. The internet reminded him of a time when he was in the Boy Scouts on a mountain top sitting with a dehydrated food packet and a crackers and jam pack, and a need for some water for re-hydration of the small food packet. He eyed a clean puddle of water in a depression in the rock surface of the mountaintop and it was fresh as it had just rained that morning. With very little water in his canteen, he saw the puddle clear and fresh and was about to move towards it when another scout tramped right through it lifting all the mud from the bottom, making the water useless. This is what he thought about every time he saw a subject muddied on the internet with extremists from both sides and the confused in the middle.

"What did you do then?" he heard her ask through the distant fog of his thoughts as he came back to reality.

"Threw my hands up, it wasn't worth it; I don't have the time. June, the internet is filled with stupidity, manipulation and grand delusions, and a need by many to manipulate or be heard and Wikipedia and YouTube are two great conduits through which these people can feed lies to the public. The Network news media today is also poor in character and lacks the objectivity and the quality of the traditional Network news of the past. It is culpable in driving people to alternative news on the internet and to what one might call steering news, taking people to information that they want to hear and not what they need to hear. As a result, we will see more ignorant violence in this country," he hesitated and thought, for part of a second, to be careful not to make it worse with June. "Once you open that door you open yourself up to a knowledge minefield and all that it can create. I'm not trying to scare you completely away from the internet or water down the criminality of specific groups and I'm not saying that the Russian mob is not violent, we know that they are and they have supplanted the Italian mob in the US but they are not stupid enough to go after compliance officers, and why would they. To quote a Russian familiar with violence on a grand scale, Stalin once said the greater the catastrophe the easier the deniability. Deniability is an easier way to go too when dealing with accusations. Why use violence on something small that is deniable. Violence would only add credence to the accusations. In the end, don't believe what you read on the internet or simply take it with a large dose of salt."

"But we catch their money laundering," she said as he could tell she was giving into the fact that their reaction might not be extreme.

"On such a comparatively small scale that they just walk off and go elsewhere, employing deniability as they go until the FBI gets them," he finished, feeling that her paranoia and fixation were really abating this time. It was work but worth it.

"What about the Chinese?"

"Geez, what about the Chinese? Have you been reading spy novels lately?"

"No, but that private placement written in Chinese giving them green cards for money; and that girl just did not care that she broke every rule. We found that one in email too, what else are we going to find when we look closer at the Russians?"

"Listen, that deal was bad, plain and simple it did not represent a legitimate EB-5 investment. The girl was completely off the rails and still is probably, wherever she is, and she will get weeded out. That was a bad hire. And with regard to the Russians, we just had that conversation. If we find any money laundering, which it appears we have, we will research it as we are doing, file the proper paperwork and engage home office."

"What is Made in China 2025? And you just mentioned a Chinese social credit system, which I heard about."

He looked at her for a second, "It's the reshaping of Mao's 2049 Century Plan and the social credit system is just the way they keep their population in control. Why are you focusing on that?"

"They want to take over, don't they?"

He hesitated again, "Well, in a manner of speaking, yes," and thinking to himself, '…… they along with Russia.'

"Why would they reshape Mao's plan as you say."

"What have you been reading?"

"I overheard Hooper talking on the phone the other day while I was waiting for some documentation and he was talking about the Chinese using our capital markets to raise money for blacklisted companies which is deadly, he said, and gives them an upper hand. How can they do that?"

He hesitated again, "Because no one is stopping them. They want that capital movement. Listen, Hooper's the most intelligent guy in here and he's going to fling this stuff out in a manner that makes it seem like it's a fait accompli, whatever conclusion he came to about the Chinese while you were sitting there. And you didn't hear the other end of the conversation, unless it was on speaker which he doesn't use."

"Is this why they are changing their plan from 2049 to 2025?" she asked disregarding his softening of Hooper.

"Very good. It is interesting because the Chinese are extremely patient and the reshaping of the Century Plan and cutting it by twenty-four years signals either loss of patience, a decree to the masses or a sure proclamation to the world that they know something we don't or all of the above. Geez June, you have me thinking about this now."

Her eyes just looked at him and waited for a better answer.

"Look, we deal in finance and the policing of legal money movement and investments which is going to intensify anything we hear with regard to organized crime or international intrigue involved with money. We are going to be more sensitive than most and you in particular because you are always in the weeds with this."

"Well, it feels like we're under attack."

"We've always been under attack, whether it's the Italian mob years ago or the Russian mob today or the Japanese of yester year or the Chinese and Russian governments of today."

"I guess you're right."

"Good, let's get this new Sar done and then organize our approach to cleaning up what we have once we find out the extent of it," he said calmly, realizing he had included the Russian government in the conversation without her noticing it and thinking to himself, 'damn, now she has me going.'

CHAPTER 15

LITTLE LUCIA

Jake left June to finish the S.A.R. with what they had in hand along with his concern not to delay and to get the 'ball rolling.' He also left it up to her to add what she deemed necessary and prep it for delivery and transmission. She would email it to home office and overnight the actual paper, as she had done with the first one after Helen had finished with it.

He headed, again, back up the hall to Helen's office.

Stepping into the doorway and grabbing the handle of the open door, for a second, for feigned support, Jake grinned as Helen looked up from her desk.

"How's June?" she asked after a second and seeing that Jake had been, possibly, dealing with her fears.

He closed the door behind him and smiled, "She's seeing Russian mobsters behind every tree and thinks the Chinese are going to do something rash to take over America, and she's got me wondering too."

"You need to get her away from that computer," laughed Helen.

"She knows she gets carried away and I think I calmed her, I have her finishing the Sar and getting it out. It'll keep her focused. Were you able to talk to Henry some more?"

"I walked down after you left and all I could really get out of him were fat jokes directed at me."

"But you're not fat."

"Just his way of trying to annoy me, he likes to do that."

"So, nothing."

"Well, not necessarily. He said Jenkins really can't roll the dice and that Phelps isn't much better. He likes creating intrigue and that's nothing more than maybe saying they like to 'play the ponies' and they're apparently bad at it and may be in hock. He did add something else though. He said, 'perestroika is a bitch', whatever that means."

"Who knows, something other than the fact that they are probably involved with the Russians beyond the average client/rep relationship."

"Yeah, well you know Henry. He'll never tell you. He'll make you work for it."

"Did you get that list to Josh?"

"Yeah, just a little while ago."

"Okay, I'll add on to it later and 'reply all'."

With a little bit of a laugh looking up at Jake, just as she clicked away what she had been reviewing, Helen asked, "And what's this about the Chinese? Did you have the same conversation we had?"

"Oh, she overheard Hooper pontificating about the Chinese manipulating the capital markets for nefarious reasons."

"What?"

"Hooper scared her about the Chinese while she was sitting in his office and he was on one of his marathon phone calls. That Private Placement we had from Lin Loo added fuel to the fire after the fact. She thinks the Chinese are going to take us over."

"Well, that's probably their plan, with the Russians not too far behind. I hope you didn't mention that scary book about warfare."

"No doubt but she feels, from listening to Hooper, that the final play may happen soon with the Chinese and she's got me thinking about that now. And I didn't mention that book."

"Thinking about what?"

"'Made In China 2025'. We discussed it briefly. Why would they say that?"

"They want to be top manufacturing dog in a few years as you said and they are more than on their way there, I agree. They'll probably pull a cyber-attack on our capital transfers at some point," and she grinned"

"Ah, great thought," he said with an agreeing frown, "but this is more than that, getting back to our earlier conversation and that scary book Unrestricted Warfare. I had a professor in college for Chinese Foreign Policy and he set my ship ajar at a young age with regard to the Chinese. The guy was part of the Nixon administration but wasn't into Ping-Pong diplomacy, he was more cautious."

"What? Ping-pong?"

"It's a generational thing, we played them in Ping-Pong. Mao invited the team to China and Nixon jumped at it as an entry to diplomatic relations."

"The team?"

"Yeah, our Ping-Pong team, it's still in the Olympics although overshadowed by Beach Volleyball."

Helen laughed, "Yeah Beach Volleyball; it got me to stop watching."

"I hate it. They seem to break to it every ten minutes, or in the middle of something exciting."

"Well, that about sums it up," she laughed.

"Junk like that has ruined the Olympics. I turned on the 5,000 Meter race to watch two guys who had trained together under a distance runner by the name of Salazar. One ran for the US and the other for Great Britain, but they worked as a team. It was beautiful to watch them set up in the beginning of the race and just as I was waiting for their next move, they went to Beach Volleyball. That's worse than putting Heidi on at the end of a football game."

"Heidi?"

"Ah geez, I am getting old. It's a long story. Anyway, June thinks the Chinese may do something rash short of war and she's got me thinking about it again. They had a hundred-year plan and those people are patient and they use patience to win. Why would they shorten their plan or say they had even if they could? It doesn't fit, thinking about it some more; United Front Policy and all of that," he concluded as though he were having a thoughtful discussion with himself as he looked at the floor near the end of his statement.

"Now you're confusing me."

"It's June's fault," Jake grinned now looking at Helen.

"Yeah, I'm sure. It's this job; it'll make you crazy if it doesn't kill you."

"Yeah," laughed Jake as he finally took a seat in front of the desk, "that's what June's afraid of. We need to review a bunch of email and see what these guys are up to."

"With our new electronic filing system, I'm able to check their case notes too, which I was just taking a look at before you walked in."

"Good idea, I hope they're better than the average, and maybe they did slip up in their notes if they are up to something. Don't get too bogged down with those though, the emails will be our best bet and no doubt we'll get quite a bundle of them."

"Well, there may be a mystery character in the notes that I've looked at."

"Mystery character?"

"Yeah, Lucia. Her name pops up as what I would guess to be another advisor. They'll say 'Lucia mentioned…' this or '…mentioned…' that and what she mentioned is not of great enough importance to really point it out in any kind of notes. And sometimes her name is in a sentence that just doesn't make sense, or there's a number with it that doesn't make sense."

"Geez, are you talking about a code? You've really been reading a number of these."

"Who knows. They aren't sending these notes to anyone it's only for them so maybe they're sticking in reminders for themselves on minor issues. Oh, and it's Little Lucia, forgot about that," added Helen.

The little hairs on the back of Jake's neck stood up, "Can you pull up one of those notes," he said with haste in his voice.

"Yeah, sure," said Helen looking at him nervously, "why the rush, what's with Little Lucia?"

"I knew Lucia," he said without even thinking about it.

"What?" she asked still typing on the keyboard.

"Yeah, she was a synchronized diver and swimmer at the 1939 New York World's Fair."

"What?"

"Little Lucia, why are you looking at me like that?" he stated as though knowledge of Little Lucia was common.

"Well, you've left me behind here a bit," she said as she stopped working on pulling up the notes.

"I sent her a postcard from England a bunch of years back," he said having been jerked back in time to another place by the mention of the name.

"Now this is getting stranger. You're scaring me more than June when she goes someplace else."

"It's scaring me. The odds of Little Lucia showing up in reference to the same person I'm talking about is slim to none but it appears it may have; this is beyond fortuitous."

"I'm still lost."

"Little Lucia is a book about a little girl named Lucia and it was written in the 1920's, and I knew the woman who the book was based on. Who knows if it's the same person, or even the same character, they are referring to."

"This is more than odd if it's the same person, and why would it be?"

"Well, they may not be referring to Lucia herself, but then it may be."

"Who was she besides a synchronized swimmer from the 30's?"

"She had an interesting life. She had an affair with Leslie Howard and she had a fairly comprehensive home library of films she took of Margot Fonteyn on stage because they were friends," he said while looking out the window and thinking.

"Neither of whom I have ever heard of."

"And that is a shame," he said looking back at Helen, "Leslie Howard was a popular actor in his day. You may remember him as Ashley Wilkes in Gone with the Wind. He was killed in 1943 when the airliner he was on was shot down over water by the German Luftwaffe."

"No Kidding. How did you know she had an affair with him?"

"She told me. As I said, I knew her. I became somewhat of a confident of hers in her last years. Knowing about that affair is why I had sent her that postcard from London. I still feel bad about it today," he said looking out the window again.

"Why?"

Looking back at Helen, "Because I was going to stop by and see her before leaving for London on business, it was several weeks before Christmas, but I thought I'd be back and see her just before or after Christmas. I sent her the postcard and signed it Leslie Howard as my way of telling her that I was thinking of her knowing I would see her again, but I never did."

"Whaddaya mean?"

"She died while I was in London and I have never felt right about that. I didn't get to say goodbye."

"But you did, in the postcard."

Jake smiled at her, "Thanks; that does feel better to hear someone else say it."

"Now who is the other one, Margot....?"

"Fonteyn. She was one of the greatest ballerinas of all time. Lucia had an interesting life and was strong headed and tough to get to know. Her first husband was a fighter pilot in WWII and a rather handsome and dashing guy, she showed me pictures, but she left him right after the war and moved on. She was an independent soul and smoked Lucky Strikes, and didn't suffer fools. She was a beautiful woman in her day and the type that men would try to obtain partly because she was unobtainable."

"Don't let them hear you talk like that today."

"Yeah, well no one controlled Lucia or told her what to do. She was one strong individual."

"Well, why is she in the notes if it is her they are referring to?"

"She was an international traveler with broad contacts including the Russians, no doubt. But we are talking about the 1930's and the 1940's after the war, so unless it refers to a specific relationship that is secret but yet powerful enough to travel through the decades it may be a reference to the book. They may be using the book to generate a simple code and I am assuming that the book is hard to find, if one can find one at all, and that may be helping to hide the center of this. A book that is almost impossible to find as the reference book for a code or cipher of some sort would be an added layer of security."

"This is starting to sound like a spy novel."

"Yeah, too much so."

"Do you think Mutt and Jeff would really be this deceitful or clever?"

"Who knows these days and they may be letting someone direct them if it's extremely important. Pull up some of those notes and let's have a look."

She went to work and clicked on one and scrolled down, "Here, here's one," she said as she turned the screen around and he readjusted his glasses and leaned forward.

'Little Lucia was in the sun last time I spoke with her,' he read, "That's innocuous and could refer to someone who exists. Find one that doesn't quite make sense if you can."

Helen pulled the screen back around and scrolled, stopped, scrolled some more, then stopped "Yeah, this one is strange," she said as she moved the screen back around so Jake could read it.

'Little Lucia is windy and tight but the cloud was full of rain,' he read aloud, "Geez, what the hell is that? We need a cryptologist. Why in God's name would they put code in case notes?"

"Jeesus,… to share them, not just for themselves!" stated Helen, surprising herself with her own sudden realization of something.

"Whaddaya mean?"

"June sent me a memo from home office a week or so ago about case notes and I forgot about it until just now. You know how she sends home office memos out to us individually if she thinks it may apply to our work, well this one was on case notes. The system will allow authorized access using a telephone number, they call it a weakness we need to be aware of."

"Who has authority to give access?"

"The original author of the notes."

"Oh great, the heart of this thing may be in the case notes. Okay. Once we get those emails lets vet them and break out the ones that make us nervous so we can review them quickly once we have the software for interpreting them. Then match the dates of the email to case note dates referencing Lucia, one day before the case note and one day after and the date of the case note."

"Then what?"

"Well, that'll take us some time and we are just going to have to improvise as we go along," he looked out the window again then back at Helen. "I'm going to have to see if I can find a copy of Little Lucia and see if we can figure anything out. If the name Leslie Howard or Margot Fonteyn show up we're done because I don't know a helluva lot about Lucia's life," and he grinned.

"You really think that could happen?"

"If it did, I'd retire. No, they may be just using the book, but when I first thought of it and then the Russians and Lucia's connection to the ballet my imagination carried me away."

"You've been spending too much time with June."

He laughed, "You may be right."

Jake returned to his office and added a comment to Helen's request to Josh for email from specific addresses and then hit 'reply all'. He worded his comment in a way that complimented Josh, to the degree that he knew the man would pump his chest a bit. He also worded it so that Josh would understand the importance of the requested access, but yet kept it in check to keep June from getting nervous. It was all a grand juggling act.

CHAPTER 16

SOCIAL DICTATIONS AND RUSSIAN INTERPRETATIONS

Two days later, while Jake and his team still had something on their hands which was unsettling in its growing complexity, Josh had other concerns. He probably understood that there was more than isolated money laundering going on in his office, but he had more concern for entertaining a group of sexual harassment seminars. The state was requiring everyone to attend one of them, June having attended the first one of two in the morning. As Jake attended the second one with Helen, while June was busy back in her office, the only thing he could think of was the hot potato they now had; but his ears did perk up on several comments from the seminar presenter until he had just had enough.

He raised his hand after the teacher of the seminar/class stated that '…unasked for compliments should be avoided.'

"Yes, in the back?" she pointed at Jake as Josh turned to see who it was and when he did his face dropped. He knew Jake was going to say something he wasn't going to like.

"I compliment both men and women on how well they look every day. Are you telling me that I can't do that?"

Helen smiled and lowered her head knowing the man she worked for was a people person and one who took care of his team and she was so happy she worked for him.

"Yes."

"But it makes them happy."

"That's what you may think. Did they ask you for the compliment? They may be upset underneath and afraid to say anything."

"Are you serious? You want us to shut down our humanity?" he asked as he felt a slight hesitation in the presenter as though she didn't believe what she was saying.

Helen smiled even more. She was glad someone was saying something.

"Yes, you can't make comments that are unsolicited."

"Geez, can we smile at each other or nod to each other when we pass in the hall, say good morning, things like that?"

"You cannot make comments or give compliments, or salutations, to people that are not asked for. You don't know what they are thinking," concluded Josh in a disagreeable tone after having turned in his chair in the front of the room to face Jake in the back.

"'Oh, it's so far, the other way my country's gone.'"

"What's that?" she asked in a friendly tone.

"Oh, nothing, just a song by a guy named Jackson Browne, 'Across my home has grown the shadow of a cruel and senseless hand though in some strong hearts the love and truth remain.'" He knew the next line but wouldn't bother: 'And it has taken me this distance and a woman's smile to learn that my heart remains among them and to them I must return.'

"That sounds honest, we can talk after the seminar."

"I would love to," replied Jake seeing a kindness in this woman.

━━━━━━━

People funneled out as the seminar ended and Josh went up to compliment the presenter while Jake sat and waited, and Helen left. He sat looking to the front and at the presenter, waiting for Josh to leave.

As Josh left, he gave Jake a look that said he wasn't happy. As he passed, Jake shook his head to himself and smiled remembering Josh's preaching to leadership to express what is on their mind and never hold back. Josh really didn't want to hear anyone else's opinion; he fit well with the times.

"My name's Jake," he said as he walked up to the presenter and extended his hand.

"I'm Elisa, nice to meet you," she said as she shook his hand, "You may guess that I agree with what you were saying."

"I figured, sorry if I sounded aggressive."

"You were okay and I'm glad you spoke up. The state had this seminar put together and we were lectured not to deviate and not one of the other presenters was a man and most of us are Black, by-the-way," and she smiled in a way that told Jake that she knew what he was thinking.

"You're kidding."

"No, it was rather embarrassing as we knew what they were up to as we gathered in our group to receive instruction on it. I figured you would appreciate that," she laughed. "I also like Jackson Browne."

"Elisa, it's a mad, mad world we are getting launched into."

"And madder it may get. Do me a favor would you, just between you and me."

"Sure, what?"

"Don't change. I know who you are and God help us if you and others like you go quiet. I don't know what's coming but I have two teenagers and I don't want them shut down either."

"Elisa, I can't change," he grinned, "and as someone I once knew said, 'You can't chase me away with a chase'n away stick'. You have boys or girls, or both?"

"Two boys, fifteen and seventeen and I'm worried. I don't want them put in a box and marginalized because they are boys."

"Well, from what little I can see, their mom will give them the right tools and personalities to weather the storm."

"I'm hoping."

"We can only put one foot in front of the other and do the next right thing. If enough of us do that we will get through this extreme swing of the pendulum. I lived through the social revolution of the late sixties and early seventies, and Vietnam."

"I didn't experience that but there seems to be a selfish violence to this. That was about peace."

"It was, for the most part."

"This new generation thinks they are being selfless but their self-ishness marks most everything they do. I am not bringing my boys up like that."

"That they are Elisa, but your boys will be fine. We do seem to be in a battle for what is right and what is equitable as well as for free-dom of speech. We're trying to be pragmatic in a place and time that won't allow it. If they don't like what they hear or see they try to shut it down. My God, they've even censored Bugs Bunny for Pete's sake. I like Hepburn and Tracy and they even blurred out Hepburn sticking her tongue out at Tracy in a funny scene out of Adam's Rib, which is not funny now. They can't shut me down and, apparently, they can't shut you down either and your boys will have the same strength that their mom has. We will make it and so will your boys," he said but think-ing that in reality he was glad that he was walking towards his sunset. He was seeing too much selfish destruction and censorship, and, as a student of history, he was nervous right down to his bones. This type of social control had already occurred several times in the modern era with devastating effects, and he knew that he would defend, with his life, the right for anyone to say what they wanted even if he dis-agreed, but that type of thinking had become uncommon.

"I'm glad I got to talk with you," she smiled.

"It sounded like you needed a relief valve."

"I did, thank you."

"Where are you off to from here?"

196

"The end of the day for me today; back to headquarters downtown."

"Does the seventeen-year-old know where he wants to go from high school."

"To Chapel Hill for journalism," she said as she started to pack up the papers on the lectern.

"That's specific…we need some good journalists."

"That's what he says," she beamed as she stopped and looked at Jake.

"Sounds like his mother did give him the right tools for the future."

"Thank you Jake, I guess I needed to hear that. I'm still nervous."

"A mother's prerogative but he'll be all right and he might be part of the solution. Some of these so-called journalists today can't get even two of the five W's, which I learned in high school, into their stories. Hell, I learned to get all five into the first paragraph."

She laughed, "Who, what, when, where and why," she said as she removed her flash drive from the presentation computer at the side of the lectern.

"You know!?"

"Oliver!"

"Who?"

"My son, he filled me in," she said as she stopped again and looked at him.

"Now you've made me feel better. We'll be okay. There should be enough Olivers out there to make a difference."

"Thank you again."

"Listen, I'll leave you alone to pack up and get out of here. Tell Oliver …, tell him thanks."

"I will," she said as Jake turned and left. She knew what he had meant.

A week later Jake had the Russian translating software in his hands.

They were ready to line up emails for review. The emails that Helen had already put in chronological order, with the "Reply All" email threads in Russian attached, would be reviewed first.

They still had not received all the emails that they had requested, using Josh's authorization, but they had enough to start. Once they received the rest of the emails, they would run them through the same review process. They would as well compare them to the case notes and match them up to 'Little Lucia' references one day before, the day of and one day after.

Jake had found one copy of Little Lucia, and another book, Little Lucia's Island Camp. They were online in a family bookstore on a farm in upstate New York and he ordered them both, for good measure, with expedited delivery. They were the only copies he could see online and they had been published in 1922 and 1924 respectively. He was able to determine that there were two other titles in the series, which had been published in 1923 and 1926, but he was hoping that if there were a direct connection, he would have the book that would help him determine that and maybe decipher what they were saying, if anything.

They had several pieces to put together with this investigation while handling everything else that they dealt with on a day-to-day basis.

They certainly could have used Google's translator but they didn't want to jump into that pool as Jake said. It was better to have waited for the approved software, which they each now had in use as they each reviewed the emails on their own first. Jake had wanted them to read the emails separately so they would not influence each other's first impressions.

The first email they each looked at, in chronological order, was directed to Phelps with directions to look into an ETF for the writer and it wasn't a utility. It was an unexciting email until they each engaged the translator software and looked at the accompanying emails, to and from the Russian addresses, that had preceded the request and were now attached as part of the thread. It became a little more interesting as they read through them from the bottom of the email up to the last one sent at the top.

Email from Dimitri to Randy Phelps:

Randy,

Can you review the Vanguard FTSE developed markets ETF for us if you will.

First attached email in Russian, from Pavel near bottom of email:

Greetings Dimitri,

Have we determined where to put the money of Michail Arkanov in response to his electronic note? It needs a home as soon as you have time. Any home is good. You know how impatient he can get.

Goodbye until next time.

Pavel

Second attached email in Russian to Dimitri in reply to Pavel's response to email from a third source:

Pavel has understated the importance of this. I should not have to say more.

Viktor

First Email in Russian to Viktor, Pavel and Dimitri from Michail was not in any of the replies after his initial email which would be found later in another group from Latham:

Jake had already read the email thread among several others that were similar when he walked into Helen's office.

"You've read these I assume," he said with as sheathe of papers in his right hand as he closed the door behind him with his left and then took the seat in front of her desk.

"Yes, pretty enlightening aren't they."

"Yeah, but not completely. Check out Michail Arkanov, in the first email, for life insurance will you," he said as he held up the two pages with the email that contained Pavel, Dimitri and Viktor's comments. "I'll have June run over his investment account. He is one of the three on the FBI watch list," he said as he handed the two sheets across the desk to Helen. "Even if he is moving funds around, we'll need to find the source and see if it can be tracked. I'm sure they've covered their tracks if there are any. I need that damned book Little Lucia. I know it's a long shot but I feel it in my bones, there must be a connection."

"Well, I pulled up the Little Lucia references and more than a few of these emails fall within the three-day period surrounding the reference."

"Do you have the notes on the days surrounding this request for information on the Vanguard ETF for Arkanov?" he asked nodding to the two sheets that Helen was now holding.

Glancing quickly at the top sheet, "Yeah, I know this one. There is actually a Little Lucia reference three days before the original email went out with reference to yet another email. Then there is a Little Lucia reference the day after it was received."

"So the connection date broadens with other emails, past one day on either side."

"Yes, but I haven't found the other email referenced and it may be among the ones we're waiting for."

"If that book is being used as a code key, we'll need to figure the damned thing out or we'll have just assumptions with another Sar."

"Those Sar's are getting to be like Monopoly Money," she laughed.

"Funny. The second Sar may be enough as it will probably all tie in."

"I wonder what June's dreams are like right now."

"You don't want to know."

"I bet she's running a lot."

"Not funny," he grinned, "One way to get into shape, I guess."

"I wonder if they're in full color Panavision or black and white."

"Definitely film noir."

"What?"

"Nothing, but I am not going to fill her in on the Little Lucia books and the fact that one might be a code key. I'll wait to see where we are and drop it on her last minute if true."

"Oh, that'll be interesting. I can already see her eyes bugging out. You need to do it during a group lunch with salad. It's funny when she doesn't realize she's chewing something with her eyes bulging, and salad works pretty well."

"Ah, team love," joked Jake.

"You know I'd do anything for her."

"Yeah; I know, and it is funny. Can you pull this guy up now?"

"Yeah, give me a minute here," she said as she turned her attention to the computer.

Jake sat, while she clicked away at the keys, and skimmed over a few of the other emails that he had already read to think if there was anything else he needed to bring up at the moment.

He heard her slam the enter key and within a few seconds, "Here we go, he had a universal life policy, straight forward."

"Had?"

"Yeah, he cashed it out after, let's see…four weeks. He pulled out thirty-five thousand minus penalty. He didn't MEC it by overfunding it but he took the penalty because he signed the receipt immediately on issuance and ran past the ten-day free look period. If he had overfunded it and allowed it to turn into a Modified Endowment Contract it might have popped with the IRS through our reporting."

"Well, a penalty is the cost of doing business. Thirty-five thousand isn't huge but I wonder how many polices he had elsewhere pushing them right up to becoming a MEC?"

She hit a key and then enter, "It transferred out. I can't tell by this system but I bet it went to one of our brokerage accounts for further integration."

"Great systems. Hell, Little Lucia as a code key is high tech in comparison. Too many holes in our systems, and underwriting never talking to the field although they see everything. Just a joke. If it shows up in brokerage it won't tell us where it came from damnit; we'll just have to assume that if it's the same amount as the cash out we'll know," he complained to Helen knowing she already knew this but he needed to say it out loud in frustration anyway.

"Uh-oh, query."

He grinned, "Yeah, I use the word query too much and that shouldn't be the case, we should have it all at our fingertips. Well, at least we have access to almost the full brokerage view although I may have to query them about some of the aspects of what we find," he grinned again, "I bet it went into the Vanguard ETF. Can you look for this guy in the brokerage system?"

"Yup, heading there as we speak, it'll take a bit. Ah, whaddaya know, here we go, one second."

"What do you think the odds are we get the buy and then see half of it sold a few days later and cash out with one of our checks."

"I'll be," she said as the screen came up on the man's account holdings, "fifteen thousand in the Vanguard ETF. Let me look at his trade blotter."

"You'll see cash out."

She struck the enter key as he finished his sentence and then looked, "Yup, you got it. Liquidated eighteen thousand and change, closer to nineteen thousand. Add that to fifteen thousand and add back in the penalty on the life policy, and the low commission on the ETF, and you've got it."

"Okay, can you print that out, scan it and send it to me. I've scanned these hard copy emails and sent them to you in one document. Here," he said as he handed the rest of the papers he had across the desk, "keep these in a paper file. Don't dial June in yet, although she has seen the emails. I don't want to dump on her, but we will once we find more history, a pattern and whatever else we can find. Let's hold off on this third Sar for a bit until we get more on this. I'll query home office on the specifics to connect the life cash out with the brokerage buy."

"You got it," she said as he got up to leave.

Next, he headed for June's office, more to make sure that she was fine.

He knocked on the open door and her head came up from the computer screen, and he could see that she was tense.

"Everything okay, any more irregularities?"

"Yes, they go back a year; I checked past six months."

"You know that if we found a couple, and these clients have been here for a year or two, we'd find more," he said trying to allay her unwarranted fear. She was fine when she was slightly nervous but when she became overly so she started to make small mistakes and the realization of her own mistakes made her even more nervous. It would snowball and he had seen it once before when it got out of control, and that was with regard to an office audit and had nothing to do with the "Russian mob".

"Yeah, yeah, I know but there are a lot."

"How many is a lot?" he asked as he shut the door behind him but remained standing.

"Went back past six months as I said and then out a year, and there are thirty-four of them with two clients…both Russian."

"Well, the second Sar is already in. How much was in the final Sar, the six months we discussed?"

"Yes, twenty-two of them. These others, of course, are just from the extra searches out over a year as I said, but they increased irregularly over the year to now."

"Okay, shut it down. Document everything you found and put it in a separate file from the Sar as a follow-up to the original report. Put a bow on it and we'll give it to the investigators who may contact us on the second Sar, if they do. Helen and I are trying to figure out the Russian emails and once we understand those, we'll all sit down together. Right now, we are good. Just go back to your regular oversight for now, you don't want to get behind; this thing is already chewing into our limited time and we tend to have twenty plates spinning on poles at any given time," he said softly, using the spinning plate analogy he had once explained to her as coming from the Ed Sullivan Show when he was a kid. It made her smile while he tried to put her back on the calm systematic tracks where she needed to be. She didn't need to be disturbed with what he and Helen were finding, not yet at least.

"You have any questions?" he continued.

"No, but what should I do about trade approval after review for these clients. We now know that these clients are churning or being churned now with ETF's. I've been approving them too. I don't think I paid close attention because they were utilities," she admitted.

"I know, do nothing, just approve the trades, moving forward, with a note that we are watching the client. It's not that egregious in appearance and we have the Sar in so technically we are waiting for direction…and I don't want to upset the apple cart just now and warn the clients. Geez, utilities."

Her eyes came from her screen, looked at him with some intensity and he thought twice about what he had just said.

"Is there a lot more going on?"

"No, not a great deal at this point. Some of the emails do point to possible collusion with the reps or maybe a quid pro quo," he had to tell her something for now. "Don't worry about it. If it becomes bigger than it looks, we'll turn it over to home office and wash our hands of it."

"A quid pro quo? Like working with an accountant and swapping clients?"

"No, this is a bit different, but nothing to be worried about," he said thinking of Henry talking about the ponies and dice. Was there a quid pro quo between one or two in debt gamblers and their mob connected clients? This had begun to formulate with Jake. He was hoping that it wasn't the case.

"Besides approval for future ETF trades what about switches for mutual funds coming from these reps with these clients? They won't stop until we stop them."

"Good point, get me the switches and I'll sign them so it's under my license. Let them know that you are giving me some of your work-load and I'll take some switches from other reps as well so they can see that. I don't want them folding up shop before we have this fig-ured out. And as the obvious mechanism for their integration is the use of ETF's I'll start countersigning the trade blotter with an adden-dum in addition to your explanation."

"It sounds big."

"Probably not, I'm just making it sound that way," and he smiled at her hoping she would take it as a bit of an over exaggeration on his part. When they needed her detail on this, he would drop it on her in a team setting so it fell on all of them. He would also do it at a time when it could be wrapped up quickly.

"Send an email to Phelps and Jenkins. And pick three other reps with moderate trades and add them to the email and let them all know together that in an attempt to spread the workload, I will be taking their switches until further notice."

"Okay, I'll do that now. I know the three I can add who won't cause you to get an undue load of switches. Most of their trades are new and not switches."

"Okay, cc me and as soon as Helen gets more from the emails we have, along with the ones we are yet to receive, we'll put it together and see if there is any connection with other clients," he said knowing those other clients were on the FBI list to watch or 'to keep an eye on' for a total of eight Russian clients to be aware of. He hoped it would not spread past the eight noted by the FBI as such a revelation would bring the FBI closer to his office.

"Yup."

"Gotta run, I'll look for that email," he said as he moved back towards the door, "I'll leave the door open," he added knowing that showing lack of concern for privacy might help relax her.

CHAPTER 17

REPRIMAND, REWARD AND GUIDANCE

W hen he got back to his office the first new email in his oner-ous queue, as he would get close to two hundred a day, was from home office Complaints Review with 'Walter Crouchtiker' in the subject line.

"Oh, crap," he muttered to himself. "That's all I need on top of everything else."

The complaint dealt with life insurance, and thank God it didn't appear to be any names that he was familiar with at the law firm where they had had problems.

The client was under the impression that he was buying a retire-ment account and had come to find out, from his accountant, that he actually had a life insurance policy.

"Geez, how does someone not realize that they are buying a life insurance policy? Walter!" he said to himself.

Jake knew that '...the guy could sell ice to an Eskimo,' and the old expression was truly applicable. The guy should be in theater.

He got Walter on the first ring of his cell phone, "You have any good retirement accounts that might cover my life too."

"Why sure Captain."

"Geez Walter, you just can't help yourself."

"No, I help anyone I can."

"And everyone it appears, with the flavor of the day."

"What are you selling?"

"Not ice cream but it would appear that you are, in a form."

"Getting philosophical with me!?"

"Never, but it would appear redundant."

"How so?"

"Stop doing the wrong thing for the client. You cannot sell life insurance as a retirement account."

"It can be."

"No, it can't, I've told you that, and we have a client complaint that says you'd better stop today. Now I have to deal with this one. How many more are out there?"

"I don't know, I've sold a few. They signed for the policies, so they know what they are."

"Yeah, well, you did such a good job that the client complaint I'm looking at states that he still thought that it was a retirement plan even though he saw the words Life Insurance in the receipt he signed. You do too good of a job at selling."

"Well, you see!"

"See what?"

"I'm good."

"And maybe at the wrong thing. For someone as smart as you are you don't know the first thing about what you are selling people."

"Sometimes that helps."

"Oh, that's good. The car has a great paint job but you don't know how it runs or if it runs."

"I wouldn't use that analogy."

"What would you say then?"

"Sort of like the Golden Goose."

"Oh, that's good too. Well, we know they lay eggs."

Jake could hear Walter snicker on the other end of the phone, "They are all expected to hatch."

"Yeah, and what, scare the hell out of the client when they are expecting a golden chick and wind up with a two headed snake."

"That's scary."

"Stop it Walter. I have to clean this one up and fix the client. Of course, it will come out of your pocket. I would suggest that you go back to the client's you sold these to as a retirement account and confirm with them that this is a life insurance policy first and that they can use the cash value in retirement if they no longer need the life coverage. You will need to resell them."

"Whaddaya mean my pocket."

"You will be charged back your commission on this."

"You can't do that."

"That's the way it works. You sell a lemon you have to give the money back."

"I'm not a car salesman."

"No. I wouldn't give you that compliment. You'll have another letter of reprimand in your box that you will need to sign and return to me."

"Okay Captain."

"Don't patronize me just do what you need to do. I was in this business before you were born."

"Okay."

"I also want a list of the clients that you went back to on their policies."

"Okay, when I can get to it."

"Do it now Walter. This is how it works. Any complaint that comes in on these 'retirement accounts,' without verified follow-up that you spoke with the client to reconfirm that they understood their Life Insurance policy, will automatically go in the client's favor without argument."

"That's not fair."

"Geez Walter, now I've gotta go. I have miles to go before I sleep."

"I don't think you ever sleep Mr. Frost."

"Nor do you and that may be part of the problem. Goodbye Walter," and he hung up to get back to his email queue, which had continued to grow in front of his eyes as he spoke with Walter Crouchtiker.

As he clicked on the first email, he saw a shadow come across the frosted glass wall between his office and the hallway, and then there was a knock on the door.

"Come in."

It was Jim Parker.

"Hello Mr. Bowen.

"Glad you stopped by, what can I do you for?"

"I got this letter from the people investigating the Ukraine policy."

"It's the 'Ukraine policy' now?" smiled Jake reaching for the letter Jim was handing to him across his desk and noticing the return address of the international investigation company hired by his company, "Grab a seat."

"They said that they may not need to interview me."

"Good news," Jake said as he pulled out the correspondence while Jim seated himself.

They sat quietly for a moment while Jake read the letter and then smiled, "Good," he said as he folded it back up and put it in the envelope before handing it back to Jim. "This means that they are pretty clear on what happened and that they don't see it involving any collusion on your part. You probably won't hear from them again other than a letter stating briefly the determination that they came to and referring you back to the firm for a more comprehensive explanation, if you needed one."

"I don't think I'll need one."

"No, I don't think you will and further to this I have spoken with Josh about your enlistment in the Air Force."

Jim looked shocked and froze for an instant, like a deer in the headlights. It was becoming a notable reaction around this office, thought Jake for a second.

"Don't be worried."

"But he gave me my chance here."

"Ah, well, we won't get into that one. You were built for better things and Josh sees the wisdom in that. So, when do you need to report?"

"In a month I'm assuming, at least that's what the recruiter said. I need to go to MEPS next week for two days for aptitude testing and medicals."

"Okay, good. We can close this Ukraine matter up and get you straightened out and out the door with time left to spend with your family and friends before you report."

"I'm sorta nervous about MEPS."

Jake had tried not to recognize it when Jim mentioned the testing, "Do not equate your Series testing with the military aptitude testing. You had to study specific information for the Series exams and you did not have time. The military aptitude tests just determine your basic abilities and I have full faith that they will prove what I already know, that you need to go to pilot training."

"Thank you, Mr. Bowen."

"Don't thank me, it is who you are and you will do well. Don't forget, the deal is to let me know how you are doing along the way."

"I will and if I can ask you questions along the way…?"

"You can but once you walk through those Air Force portals you will know more about them than I do. Airplanes, you can always ask me about them. I'm going to start processing you out now that the interview is moot and if they do need you, they will bump into me and I'll take care of it. How does that sound?"

"Sounds good," he said while his demeanor changed as he became more positively animated.

"Okay, get outta here and get yourself straightened out, and I'll have Barbara in licensing start your termination and processing out."

"Thanks again," he said as he got up with letter in hand and headed for the door. Then he turned just before leaving, "I'll carry you as my co-pilot when I start flying, if you don't mind."

"I'd be honored," smiled Jake with warm sincerity, "now get out of here."

Just as he went back to his email another shadow came across his frosted glass wall and it was always for him when it seemed to be in a rush, and also because he was the last office at the end of this corridor. He waited a second and Emma popped around the corner. She had been part of the financial planning staff now for six months.

She stood in the doorway, a beautiful, smart and athletic young girl of twenty-four who, as it happened, went to the same university as he had, after attending preparatory schools in Europe. Also, their birth dates were two days apart and he gave her favor, and had a hard time trying to hide it from others. She was the same age that the daughter, that he and his girlfriend Charlotte had wanted, would be. He had always wanted a daughter to teach how to hunt and fish and be her own person. They had come close and thought that they would have her but in the end they did not. Emma, in a way, represented the daughter that they never had and he felt Charlotte would feel the same way if she were to meet her but then Charlotte was in Europe a great deal of the time, and that was another story.

"What can I do you for?" he asked with a warm smile.

"I just came by to invite you to lunch tomorrow, if you can. I have a couple of things that I'd like to bounce off of you if I can."

"That sounds good, how about noon tomorrow in the lobby, I'll calendar it. Everything good?"

"Yes."

"How's that young man of yours?"

"Fine but that's part of it, if I can get your advice."

"You got me tomorrow."

She had a glow on her face now, "It'll be a nice lunch."

"I'm looking forward to it. Noon."

"Okay, see you tomorrow," and she was gone as fast as she had appeared.

They had lunch the next day at a Spanish restaurant off of Lexington

Avenue that Emma favored. It was an escape for him to a better place briefly and away from the juggling of problems with a large problem looming that was still just an enigma. She talked about her job opportunities and asked his advice. She spoke of her boyfriend as though asking for approval from an older man who might be wiser. All he could say was, "does he make you laugh and feel safe?" She had said yes and smiled and he didn't have to say any more. He gave her advice on the financial planning business and refortified her belief in her abilities. He had never seen someone so young just blow through the Certified Financial Planner tests and requirements as she had. He was proud as maybe an uncle would be knowing that she wasn't quite his daughter but he felt his daughter's spirit smiling warmly at him as he gave Emma advice, and he would take that and tell Charlotte about it. He would tell her about it but very carefully in a way that she would feel joy, and not sorrow over never having the daughter she had always dreamt of. He felt the spirit of their daughter in many ways at different times and tried to share a little of it with Charlotte in an attempt to bring her along and give her at least that spirit of their daughter that he was beginning to know.

CHAPTER 18

THE CODE AND A WILDMAN
INTERLUDE

"I got the rest of the emails," said Helen as he entered her office after his lunch with Emma and still a bit groggy from having a full meal at midday, as he usually had only an apple or a banana to keep him going.

"Did you have a chance to look them over?" he asked as he took a seat in front of her desk.

"Yes, and I applied the software to several with the attached emails in Russian."

"And?"

"Interesting. I cut and pasted a list together with translations and referenced emails along with the chronology."

"Geez Helen, what's in that coffee of yours?"

"I probably shouldn't drink so much of it. I bounce off walls enough without it."

"Glad you see that. I've actually seen you bump into things in a hurry and keep moving without noticing," and they both started to laugh. They were getting a little dizzy and stupid over this Russian connection with Phelps and Jenkins.

"What's your quick read?" he asked as they collected themselves.

"Well, they are moving money and it is obvious that we are not the only destination, and there seems to be need for haste. There seem to be some missing pieces as well. I get the feeling that it's more than just Phelps and Jenkins taking money in and spreading it around. Before you walked in, I was looking at their case notes again and in particular Phelps. He definitely has markers around the dates of the emails with Russian attachments, more so than Jenkins."

"Any feel for what they may mean?"

"No, not really. They're vague. It's Little Lucia again, and again it's a marker, sometimes with numbers, following in reference to one item or another that makes very little sense in the context of the note itself."

"Book code?"

"No, all numbers are two digit and split from each other which implies separation, and there aren't enough of them in any single note to form anything of significance. I just don't know, but there are no three number sequences and the two digits are few and far apart. It can't be a book code unless the numbers are just book pages, which makes no sense."

"Okay, there has to be something in there."

"Do you think Phelps and Jenkins are that bright and cunning?"

"No, but as I had said, they may be getting this from their Russian clients off line, which means this thing may be bigger than we think, obviously reaching other investment houses."

"Any other thoughts on Little Lucia?"

"I've been going over what I knew about her to the point of distorting it all. There is nothing there except a life of intrigue sixty or seventy years ago. The only conclusion that I keep coming back to is that her life was too far in the past and too secretive for someone today to play off of it. No, it has to be the books and I am still waiting for the two that I could find that I told you about."

"I looked on line for those books too, to see if I could pick anything up in relationship to them or the author Mabel Robinson."

"You have been busy. Anything?"

"No, she and her partner Helen Hull both taught at Columbia and were lifelong partners. They were both writers and that is about it other than the fact that they were engaged in women's rights issues and wrote about women. Also, besides writing children's books, Mabel had written a book on writing for young people which is highly considered."

"Okay, it's gotta be the books then."

"Oh, I found a third book and ordered it."

"You're kidding."

"No, Little Lucia's School published in 1926."

He grinned, "Keep drinking that coffee and let me know what you paid for that book."

"No, I'll keep the book and give it to my nephew, you don't owe me anything."

"Well, I guess we are waiting for those books and if we can't find anything, we'll move forward with what we have. Have you been able to talk with Henry again to see if you can get him to give a little?"

"Yes and no. I spoke with him but he's having too much fun with this, especially the more I try."

"Any fat jokes?"

"Of course," she laughed.

"Maybe we should steal his thrown and hold it for ransom."

"That chair is his sole purpose for coming into the office. He needs to sit in it. King Henry. It might not be a bad idea. Sometimes I walk in when his door is open and he is in a trance in that chair like he's in the captain's chair on the deck of the Starship Enterprise."

"Maybe he is. Keep trying if you can. We need just a little more to let us see what we're missing."

"Not to change the subject but Epstein is complaining about the thirty thousand that the company has kept from that large outside variable life policy he wrote."

"Christ, I explained that to him. He got it. He didn't like it, but he got it."

"He stopped by because you were out to lunch. He came with those wild eyes of his and told me he wanted Josh to speak with him."

"Josh is frightened of him."

"I know that but what am I going to say."

"I get it now. He just wants Josh to recognize him. It's simple and this Director just doesn't get it. Okay, I'll get Josh or one of his delegates to talk with him."

"You know Josh won't."

"Okay, Doris then. She's the CFO."

"Oh, that'll be good. You know that they are all frightened of him and think he's crazy."

"And you and I know Dave. He's a good guy who is just too intense for most people. Maybe Doris needs a dose of reality. I'll get her in front of him."

"She may freak."

"I sort of hope so," and he smiled at Helen. "Okay, let me go take care of that," he said as he pushed himself up from the chair, still heavy with lunch.

———

He was still thinking of the Russians later that day when he convinced Doris to see Dave in place of Josh. The guy was rarely in but was '... in today', Jake had said to Doris as he told her that they really needed to quell this before it became a problem. After all, he told her, it did bring twenty thousand dollars, out of thirty thousand, into her books for the cost of local oversight of the policy.

Jake knew that the company had to make money on the policy. He also knew that most, if not all, of the oversight would take place at the opposing firm. But it was the pound of flesh that Dave Epstein had to pay to get his client the outside variable policy not sold by his firm, and both he and Josh knew this. Doris did not know this and was visibly nervous when they entered Dave's office. On top of his intensity and nervous energy Dave was probably the wealthiest agent in the office and he knew what he was doing with his structuring of life insurance for large estates. He wasn't just a salesman. He was actually an estate planner first and was concerned about doing what was right for his clients; even though it would cost him, as in this case.

Doris did not say a word other than responding to Jake's introductions. She sat in the far seat, nearest the wall, of the two seats in front of Dave's desk. She was hemmed in with Jake sitting in the seat next to the door and Dave in front of her, behind his desk, with his face highlighted by the faint glow of his computer screen. They had just pulled him away from the concentrated intensity he was giving to a complicated life illustration on his computer. This would be good. She had a hand full of papers, which she had quickly printed off of the computer file showing the commission that was taken, by the firm, from Dave's policy commission from the outside company.

Jake was not going to say a word; it was up to Doris, but Dave jumped in first.

"Why are you taking thirty thousand dollars of my money?" his eyes bugged out as if he was coming over the desk at Doris.

"Ah, umm, ah, well it covers our costs."

"Whaddaya mean?" came Dave with his voice rather high.

Doris went back in her seat until she could not push herself back further, "Well, you can see here, where the firm debited the commission to cover our costs," she said as she held up the debit blotter from the file papers.

"What does that mean? It doesn't mean anything! Why did you take my money?"

"Jake?" asked Doris as she glanced over at Jake with some terror in her eyes.

"What? You're explaining it." He loved this.

"Well...well, it's our money." Jake heard her say the wrong thing.

"What do you mean your money? That's my client. I've had that client for twenty years. You don't know who he is; why should you take his money?"

"Ah…so we can pay Jake and his team," she said glancing sideways at Jake without taking her eyes off of Dave as though he might come across the desk and pounce while she wasn't looking.

"Don't look at me," Jake responded knowing Dave knew all of this and had finally accepted Jake's explanation a week earlier. He was still upset that Josh was not sitting in front of him explaining this.

"That's a lot of money!"

"We only get twenty thousand."

"That's a lot of money! Jake gets that?"

"Well, no. The office does."

"Well, how much goes to Jake?"

"Well, none."

"You just said it went to pay Jake and his team."

"Well, that's a figure of speech. It doesn't go right to them but it helps us pay them to review your policy on a regular basis."

"So, you are paying them more than they were getting?"

Jake loved this. Thrifty Doris was nervous and needed to defend her cheapness.

"Well, no. They are getting paid the same."

"That doesn't make sense," he said with some force as his eyes bulged more and some spittle came to the corners of his mouth. Dave was in full stride with the demeanor that scared those who did not know him. "Well, then were does it go?"

"To the office."

"For what, for Josh?!"

"Well, yes, some. The cost of the office…"

"Doesn't make sense, I'm pretty busy!"

"Okay, okay, we'll go if you like."

"Yes," he said as his face fully lite up with the light from the computer screen as he went back to the life illustration he had been working on when they came in.

"Okay, Dave, see you later," said Jake as he bumped Doris on the arm and nodded towards the door. The man just went calmly back to work from a bulging eyed maniac and this unsettled her even more. Jake had to bump her again on the arm as she was frozen.

Dave kept working while they got up. He didn't stand to say good-bye or attend to any basic courtesy. Jake knew that he didn't mean anything by it. He was just back in the intensity of his work world and they weren't even standing in his office. That was just Dave. Jake knew that under that veneer was an intense guy who would give you the shirt off his back, if you needed it, without thinking twice and not wait around for acknowledgement.

Jake stood aside and let Doris out first, then quietly shut the door behind him and they were quiet until part way down the hall.

"Well, that went well, don't you think," said Jake trying to break the ice.

"Did it? He's scary!" she responded still looking ahead as they walked. She looked like a kid who just went through a real haunted house on Halloween and survived.

Jake grinned; it was funny he thought. He had needed that.

Later that day Jake ran into Dave walking across the lobby and Dave stopped, eyes still bugging out a little and stated more than asked, "Was that okay Jake? It wasn't too much was it?"

"No Dave, you were just right."

"Okay good," and he was gone again down the hall to his office.

It was all about Josh not recognizing him and Dave giving Josh a piece of his mind, through Doris, for not coming to his office. Jake had known he was going to go off on Doris. They didn't have to talk about it with each other.

It was interesting how two of the most frightening people, and one, Hooper, being the most annoying as well, to Josh were both liked by Jake and Helen and two of their favorites. The man just did not understand people. He would joke about people behind their backs like a high school bully or prankster and completely miss the person. Jake particularly liked his attacks on what Josh called WASP's, a term Jake hadn't heard in years. Josh's caricature of so-called WASP's was in turn a perfect description of his own character and his revealing superiority over others, which he would unknowingly parade about on occasion. The man, as smart as he was, was people dumb and a bit of a narcissist who would show subtle traits of jealousy on rare occasion. He thought he knew the lives behind people from their surface but yet had no idea what they had been through in their lives putting his own personal experiences in a realm greater than theirs. He just didn't know.

CHAPTER 19

A WIZARD AND A BAD TRADE

"So, how did it go with Dave?" asked Helen as Jake entered her open door.

"Need I tell you?" he grinned as he closed the door and took the chair in front of her desk.

Looking across her desk at him, "I'm sorry I missed it."

"Yeah, it was beautiful,"

"Spoke with Henry, by-the-way."

"Anything besides a fat joke."

"Yes actually. We got into a back and forth and I went after his thrown, and he said he wasn't the only one in the office on a thrown. When I asked him what he meant he just said that Phelps and Reynolds were only jesters."

"So what the hell did he mean by that?"

"I don't know, he just told me to 'follow the yellow brick road to find the truth. There is only one place to find a brain, courage and a heart'. Then he gave me that grin of his."

"Geez, there's someone behind Phelps and Jenkins!"

"What?"

"Henry's playing a game. The Wizard of Oz was not what he seemed.

He was a simple carnival barker behind a curtain," said Jake as though he was talking to himself and in thought.

"Like a dog? What's a barker?"

"Oh, a carnival barker. The guy who stands in front of a show, like the bearded lady who juggles twenty baseballs, and tries to bring people in to see her."

"What?"

"The guy who, in the old days of carnivals, would yell at the crowd as they passed, trying to entice them to enter the tent he was standing in front of and pay for the chance to see an oddity or show of some sort. The Wizard in the Wizard of Oz was a carnival barker, in reality, who wound up in OZ and gave them what they wanted, which was a grand Wizard who knew all and could do all with fear as his main power."

"You got all of that from what Henry said?"

"Sort of," he said as he looked at her and grinned, "I think we have a third person in this office involved who we have no idea about yet."

"That's sorta creepy in a way; should we tell June?"

"Don't be funny. It's gotta be in the notes someplace…or maybe not. Maybe we need to hold Henry's chair ransom."

"He'll never say anything unless he sees someone get hurt. He wants us to figure this out but he's not '…going to tell', as he says."

"What?"

"When he hits me with his fat jokes, he finishes sometimes by saying, '…are you gonna go tell now.' It is funny but I think he is the type who would never tell on anyone."

"Okay, we can figure this thing out. It may just come down to one of those books or not at all. I don't want you spending too much time on this until they arrive. Put as much together as you can as you go through your day until we make a final decision of how far we go or cannot go with this. It's worth repeating, we just have too much other stuff on our plate from day-to-day to get completely wound up in this."

"On another topic, Tony Colantoni had a trade problem with one of his larger clients."

"Oh no, what now, another one of our firm's great safety triggers go off and screw another client."

"Yeah, how'd you know

"A feeling. I dealt with a little trade hiccup with him last month that really wasn't worth mentioning. He's the only guy in this office buying and selling large round lots of stock for some of his clients. Stock, now there's a novel word we don't use around here anymore. What happened?"

"It was when you were out to lunch, his office called. I forgot to tell you with Dave the madman on the warpath. They got a stalled trade and are trying to take care of it with home office."

"I'll go see him. He won't get anywhere with them. They'll make him do a trade correction."

"On ten thousand shares of a twenty-two-dollar stock at the market."

"Oh, Christ."

"Yeah, they blocked the trade. He's liquidating part of a large position for a guy who was once a principal with the company in question. He sold ten thousand at the market when the market opened. Then an hour later the client wanted to dump ten thousand more so they put in another ten thousand sell at the market with the stock stable, and the firm held up the execution thinking it was a dup in error."

"They can't do that. The guy puts in an order the firm is required to get best execution which means immediately. If he duplicates the order that's his problem and it goes to his errors and emissions."

"I figured as much and he's trying to get home office to fix it, as by the time they shook the people loose downtown to finally do the trade the market had moved."

"Don't tell me."

"Yeah, it moved down a dollar fifty or sixty or something close to it. He said he'd get it fixed and get back to us."

"He'll never get it fixed; they'll stick him. They must be out of their collective minds. They are putting so many roadblocks in the way of the client and the rep to protect them from themselves that they are causing damage, and it'll only get worse. I feel like reporting my own firm to FINRA. I'll go talk to him. It seems it's pick on Tony week with everything the guy's had to deal with. Anything else that's lurking in the shadows that came your way while I was at lunch? I oughta go more often."

"Well, no. Nothing important."

"Like a trade stop on ten thousand shares."

"Yeah, well the Russian Connection has occupied my mind lately, besides Dave's wild eyes."

"Oh, 'the Russian Connection', I like that," he shook his head. "Okay, let me go see Tony now," he said as he got up and turned for the door and then stopped and turned around, "By-the-way, before I forget, Mr. Parker is out the door. They don't seem to be interested in interviewing him about the Ukraine Connection," he grinned, "so I started his paperwork to give him some time before the Air Force gets him."

"Does Josh know yet?"

"Yeah, I told him over a week ago; sorry I forgot to mention it. And he told me the guy was part of his number and a financial planner."

"Part of what number? He wasn't getting any production in."

"Diversity number."

"Are you kidding?"

He looked right at her straight faced, "Does this face kid!?"

"God, besides messing with these reps he's going to get a law suit."

"That's what I told him. In the end he saw it my way and Jim will be safely on his way. Let me go and see what's going on with Tony's trade, or should I say no trade," and he turned and headed out the door towards Tony Colantoni's office.

Jake knocked on the open door to Tony's large office suite, with two attached offices off to either side of the main office.

"Is he in?"

Tony's son Chris looked up from his computer screen, "Sure, you can knock on the door; we had a nice trade," he grinned.

"I heard," replied Jake shaking his head so that it was barely noticed.

"Yeah," came from behind the door after he knocked.

He opened the door and stepped in to see Tony on the computer at his standing desk.

"Where are we with that trade and how's the client doing?"

"Jake, what the hell!"

"I know."

"This is just a rinky-dink shit show here sometimes."

Tony never minced words, nor did Jake so they appreciated each other. Tony at one point had told Jake that he was from the Bronx and he appreciated people who weren't 'bullshit' and he appreciated Jake. One of the best compliments Jake had received and, as tough as Tony could be, he had honor and had never given Jake the wrong information.

"I know, it's a life insurance company first Tony; trading scares them. Where are we with making the client whole?"

"Sixteen thousand and change! They want me to file a trade correction on my insurance."

"Not gonna happen," Jake was starting to steam. The firm had screwed up with one of their idiotic safety features and harmed a client and a rep in the process. They actually contravened the law which required 'Best Execution.' This was a Securities and Exchange Commission law and neither the SEC or FINRA would be excited with what had happened, and they were trying to cover it up with a rep trade correction. "I'll get hold of the head of trading; give me the client information would you. And don't file a trade correction."

Jake would wind up having three calls with the head of trading who tried to say that it was normal procedure to hold up a trade they thought might have been duplicated in error. He tried to tell Jake that their clearing house, for executing the trade, followed this as their normal procedure. The man was actually lying to Jake which got Jake to raise his voice. He knew the clearing house well and knew that no such procedure would ever be carried out by this well-established company. Jake finally got the head traders' boss and he admitted that it wasn't the clearing house but the firm. He said they put 'guardrails' in place to protect everyone.

"You put guardrails in so tightly that my rep and his client ran out of road. You cannot do this. If any of the governing authorities see this you will be screwed; this is NOT best execution."

It reminded Jake of his own Health Savings Account or HSA. Two years earlier he had asset allocated all of his funds in the account to different mutual funds and then clicked the button in the account that said EXECUTE TRADE. The trade never was executed it turned out as there was a 'failsafe' button that was on another site page that he needed to go to and click on to verify that he did indeed want to make that allocation. He missed two years of a bull market, with a small account, due to this. He had thought that he had set it up to fly on its own for the next couple of years and left it. As they did not send out statements, he never saw that it was sitting in cash. There was no clear instruction on the site about this safety trigger and many people were caught. Jake could hear the rep on the phone backpedaling when they spoke. He was backpedaling in a way that told Jake that the rep spent too much of his time dealing with irate account holders such as himself. Safety in the name of protecting themselves from litigation was becoming such a big factor in the investment world that clients were actually getting hurt. Control was not only being taken out of peoples' hands in society in general, in the name of safety, but it had moved to investments as well.

Jake had thrown down one of his cards with his potential threat to the trader over Tony's stalled trade but the firm acquiesced and made the client whole and kept the rep's record intact. It took a week of calls, eventually, and Jake did not make friends with some of the people in trading and word would get around, but sometimes this had to happen and you gave up a bit of that good equity you had built up with home office. He was getting tired of fighting with the inherent problems such as this one, which needn't have to happen. Well, he wasn't dealing with a wire house or the old type of stockbrokerage firm that he had grown up in. Everything was becoming too controlled and automated, and dangerous. He found himself helping the firm make corrections to everything from their procedures in certain situations to their interpretation of the law. He shouldn't have to do this. It could be a scary place and he still had the Russians.

Their hiring and rep maintaining decisions were frightening too. They hired not only those who they thought capable but they gave preference to many who were not, simply due to their race or sexual preference, which he had brought to Josh's attention as a concern. Jake saw this as not only unfair to all those who came looking for a position as a rep, no matter what the color of their skin, but he also saw it for the danger it created in disenfranchisement and potential law suits, besides adversely affecting the firms' bottom-line. And this too, he had mentioned to Josh. 'A brave new world', as one famously stated. At least he got one kid headed on the right path which gave him a smile before he again remembered that his big problem at the moment was the Russians.

CHAPTER 20

THE CODE BOOKS START TO ARRIVE

He received the first book he had ordered less than a week later, at home. It was Little Lucia. Now he could see if there was any connection.

When he opened the book, it opened right to the dedication page, yellowed and brown since this Fourth Edition printing in March, 1926. It was dedicated To: THE REAL LITTLE LUCIA. He held the dedication page open and stared and smiled and remembered the Lucia that he had known. The strong, feisty, aged Lucia who smoked Lucky Strike cigarettes as though they were made just for her. A little girl who had grown into a woman of substance, who left her mark quietly on the society and times that had surrounded her youth and later years until she became an old woman tucked away in a home. She was still inside that older shape and she knew that he understood who she had been and he respected the trust that this realization had established.

The story opened with Little Lucia breaking her leg right at the start of her summer at the beach and that, at four and a half, she was upset that she would not be able to do all of the things that she had planned to do that summer; a precocious little girl. She would be bedridden for the six weeks of the summer before she would then have to return to the city. This is what made her cry, not the experience of the pain and fear of a broken limb at that age. It sounded like the older woman that he had known. She was energetic and engaging as a small child, years ahead of her equals.

He decided he would read the book first and then read the selected notes that Helen had compiled.

He knocked on Helen's open door the next morning, as she had her focus on the computer screen off to her left and hadn't noticed him walk up to the threshold, "Helen, I got the first book yesterday."

She shook her head and looked up still mentally engaged with what she had been working on, "What book?" she asked absently.

"What book do you think?"

She hesitated for a second before he got her full attention, "Little Lucia, you got it! Which one?"

"The first one, Little Lucia. Can you make sure that you have every note that you think may be related to the subject in the file you sent me. I'm sure every one of importance is there but just double check. I'll read the entire book tonight at home and then hit the file first thing tomorrow morning and see if we have a key of sorts."

"Yeah, I wanted to double check this morning anyway so the timing's good."

"Don't tell June. I'll wait until I read the book and look at the notes in the morning before letting her in on it. No need to have her worry unnecessarily," he grinned with subtle concern.

"I agree," she laughed.

That evening the second book, Little Lucia's Island Camp, was waiting for him and he had a file of all of the printed-out notes, as he had decided to do some of the reference investigation work at home. He had his work cut out for him but, in a way, it was a puzzle and he looked forward to spending an evening with it.

This second book had a copyright date of 1924 and was the original addition and, at some point, had spent time in the Osterhout

Free Library in Wilkes-Barre, Pennsylvania. Both the inside of the front cover and the inside of the back cover were decorated in the modern art of small children with pencil swirls of different width and depth and shade suggesting that several children over the years added their expression to the art. Dorothy and Raymond tried to write their names in large elementary script at different times in the book's history. The book was yellowed and stained around its outside edges and wrapped in a red hard cover. But the interior pages had been kept relatively pristine, with the occasional stain, and an overall rust color from age. Similar to the Little Lucia book this book had black and white illustrations that seemed to be from woodcuts, although it had more illustrations than the Little Lucia book.

Jake just looked at the books for a bit and reflected on the simplicity and joy of his own childhood, and the children's reading room in the Englewood, New Jersey Library which sat on the hill leading into town. It had pink white apple blossoms outside its oversized open windows in the spring and he could almost feel their sweet scent on the light breezes of those childhood springs. He smiled and for a moment was removed to a wonderful place still in his heart and now part of his soul.

He pulled out the paper notes and started with the obvious, or Little Lucia, which was referenced in the notes. He came up with nothing.

He tried to determine if the number references, and phrases attached to them, somehow aligned with the book, and nothing. He just could not see what it was. Maybe the reps were smarter than he was giving them credit or maybe these books had nothing to do with the reference to Little Lucia, but they had to. There was no book code possible in the single two digit or, on occasion, set of two two-digit numbers in the notes. They appeared more random than anything else. He checked the phrases with accompanying numbers against page numbers and nothing. Or maybe it was right in front of him and he just couldn't see it.

After two hours he moved to Little Lucia's Island Camp. Maybe there was a connection here and maybe it would get him to look at the situation in a fresh way with a different story. He was getting so caught up in it he would probably complete his investigation before returning to the office the next day.

Little Lucia ended with a collie puppy of no name in Little Lucia's arms. Now, in Little Lucia's Island Camp, the dog had a name, Laddie. Jake smiled and at the same moment felt a brief familiarity with the name and then moved on.

He again read the book, compared the numbers in the notes to page numbers to see if there was any reference to the accompanying phrases, and nothing. There was not one set of three numbers let alone multiple sets in sequence. It simply was not a book code as hard as he tried to make it one, but there was something familiar that he couldn't quite put his finger on.

He stayed up until he had complicated his search so much between numbers and word play that it made no sense at all and the simple children's stories were taunting him in their simplicity. He dreamt of the stories that night and remembered some of his dreams and still there was no clarity, at all. But he saw the collie in his dreams and, even though as a child he grew up with a black Labrador retriever, this collie was familiar somehow. Maybe he missed having a dog since his Newfoundland had passed away. Then he thought of his neighbors Collie 'Thumper' when he was a kid and he thought he had something but that wasn't it. It was just a dream.

He shook the cobwebs off in the morning and took the early bus with the books and the note file in his computer bag. He went over both books in his head as the bus headed towards the city. He pulled out the notes and with both books in mind went over them. There was something there. He felt it, but he was stumped.

He spent a half hour that morning with Helen, going over his experience from the night before. He had walked into her office first thing in the morning as she was always in early.

"There is something there, I feel it but I just can't put my finger on it."

"Maybe we're making this too complicated. Mutt and Jeff couldn't be code masters even if they are working with the Russians," and she grinned with a bit of sarcasm.

"No, but as Churchill once said, I think he said it anyway: the 'Russians are an enigma within an enigma', sort of like those wooden Russian dolls with one inside another, inside yet another and so on."

She laughed, "I think you've spent way too much time on this boss."

He grinned at her subtle humor, "Yeah, you're right. I'll put this down for the day."

"Hey, maybe there's something in the book I ordered."

"Could be," he said with a certain lack of enthusiasm.

He still did not fill June in on his lack of findings and the interest that he and Helen had developed in the name Little Lucia, as the fear of putting her on edge was still there.

He left the books and the notes in the office that night and headed home at the end of the day, committed to not thinking on the puzzle that he had put in front of himself. But the entire way home, even on the walk from the office to the bus station, he thought of nothing else almost walking into traffic on Fifth Avenue in front of the library. It was starting to drive him a little crazy and he just could not give it up. That feeling of familiarity kept coming back and he couldn't put his finger on it.

He started re-reading Moby Dick on the bus into the city the next morning, to take his mind off the Russians and Little Lucia, and Phelps and Jenkins. He had been reading it on and off getting bogged down with the descriptions of types of whales, right where he remembered getting bogged down in high school, but the adventure was coming and with that anticipation he forged on. His anticipation of figuring out what Little Lucia meant was just as compelling as he read on about the whales, with those two old children's books churning the wheels in the back of his mind.

He walked into Helen's office, first thing, after dropping his computer bag in his office.

He stood stock still in the doorway, "You think of anything overnight?"

Looking up at him with confidence written on her face, "What's Ladeski's nickname?"

"Nickname, geez. Ah, Lad something, why, what does that have to do with anything?"

"Laddie."

"So…ah, geez. The dog?"

"Yeah, has to be," she said as she held up the book Little Lucia's School with an illustration on the front cover of Little Lucia running with her Collie dog, Laddie. "This was waiting for me when I got home last night and the cover hit me. It's simple. You've been thinking too hard. Colin 'Laddie' Ladeski. Don't laugh, Collie by the name of Laddie; Colin/collie 'Laddie' Ladeski."

"So, it's just a name reference and nothing more."

"I think so."

"So Ladeski may be involved in this and Henry knows this."

"Probably."

"Geez we were thinking too hard."

"You were thinking too hard, you need a break."

"Probably. Let's confirm this if we can; run it by Henry and see what you get."

"Yup. They're not geniuses, they were just having fun."

"Yeah, to an extent but they made those notations to remind them that maybe this guy is in charge and referenced a book that's as rare as hen's teeth."

"Maybe… 'Hen's teeth'?"

"Yeah, they don't have them,.. teeth," he said, his mind elsewhere trying to figure out where this was going next.

"No kidding," she said as he didn't pick up on her humor about his use of an antiqued characterization as he was someplace else in thought.

"Yeah, all right," he said like an embarrassed kid, giving her his attention again, "Ok, let's confirm that Ladeski is part of this thing and then figure out why and to what extent."

"We can start looking at his emails and business more closely."

"Start with that, looking at his Life business and getting what emails you can. Don't go through Josh to get any. He'd just upset the apple cart if one of his babies like Ladeski is involved, or I should say top baby."

"Okay, gotcha."

"I'll go fill June in and have her check his securities business."

"Have fun with that. This association with Ladeski will not be concrete enough for her to understand, you know. She doesn't put things together like that; they cannot be abstract," and she grinned.

"I know, I know. You're having fun aren't you."

"I can see her confusion right now."

"Yup but as it is not in black and white, she may not get too nervous, and she will probably see the concrete pieces, right off, that we don't see at first glance. All right, let me get headed down there."

"It's only three doors away, not a journey."

"It can be," he grinned and left.

Standing in June's doorway he knocked on the open door, her head again down and engaged, completely, with her computer screen.

"Oh. Yeah," she said looking up partly startled.

"How you doing?'

"Good, no more day trading utilities," she said with pushed humor in her voice and on her face.

"Good, I have something else," and her face changed and became serious again, and nervous, "I want you to start looking at Colin Ladeski. Look at his trading patterns for any anomalies."

"Like what?"

"You'll know when you see them. Also make note of any Russian contacts he may have."

She looked at him.

"Just keep that in mind, Helen is checking his case notes and emails so it won't be anything that will be overtly obvious. You have a good feel, so just keep this in mind."

"Is he involved with the Russians?"

Jake walked completely into the office, shut the door behind him and took a seat in the chair, now in front of June, before continuing, "We think so, through Phelps and Jenkins."

"Oh," she said with some fear on her face.

He then decided to tell her so she could make the connection, Helen was right, and the book connection could not be too abstract, "Listen, I didn't want to tell you until we had a better idea about this. It was the Little Lucia books… Oh, yeah, we didn't tell you. The references they made in their case notes to Little Lucia, it's a kid's book. Helen and I think we found a connection to Colin Ladeski and those references. Now I know this is a stretch but Colin is called 'Laddie' and that's the name of the collie dog in the Little Lucia books."

She smiled and turned her head a little sideways, "Ah, that's funny. No why, really?"

"I'm serious. I'm really not joking."

Her face changed. Something this abstract, related to the Russians and money laundering, and whatever else, with their top producing rep sitting on top of the pile, came rushing into June's reality all at once.

"I'll start looking," she said nervously.

"June, take it easy. We are just being thorough about this as we systematically go through everything. You know how this works. We may see a large fire but as we get closer and start to discount certain things the fire gets smaller and more manageable and it really doesn't burn," it wasn't his best analogy but it worked.

"Okay, I'll look closely."

"Any questions?" he asked as he pushed back the chair to get ready to leave.

"Well, Ladeski has been liquidating and moving funds out of a couple of his qualified accounts."

He stopped mid action, "What? His personal qualified accounts or clients' accounts?'

"His personal ROTH and Traditional IRA and the Ladeski Family Trust."

"Geez," he said as he sat down again.

"He's been calling me to liquidate for him."

"You didn't think that odd?"

"No, he's done that in the past. It has become somewhat regular recently though, but... he's a big producer, so..."

"So, it didn't register that something may be up?"

"No."

"Where do the funds go?"

"I put in for a check in his name and it goes in his box."

"How much over the past month, do you know?"

"I can check. I don't know, not really paying attention to it."

"Is he having taxes withheld?"

"No, he made that clear not to do that."

"The guy needs money."

"Why? He's the biggest producer in the office."

"Who knows at this point but it sounds like he's overextended and in a short period of time. How many liquidations over the past month?"

"That I remember, seven."

"Geez and that didn't send up an alarm?"

"No, he's number one."

"Were the amounts around the same?"

"No. Some big, some small."

"Doesn't sound good. Sounds like he's paying off as he goes."

"What's that mean?"

"He may be our gambler," said Jake now looking at the top of June's desk and thinking as he started to rub his chin, "All three could be involved with gambling, or just Laddie," he mumbled to himself and then looked up at June, "Okay, put a list of his liquidations together; dates, times and amounts, and then we'll go from there."

"Okay, anything else?" asked June with both worry and the look of forced concentration on her face as more information than she had known, or thought was out there, was now coming at her quickly.

"No, get me that information and I'll fill Helen in on it. Then we might have another lunch outside the office, or maybe in one of the sound proof conference rooms," he said as he pushed up from the chair in front of her desk.

She gave the screen her full attention and started to punch keys as he turned to leave, "I'll close the door behind me," he said without turning as she nodded in confirmation, her eyes on the screen in front of her.

Within a minute he was standing in Helen's doorway. She looked up and he grinned, stepped in, and closed the door behind him.

"Laddie's been liquidating his personal accounts, including the family trust. He seems to be spreading the liquidation over three qualified accounts and I'm sure the ROTH is probably heavily drained as he's not declaring taxes on the other two."

"June?"

"She's been doing the liquidations for him."

"Smart. He knows she'd be a little bit awed because he is number one and she post approves trades. He needs the money badly."

"Yup and I think ol' Laddie boy may be tied up in gambling."

"All three of them?"

"Don't know yet. We'll have to figure that out."

"How's June?"

"Nervous of course."

"The Russians?"

"Yeah, I'm thinking. It has to be them."

"You think they have our reps in hock?"

"That's what I'm thinking but I hate to go there. That would add another layer to this whole thing, making it more dangerous."

"Were you sure to tell June that."

He grinned at Helen's humor, "The gambling, not the danger nor the possibility of the extent of Russian involvement."

"How do you think it may be working?"

"I don't know but Ladeski may be in debt to the Russians, and part of the deal, while he pays them off, is to launder money."

"Yeah, but tweedle dee and tweedle dumb are doing that."

"Ah, they've graduated from Mutt and Jeff."

"Yeah, because they aren't the brightest guys. I can't imagine that it gets more involved than them doing a favor for their clients."

"What if Ladeski is the target and he's getting the boys to do the laundering because it might be too obvious if he did."

"And what would they gain?"

"I don't know for sure. Let's check their new clients over the past year and then compare those clients with the clients they were bringing on over a year ago and back three years. Let's see if they were referred and see if, on average, they have a higher net worth than the clients from the previous year and then the year before that, and when did they bring the Russians on board? It has to have been over a year as June's pulled up utility churns out a year for a couple of them."

"Quid pro quo!"

"Ah, you do listen to me."

"God, I've heard you say it enough. That and 'query'"

He grinned, "Good, at least I'm having some effect. Let's try to get all this together and see if it gives us a clearer picture other than guessing."

"Okay, boss."

"Oh God, not boss. And to think, all from a kid's book."

"Yeah, why would they make any stupid references like that, that would make anyone wonder outside of the Russians?"

"The idiots let their Russian clients into the system and it was their way of telling them that they were on top of it for 'Laddie'."

"Cute."

"Yeah, the Russians are cute too."

"Don't tell June that."

"She's checking Laddie's trading and I told her to keep the Russians in mind as she did."

"Ah, good dreaming material for her."

"Yeah, well if there is a connection, other than the concrete connection in the notes and the emails, she'll see it."

"Yes she will. She'll see a lot of things."

"Her own psychedelic," smiled Jake.

"Very good."

"Yeah, but I don't wanna stretch her too long on this one."

"I think we can put what we have together pretty fast. It's either there or it isn't."

"Yup, I agree. Were you able to pull Ladeski's emails up, the one's you can access at least?"

"I'm starting to look at them and his case notes."

"Okay, good. Let me know if you find information that we can weave into what we have on Tweedledum and Tweedledee."

"You do listen," she grinned.

"On occasion. Okay, let me get out of here, I have some other fires to stamp out."

"I'm glad I'm not you."

"Oh you wait; when I leave I'm bequeathing this all to you."

"Not soon I hope."

As he turned for the door, "No, I can't leave you and June to this madness."

"Thanks boss."

He grinned. "Thanks!" he said as he left and pulled the door closed behind him thinking briefly how long he would last with Josh and then the thought was gone.

CHAPTER 21

IT ALL COMES TOGETHER

Three weeks later everything quickly crystalized and Jake called for a team meeting in one of the two smaller soundproof conference rooms, which they rarely used.

They all carried a file of paper print-offs and June was visibly nervous.

June and Helen took a seat at the table across from Jake.

Still standing, Jake started, "Okay, we know what we have, let's get it organized. I'm going to need to present this to Josh and then go to home office. Josh will probably be steamin' so we need to have it all together so I'm not in an uphill battle with him. Oh, I'm sparing both of you from that meeting," he finished as he looked down and shuffled through his file on the table before he sat as well.

There was visible relief on June's face when he let them know he would face Josh alone but she was still nervous about the Russians and now, her job as well, "Won't he want to get rid of us?"

Helen froze and Jake, just taking his seat, looked at June for a second. She had said the first thing that came to her mind as she did on occasion.

"This is our job June. He can't get rid of us. He may not like that his top boy is deep in the doo but that's life."

"But that's a lot of the office's income."

"No doubt and that will probably change. It's not only money laundering but 'Laddie', it more than appears, has a gambling problem and an IRS problem which fuels unethical behavior as we can now attest."

In the intervening three weeks they were able to determine that Colin Ladeski owed the US government eighty-two thousand five hundred and twenty-four dollars and had been avoiding a direct confrontation with the IRS through the use of a small shell company. It wasn't a great sum in the scheme of things but it was part of a greater problem with the man. They were able to determine that Mr. Ladeski had run up a gambling debt with the Russians which Henry confirmed, with a smile, after Helen met him with what they had come up with. It was clearly unfolding that he was still gambling and at the same time trying to maintain his debt with them. Part of the solution was to engage 'tweedle dee and tweedle dumb' while the Russians allowed him to keep gambling, putting the hook in deeper. This was the downfall for the Russians as the IRS became involved when he started holding back retirement account tax monies for his increasing debt. Phelps and Jenkins were getting premium referrals and clients for laundering small amounts of money on a regular basis. And in order for this type of small piece laundering to be effective, the Russians would have to be at multiple firms; but that wasn't their problem.

Jake looked at June for a minute while Helen waited and he could see she had something else on her mind, "What else June?"

"The Russians."

"They will lose. With these three gone and the FBI notified, again, through a follow-up to our Sar's, the Russians will probably just leave. Threats or action makes no sense, it would only confirm things for the FBI."

"Okay."

Helen nudged June with her elbow, "They wouldn't want you anyway. They'd probably come after me for reading all their email, so don't get too close."

"Oh, that's good. That didn't help," said Jake.

June was tense.

"Gotta have some fun with this," grinned Helen.

June's eyes started to dart from side to side as though she were looking for an escape.

"Don't listen to her June. We are handling this professionally and cleanly so that the storm will pass quickly."

"Well, that didn't help either," said Helen.

"Okay, let's just piece this thing together and get it organized so that I can go meet with Josh and drop a dime on these guys," then he looked at June and winked and she settled down. She had once asked him what 'drop a dime on them' meant as she saw it in an old movie and he had told her it was simply to tell the powers that be the truth about someone so that the bad guys would go away. It had sounded better than 'to snitch on someone'.

They spent two hours going over all of the documents that they had printed off and discussing everything that they had seen and, for the most part, discussed over the previous three weeks.

When Jake left, June was more at ease and he knew he had what he needed to meet with Josh.

Although Josh acted as a great defender of the 1st Amendment, he was not. Although he told people to speak their minds it was dangerous and unadvisable to do so, but Jake was one of the exceptions. He had grown up in an era where free speech and open discussion were the foundation and backbone of democracy and he was not going to change. Political Correctness had finally turned the corner that Jake knew it would turn as people were being shut down from speaking their minds from campuses, with extreme left leaning political activism, to the work place. It all scared Jake a bit but it angered him more so as an amateur historian. These were the types of things that happened in Nazi Germany or Stalinist Russia or, closer to home, The McCarthy Era. Now they were happening here and making The

McCarthy Era look like a dress rehearsal for a new form of totalitarianism that had finally come. This was part of what Jake dealt with every time he spoke privately with Josh about important issues that concerned the welfare of his team, or the proper treatment of other people in the office. The man would put on a great show of liberal understanding in both public and private settings but it was all patronizing. And when Jake held him to task on issues and tried to get him to do the next right thing that would show courage, in the atmosphere being created by corporate, he failed miserably and showed his anger with Jake. He had all of this to look forward to in a meeting that would start the ball rolling to expel Josh's top producer along with two up-and-comers. Jake wandered in thought over political correctness and the fact that it was holding Josh less responsible, as this was the new world order. He was concerned that the world he now lived in wanted to live in a past of their own creation and kill all hope for the future, and Josh was part of that. He then laughed sarcastically to himself about all of the ironies, and one in particular as it dealt with one of the primary ingredients of the American character: the heritage of the American Indian. They were now the Native Americans and soon to be no name at all and then no one. The irony of all of the political correctness, when it came to the imagine of the American Indian, was that it would eventually do what the 'paleface' was never able to do and that was to rip the American Indian cultures completely out of the American memory and society. They would remain in the fabric of every American but their memory and their influence would start to diminish more and more with each new generation in a way that it never had before. Their respected heritage would be exterminated through the removal of all images of these great cultures from the Land O'Lakes butter maiden, from the Red Lake Ojibwe Nation who were proud of her accurate image, to the crest of Dartmouth College. It had become an absurd sterilization of a collective memory and one of respect. They might be left to only have a legacy of running gambling halls which will only bring a tear to the eye of the spirit of the great Tecumseh. Now they were also destroying statues in the same way that the Taliban had in Afghanistan and it frightened him in the same way but he smiled, 'they will find their own way and one would hope without completely destroying the path that had been built for them by history, both good and bad.'

The meeting was set for December 7th, which seemed somewhat appropriate to Jake, in a way. Thanksgiving was well behind them and he had a week to prepare, which was fine. He actually had more than enough time to make sure that he had everything he wanted as he would address the office situation as a whole along with the current situation with Laddie and the boys.

———

December 7th came bright and clear and unusually warm. It was a fine day as Jake walked through Bryant Park and walked across the blue carpeted platform that surrounded the yearly ice rink. He stopped for a moment and listened to the still, punctuated by Frank Sinatra singing It Was a Very Good Year, coming in over the speakers which surrounded the rink. He thought of how far he had come then he continued to walk again. As he walked off the platform and headed for Fifth Avenue, he saw the table that he and Helen and June had sat at those few short months ago and he heard them and smiled and laughed to himself, and then left the park.

He started to think of the things he had forgotten to do for the ones he had loved in one way or the other. He shook his head wondering why he was thinking of these things all bitter-sweet. He stood at the light on Fifth Avenue and looked over at Patience and Fortitude majestically guarding the New York Public Library and what it held. They were telling him that they would always protect the sharing of knowledge and ideas. They would protect it all, for all to share. He smiled to himself again and the light turned and he headed to the office and his meeting, leaving Patience and Fortitude behind to mind their perennial vigil. He remembered his mother telling him of the first time that she saw the lions as a small child and how safe they made her feel. He thought of how she taught him to be good and kind to all by example. He could never be as good as she had been but he would stand for what was right and protect those he was responsible for, that was all he could do. He was going to talk about more than Laddie and his cohorts.

Jake's meeting was set for ten that morning which gave him plenty of time to get through most of his emails, finalize his notes with anything he may have left out, and update himself with several other issues that were on his plate. He had his one cup of black coffee, no sugar, which he grabbed at Cucina's on his way through Grand Central Station. He also had time to send out an email to the office reminding everyone that it was Pearl Harbor Day. Along with the email he sent a picture of the Arizona with the American flag waving above her white memorial at half-mast. It was ironic, the memorial had been designed by an Austrian Jew who had fled the Nazis in Europe, moving to Hawaii and converting to Catholicism along the way, and then being interned in Hawaii right after the Japanese attack. Japanese Americans were not the only ones who had been interned. He smiled at the irony and the sadness he had with regard to the lack of knowledge about important events, which was now pervasive in America. He put the words, "Pearl Harbor, December 7, 1941, lest we forget. Stay safe," on the note. He kept it simple.

He knew that Josh would say something about this note he sent out on Pearl Harbor as he had heard about the note that he had sent on Veteran's Day, November 11, asking the office what 11,11,11 meant and telling them that the first one to give him the answer got lunch on him. The office had fun with it and as a result many asked him questions about the Great War. Josh did not like it. The previous Memorial Day had been another occasion for Josh's intolerance for remembrance and publicly appreciating America and what she stood for. He had sent out a photo of a young woman lying on the grave of her young fiancé killed in Afghanistan. They hadn't even had the chance to marry. She was lying prone, leaning on her elbows with her head facing the white marble stone and down in prayer, and one knew she was talking with her fiancé. He never did hear as much back on these messages as he felt he should have but the Memorial Day message was a bit different, he had heard from a handful of people. He had said, "What we cherish: our fellow Americans; and what we honor this day: those who sacrificed themselves so that we may have our barbeques." One of the leaders wrote back and she said, 'Thank you, you are making me think.' From yet another who was traveling abroad; "Thank you. I visited Dachau yesterday where I lost a family member and you so eloquently reminded me of the sacrifices made to protect us all and keep us safe, God bless."

Josh had not liked the visual. He had said it was too depressing for Memorial Day. These thoughts were going through his head about the man he worked for as he collected himself. Pearl Harbor Day had reminded him of it all.

Outside Josh's office Marsha nodded to him, "He's waiting for you."

Josh knocked lightly, twice, with the knuckle of the middle finger of his right hand and immediately heard, "Come in."

As he walked in he saw Josh still at his standing desk, on his computer, so he took a moment to stare out the windows at the buildings running up and down Park Avenue.

"Ok," he heard from behind as Josh hit the last key on his computer keyboard and clicked the mouse to send the message he had been working on when Jake came in.

Jake turned and dropped his file on the small conference table and pulled out a chair as Josh took the seat at the head of the table.

"What have we got?"

Jake opened his file and without looking down at it, "Money laundering, a big rep in even bigger debt, Russians and quid pro quo."

"Who's the rep in debt."

"Ladeski."

"Can't be."

Jake knew this would be his first response so he pulled the paper on top of his stack in the file he had just opened, put it on the table and slid it over to Josh, "He has eighty-two thousand dollars and change due the IRS. This is their notification for collection."

"This says, 'Appletime.'"

"It's a shell company set up by Mr. Ladeski to deflect the IRS for a while."

"There's got to be a mistake. He makes more than that in a month."

"It gets better. We feel he's servicing a gambling debt while still gambling."

"How can that be?"

Jake visualized the front cover of Little Lucia's School with Little Lucia and Laddie running against a winter background of children skating on a pond. He smiled to himself briefly knowing that it would never come up in this conversation, but it might be humorous to go on that line.

"Here is a consolidated version of his cash withdrawals from his qualified accounts and his family trust," he said as he slid over three sheets of paper stapled together. "You will notice rather large sums of money coming out over short periods of time without taxes being taken out."

Taking the papers in his hand and looking at the top sheet, "So, what does this mean? He's just taking money out of his accounts!"

Jake laid out additional information which made it difficult for Josh to disagree. The actions of Mr. Ladeski were the hallmark of someone in growing debt. Jake had seen it before and Josh had been educated, in one of his Directors' compliance classes, about the obvious characteristics of rep runaway debt. This was too classic of a rep who was running into increasing and uncontrollable debt, or gambling. It was accentuated by the fact that the man made seven figures a year and was still 'self-liquidating'.

"I guess we have to put him on,… what do you call it?"

"Financial Stress Supervision"

"Yes, that's it."

"It's gone beyond that Josh. He has crossed the line that that type of supervision is meant to prevent him from crossing."

"What do you mean by that?" snapped Josh realizing his worst fears, that his top producer might be in trouble beyond anything fixable. He became defensive.

"It appears Phelps and Reynolds are involved as well," said Jake realizing the hard part was coming.

"How?"

"Quid pro quo," said Jake as he moved another two pages, stapled together, over to Josh.

"What's this?"

"These are high net worth clients that both Phelps and Reynolds have brought in over the past year or so, right around the time we see some minor liquidation activity in Mr. Ladeski's accounts. They do not fit the profile of earlier clients for both men and," he shoved another stack of stapled papers over to Josh, "these emails, which we requested through you, show initial conversations with these clients which clearly indicate that they were referrals to these men from Mr. Ladeski."

"So, that doesn't mean anything. And if Ladeski was giving them big referrals, what is he getting out of it?"

Here comes the good part thought Jake, "The Russians, look at the names," Jake simply said to let it sink in before he went on to explain.

Josh froze with the last grouping of papers in his hand and looked up at Jake and hesitated, "What about the Russians?"

"As you know, we loaded our authorized translator software onto our computers and started to read a great many emails from the Russians to Phelps and Reynolds. The emails that have multiple Russian addresses on them are the emails of interest and the attached emails to other Russians are in Russian," he said as he handed yet another grouping of stapled paged to Josh. "We highlighted and numbered the pertinent translated lines in these emails and attached the numbered corresponding translations, which you may want to famil-iarize yourself with but they clearly point to money laundering for the Russians. This is additional supporting information to the reports that we have already made."

"I don't believe all of this," said Josh as he dropped the set of papers in his hands and took the stapled sheets of emails with translations and started to look through them and then stopped, "How does this all add up? Doesn't make sense."

"It makes sense when you put the pieces together."

Josh dropped the emails on the pile of papers that was starting to collect in front of him, looked down at them and then looked up at Jake with a face sheathed in anger, "You're just causing trouble, like that note you sent out on Pearl Harbor today."

The man wasn't making sense. He had just realized that he was going to lose his top producer and two of his up-and-coming produc-ers and that a broader investigation into his office would be opened which would bring in FINRA and possibly the FBI. The man was in shock and denial and it was time to nip it all in the bud and address his overall attitude and behavior before the whole team became a target.

"Listen, it is Pearl Harbor Day and it was quite important to my generation as we grew up in the shadow of WWII and Korea. FDR said it is a day that will live in 'infamy' and it can't if it is forgotten about along with the lessons learned. It is respect given to those Americans who died defending us as we also defend this office."

"Whaddaya mean defend this office? You and your people do noth-ing but cause trouble."

"Cause trouble? We burn our feet everyday trying to stomp out fires in this office before they get out of control, and your lack of sup-port has given fuel to those fires."

"Whaddaya mean!"

"You don't back us up when we need the Director to step in and do so. You should not tolerate bad behavior towards my team and myself and you have in the past. You have even gone as far as to side with some reps behind our backs and ridicule your own compliance team."

"Where did you get that from?"

"You don't need to know but suffice it to say we have been told about it on several occasions and you know you are doing it. It does not help you and the maintenance of this office."

"What do you know about the maintenance of this office."

"Quite a bit more than I should besides the compliance aspect."

"Such as what?"

"You are cheap!"

"What?"

"The Christmas bonus for example. I got ninety-five dollars and my team members fifty dollars each and their salaries and mine are much lower than the average in Manhattan for our positions."

"That's a nice bonus."

"No it's not! The lowest bonus that I received for compliance at agencies of other firms, that were less profitable than this one, was four thousand dollars. And not only that, you work the hell out of the staff and put a bonus number out in front of them that you make unreachable."

"That's not true."

"Last year the office came within one thousand dollars of a multimillion-dollar goal and you did not give them even a piece of the bonus. You boasted how profitable the office was and took everyone out to lunch and that was it. Have you noticed that you have a large turnover in this office? Have you ever figured out the cost of retraining people versus paying them appropriately, or thought about the good cost-effective work that appropriate pay and incentive generate?"

"They're just ungrateful and I'm glad people like that have left and, by-the-way, it's not a Christmas bonus, it's a holiday bonus."

"Are you kidding? Like the Christmas tree which you persist in calling a holiday tree."

"That's what it is."

"That's an insult. It would be like calling the menorah a holiday candelabra."

"Well, maybe I'll get rid of both."

"Why, and take another joy away from these people like the 'Secret Santa'".

"What about that?"

"A young lady tried to organize a Secret Santa gift giving with her group and you shut her down saying she can't use the word Santa and that it would have to include the whole office. Are you kidding with this stuff?"

"Well, Santa will offend others who are not Christian and you have to include everyone."

"Well that effectively killed it and that young lady was made to feel as though she committed a criminal act. She came into my office upset and in tears. Did you know she's Jewish by-the-way? Not only are you not compensating these people correctly but you are shutting them down from any joy. It has become so bad in this office people whisper, afraid to speak their minds about anything."

"That's not true!"

"Of course it's true and you must, at some level, know that it is or you just have no true feeling for people."

"I am morally sound and always do the right thing, and I'm happy with myself."

Jake smiled to himself.

"What's so funny?" asked Josh seeing the smile.

"Oh, nothing really, Washington once said, 'Human happiness and moral duty are inseparably connected' and I know that when someone goes out of their way to illustrate that they live both they probably live neither."

"Are you calling me immoral? Washington was immoral."

"Excuse me?"

"You heard me; Washington was immoral."

"If it were not for that man, we would not have the republic which we seem to be working overtime to try to destroy these days."

"He had slaves!"

"Everyone of wealth or land, both North and South, had slaves in those days. They knew that they needed to abolish it. The Declaration of Independence almost never came about due to the argument over slavery. Jefferson, himself a slave owner, wrote, 'We hold these truths to be self-evident, that all men are created equal...' They were laying the groundwork for us in the future to create and evolve a Republic where all would be equal and the Constitution gave us the foundation for doing just that. That was the 18th Century in British-America and it was pretty amazing and foresighted to put such words down on paper. They had taken the basis of the Magna Carta and expanded it to freedom for all and preservation of free will, and they put their lives on the line to do so. Washington had even set up pensions for his slaves and helped lead the way, along with Jefferson, to a better nation where all were equal. This Republic is a work in progress and always will be. How will the future judge us? I hope not by their standards or they will have learned nothing," said Jake almost running out of breath.

"Well, he owned slaves. You have your own opinion and you shouldn't be sending out those emails like you did today."

"What, reminding people of their heritage and how their freedoms, given to them by the Founders, are preserved."

"You shouldn't say those things."

"What about Freedom of Speech?"

"What about it? There are just certain things you should not and cannot say, things that are not correct to say."

"'If freedom of speech is taken away, then dumb and silent we may be led, like sheep to the slaughter.' Washington said that too."

"That's nonsense."

"We are already seeing silenced people go underground and meet on that wonderful thing called the internet where madness is espoused through the non-confrontational and anonymous platform of social media, and internet news and articles. I would rather have public disagreement face to face which breeds understanding, and this only happens when freedom of speech is sanctified for what it is: the equalizer of public opinion and action with rational behavior as the offspring. Apposing opinions used to meet in this country through discussion and both sides would learn. This made us greater as a people, but no more."

"A mouthful and just wrong."

"Might be a mouthful but we have a social civil war, with a degree of violence, going on where certain groups are shutting down others and this will backfire much as it has in this office."

"Whaddaya mean by that?"

"We lose too many good people over both pay and the atmosphere in this office."

"What about the atmosphere?"

"People, especially the staff, are afraid to speak their minds on anything, as I just told you. Their speech is guarded for fear of reprimand. Once you shut people down, they look for a relief valve and, in our case, it is the door to another job."

"That's not true and if you don't like it maybe you should leave."

"Maybe I should. You have always told everyone to speak their minds but, as I say, they know that not to be a reality."

"That's insane."

"Is it, you are telling me I can leave because you don't like what I am saying. You mean that but you also know that you have a complex office that needs compliance experience, even though you don't like it."

"That's too convoluted."

"Is it? Maybe you need to step down off your horse."

"Whaddaya mean by that?"

"You live in a plantation house and look down on your dominion and its minions."

"That's over the top and just not so; and whaddaya mean plantation house."

"Just being a little facetious. Maybe two hundred years from now society will look at your life and try to disavow any relationship to it and condemn it in the manner that they are now condemning some of the Founders. They may look at the flow of illegal aliens, with all of its associated hardship and violence, as a type of slavery that people like you condoned. Cheap labor clustered in groups looking for work and no one saying a word to the employers making a killing, much like the wealthy cotton growers of the antebellum South, or should I say pre- Civil War South. It is a form of enslaving people here illegally, with little choice, and at the same time disenfranchising those citizens who need the work."

"That's ridiculous."

"It really doesn't matter as it will be up to the future to be smarter than the past and learn from its mistakes and gain from its achievements. If they choose to hide it or change it instead of respecting it, as they are doing today, they will be lost."

"A lot of the past was not good and should be erased."

"So, you are saying that we should deny the bad and only celebrate what we choose to be the best. If so, you are helping to create a reality that will as well, selectively, bury the good with the bad and we will go backwards in our development, towards a greater Republic, with a made up history. This country has been the most benevolent society in the western world in the past century, warts and all, and there are many reasons for that and why we are, at our base, a good people. It is truly American to reach out at our own risk and cost and help others when they cannot help themselves and the world knows this with a strange resentment but yet a guarantee for help when they need it, which they have come to expect. Some of us truly do not know what we have, politics and the adverse effects of entitlement aside."

"We aren't so good."

"Why do you say that?"

"Because we are unfair."

"Says a man who makes a very good seven figure income at the expense of his employees. Don't you find your statement rather gratuitous?"

"No, why should I."

"It seems to me that you play the role of a great progressive because it allays your guilt."

"Guilt over what?"

"I don't know, you tell me… Listen, we have more controllable issues here which we need to look at. The state of our country and society is another stage to stand on at another time. For now, we have an immediate compliance problem."

"You make enough here so you should be happy."

"Josh, I make thirty percent less than Kathy George in our upstate office with none of the problems we handle here in Manhattan. That office probably doesn't even know we have a Russian population in the States."

"Oh, I doubt that. She probably makes just what you do if not less because she's upstate."

"You can easily find out and I am underpaid to answer your question and part of that is that I'm an old White guy who you feel has no place to go."

Josh froze for a moment, "No, that's nonsense."

"You and Doris, as the CFO, know what the pay scales for my position are and you know you have a deal. You know I am right and there is no point in discussing it right this moment."

"Right this moment?"

"Maybe we need to take it up after we deal with our current situation, although we clean up one and there are two more behind it. But this one needs to be dealt with quickly and firmly, and now."

"I can't lose my number one producer!"

"It looks like you may have no choice. This is the letter that is being FedEx'd to home office today along with the accompanying material, some of which you have piled in front of you," he said as he handed Josh the letter and then let him take his time to read it.

Finally looking up from the letter, after his face had become angry while reading it, Josh sighed, "You're really hammering them."

"Not really. That implies that I am doing harm intentionally. I am just laying out the facts in the letter and referring to the accompanying material. The faster that you and home office act on this the better it will be with FINRA and the FBI."

He saw Josh's face soften and give in as he looked at the letter again, not reading it but just looking at it.

"Okay then, take care of it."

"Do you have any questions at this point?"

"No, let's wait until home office gets back to us."

"Okay then, let me get going on it."

"Here, you can take these."

"No, those are your copies," said Jake as he handed Josh the folder that he was carrying and the rest of the papers it held, "and there is additional material in here that you may want to go over. Once you do that let me know if you have questions," he finished as he pushed the chair back and stood.

He headed for the door as Josh got up and went back to his stand-up desk and computer.

"Let me know as soon as you hear from home office," said Josh, as Jake crossed the threshold of the door to leave.

"Will do," and he closed the door behind him facing Marsha, for a second, as he closed it and he hesitated, then he smiled and nodded, "Thanks Marsha," and then headed back to his office.

He had the FedEx envelope all set to go and instead of leaving it in the building's FedEx box he had the front desk call for a pickup and dropped the envelope at the desk, and headed for Helen's office.

CHAPTER 22

THE FINAL MILE: PAST AND PRESENT

The door was open but he tapped on it to get Helen's attention as she had her head down in some papers and she was physically right on top of them, which reminded him to tell her to get her eyes checked.

"You know, you should get your eyes checked out, pretty soon you'll have them so close that the print'll rub off on your nose," he said as she looked up.

"Funny. It just blocks out everything else when I have them that close"

"Yeah, keep saying that."

"So, how did it go?"

"It went, and on top of it I told him he was cheap," and before he could finish Helen looked past him at the open door and made a pushing motion with her hand.

"Oh damn," he said as he closed the door and then sat. "Yeah, well I told him he was cheap."

"I'm sure he liked that."

"Oh, you bet. He let me know that Washington was amoral and

that America wasn't so good."

"What?"

"It's not important, he really didn't give me anything to hang on to with regard to pay or bonus except that he assured me that I was being well paid for an old White man."

"He said that, 'old White man'?"

"No, I did and I let him know about the bad bonuses and no bonuses."

"Oh, I would have liked to have seen that."

"Wasn't that exciting."

"I'm sure he loves you even more now."

"Oh, you bet."

"What about our boys?"

"Oh, he's mad but he knows they're done and there's nothing he can do about it. Just dropped the FedEx at the front desk for pickup."

"Blames us?"

"Of course."

"I love that, for all the work we do to protect that income of his and our clients and other reps."

"Yeah, all of the above but he doesn't see it because he feels the loss and not the retention through our prevention," said Jake.

"Better tell June that he knows and that he's okay, and that the FedEx is off to headquarters."

"I'll leave the bit out about approaching him about bad pay though; oh, and no bonuses."

"Good idea."

Helen detected something else as she saw Jake thinking, a little lost in himself, "What else?"

"Whaddaya mean?" he asked, snapping his attention back to her.

"Well, you went someplace else briefly."

"Oh, I'm going to have to have a heart to heart with him after we take care of this."

"Yeah, well don't push it. I don't need you going someplace else."

"It ticks him off but he knows I speak my mind, and I usually do it discretely so he's not put on the spot publicly."

"Please keep it that way."

"I will. Now off to see June and then I think I'll go out for a chilly walk."

"Okay, probably a good idea to cool off. I can see you are a little steamed."

"I thought I hid that well."

"Yeah, like a zit on the nose of a model."

"Oh, that's good. Where do you come up with this stuff?"

She laughed, "It just pops into my mind as a visual, probably the Irish in me. I see it clearly, no messing around."

"And that's what I like about you, says the old guy who ruined that young lady's night by sitting next to me in the piano club in Latham," and they both laughed thinking of that night during a headquarters quarterly meeting, as he stood up pushing the chair back and turned to the door to head for June's office.

"You can scare her a bit before you tell her, it's okay."

He turned at the open door, "You're bad. I'll give her a free ride today," and he turned and left, leaving the door open as he'd found it.

June had greeted the fact of Josh's acceptance, along with the moving of the problem to the home office, with exuberance, almost manic in appearance. She was back up and running and once again saying his words before he could quite get them out. She would have no more Russian mob dreams for the immediate future and Jake felt better hearing her like this. He worried about her but with this situation all but gone from their desk she was okay.

He left her in good shape and somewhat hyper as he headed to his office to get his black wool coat, even though it was almost a spring day in December. He never left the office, or rarely, until recently, when he started going out to the front of the building just to get five minutes of fresh air before returning. But today he would take a walk on Lexington and head south towards Grand Central Station.

The cool air on his face relaxed him as he found his thoughts going back in time and looking at his whole career, or at least parts of it spread over the years. He thought of his first job as a stockbroker and of Jim, his first manager, and his friends back then. The four of them were something and he knew it at the time. They all had a special bond with each other but time had sent them in different directions and they eventually lost touch. He was thankful for the old friendships that seemed to survive from grade school and college. They, for some reason, had more staying power.

He started to think of all of the things that he had forgotten to do. He thought of the first woman he had loved at the end of college those many years ago. He had been too young and immature to understand it though sadly he did now. He thought of that woman he had met briefly one night at Mellon's on Third Avenue thirty years earlier. They had spent that one night with each other and for some reason she remained strong in his memory. She was a photographer and she wanted a child, which had pushed him away after that night, and then she was gone, headed to South America. He had always hoped, secretly, that maybe she did have that child and that it was his.

He was thinking of this with some sadness which was not self-pity but guilt over not recognizing what, at this moment in time, he knew were more important events and situations than he had realized at the time. He was immature back then and not selfish. He had always tried to do the right thing and sometimes doing the right thing was wrong as he moved on. In the end, he had Charlotte, who he would not trade for the world. He would give up everything that he was if need be to keep her safe and happy.

His thoughts were a kaleidoscope of lost opportunity and lost intimacies that were still warm in his heart but also now just doubtful memories, when he saw her. They were two blocks from the entrance to Grand Central Station. She was one step down on the interior stairs to a chocolatier with a full glass façade, just to his right. Their eyes met and she stopped as did he. She looked right at him as though she knew him and had been searching for him, and everything around him went away; and it was as though there was a light around her, a strange type of aura that captivated him. She was thirty years younger and he knew her as though she was from a past long gone and they had been searching for each other and had finally both been found. They were briefly frozen in time with each other and as he walked by and towards the entrance to Grand Central, and started to mingle with the crowd heading into the Lexington Avenue entrance, he knew he had to turn and go back. He had hesitated because he was much older and he hadn't wanted to startle her, but that should have nothing to do with it. Any perceived impropriety had no place here. There was some sort of connection which would override any awkwardness he felt about age. He just needed to know what it was about and he knew she was wondering the same thing. He remembered Jaworski's Synchronicity which he had read a lifetime ago and which directed one not to pass up such opportunities presented by fate. He turned and headed back, but she was gone, she had vanished into the crowd.

He returned again the next day at the same time hoping she might once again appear but she too became only part of his memory of an event that had left him sadly happy. Who was she? It didn't matter at this point; they had made a connection like a long lost father and daughter or a love from another time. It left him in a place to better judge where he currently stood and where he stood was not where he should be. He would give Josh an ultimatum and Josh might take the opportunity to get rid of a troublesome old White guy who could be a legal problem, and a guy who was developing closer relationships with his reps than he himself was developing.

He walked past Grand Central, clearing his head, and crossed 42nd Street, then turned up 42nd towards 5th Avenue and the Lions in front of the library. He had a need to see Patience and Fortitude. Those two lions always put a smile on his face and set him straight. He would look at them, as they guarded the library and what it contained for everyone, and see things more clearly as he always seemed to, simply in their presence.

He came up to 5th Avenue still thinking of the young woman he had seen and felt the previous day, and he stood just off the corner as the light was against him. Then it happened. A young woman, looking down at her cell phone, walked right past him, heading across the street, as an old Checker came storming across 42nd. Without thinking, his hand came up and he grabbed the young woman by the back of the collar and pulled her back, just in time, to a cry of "My God," from a woman standing next to her. She was safe and confused. The woman who cried 'my God' looked at the young confused woman and shook her head, "You almost got clobbered by a cab," then shook her head again and smiled at Jake, and everyone crossed as Jake stood still and watched them. The young girl continued on not saying a word, not even acknowledging that she had just been saved as she had her head back down in the phone. And then, as Jake started to cross, a bike blew through the light and almost hit him. It was time to leave the city. Bikes were all over the city now and they had no place there, 'it was New York not Beijing' he thought. He remembered that long before email there were bike messengers who traveled at high speed back and forth, all over the city, delivering documents and financial grams and anything small enough to go on their backs as they used pedestrians as obstacles in their high-speed obstacle course to and from deliveries. He had been standing across the street from Port Authority in 1980 when one of these messengers came the wrong way down 8th Avenue and knocked a woman, in a business suit, to the ground. The police were there quickly and he later learned that she had been killed. No, Manhattan was no place for bikes but they were now growing in number along with motorized skateboards. One of those skateboards had almost hit him and the rider had laughed as he whizzed by within inches on 42nd and Broadway one morning on the way to work. He had regretted that he hadn't moved his briefcase, at the last minute, into the path of the oncoming board. No, the city was changing, basic values were being lost and crime was coming back with this new mayor. Time Square was now a tourist park missing the busy traffic that he was comfortable with, and it was a place that he avoided once again. People did not seem to be paying attention to the city around them. He had walked into or been walked into by too many people looking down at their phones. It was becoming a world of automatons. It was time to leave. He had even asked his team and the operations people not to wear headphones or earbuds in the city because people had died wearing them in lower Manhattan when a terrorist drove his truck down a pedestrian track. They hadn't heard him coming even though people were seen to be shouting at them to get out of the way.

He approached Patience and Fortitude and walked to the middle of the steps and looked from side to side at both, smiled, and said, "Hey fellas, I'll miss you every morning. Take care of the place would ya. I know you will." A tourist looked at him, as she passed with her family from the mid-west, and looked at him as if he were crazy but he could swear he heard both Patience and Fortitude acknowledge him. As a tourist she would never experience that.

Then, as he turned to leave, he stopped and thought for a second, 'A Checker? They've been long gone, what was that doing here?' He shook his head, smiled, and headed back to the office.

The following week Jake was working on an ultimatum. Either his pay goes up at least three percent to the base for this position, which was ridiculous anyway, or he would leave.

In the middle of this letter, and debating it with himself as he loved his work and his team, he once again thought of such an ultimatum giving Josh an opportunity. He knew that it could be, and probably would be, an excuse for Josh to get rid of an old guy and one getting too friendly with his reps, that is if he thought he could squeak by on compliance without him. Josh knew that Jake's team was now the best in the system and well oiled. Jake, understanding this, knew he would probably go and he thought more about it, while looking at his letter, when the phone rang.

It was Josh, they had a new rep that Jake had not been informed about, which was not atypical. He had been a Russian immigrant during 'Magic Carpet' and one who came with a book of clients, having been in the business for seven years. It was odd to get a call like this but he responded and headed to the large office, in the back, that had been vacated a month earlier but would now house this new rep.

His name was Lev and that's all Jake needed to know for now, said Josh. He wanted to meet Jake because he wanted to meet the head of compliance, which had never been requested by any new rep before.

Lev smiled condescendingly from the doorway of the large office, as though sending a warning, when he extended his hand to Jake.

"Nice to meet you Jack," he intoned with a still heavy Russian accent that reminded Jake, briefly, of Bullwinkle Moose, making him grin without thinking.

"It's Jake, nice to meet you as well," said Jake with purposeful reserve as he extended his hand.

"I hear you are historian," he said pointedly with a heavy accent on historian.

"Jake looked at Josh."

"I told him you liked history when he asked me about you last week."

"Oh," said Jake looking back at Lev, "Yes, I read about mostly 20th Century history, the World Wars and more."

"Your Marines on Saipan!"

Jakes eyebrows went up. Why in God's name would he mention Saipan, "Yes, it was a bloodbath quite frankly, like most of the Pacific islands."

"My Japanese sensei at my dojo say your Marines slaughtered all Japanese civilians on Saipan."

Jake felt his blood rise, the guy was pushing him; well, he was going to get what he asked for, "The Japanese troops were using civilians as human bombs because they didn't care as they were not considered true Japanese, not being from the main islands. The Marines were horrified. The civilians were also led to believe that the Americans were monsters and would rape and torture much the way the Japanese behaved in their conquered lands, but it was the opposite. It was the opposite of what Russian troops did when they raped and pillaged Berlin at the end of the war. Japanese civilians were throwing themselves off what is now called suicide cliff above Marpi Point in Saipan while the Marines tried to calm them over loudspeakers. It was deplorable of the Japanese troops to create this situation. They were simply barbaric. Maybe you should look at some old newsreels as they filmed a great deal of it. I'm sure YouTube has it and maybe inform your sensei, as he has lost face in my opinion by making those accusations," Jake finished, seeing Josh in the corner of his eye uptight and nervous at this point.

Lev smiled sarcastically, "Ah, but we Russians came in and ended war with Japan."

Jake's blood really came up, "You what? Yeah, you invaded Manchuria five days before the Japanese surrendered after we had already dropped the bombs. What was it? Oh yes, Manchurian Strategic Offensive Operation or land grab and grab whatever you could."

Lev shut up and just grinned but Josh spoke up.

"Yes, umm, ah, Jake and his team are here to help you maneuver the mine fields of compliance."

"Maybe wrong choice of analogies for compliance regulations," said Jake, his face stern.

"No matter," said Lev with a threatening grin as he turned without so much as a goodbye and headed into his new office, then stopped and turned, "Oh, and there is no such thing as Russian mob." He turned again, and headed for the desk.

Jake looked at Josh who refused to meet Jake's look. Then, without a word, Josh followed Lev into the office.

Jake just walked away. Maybe his letter had perfect timing to it. He would put the letter in Josh's mailbox on Friday so that it could be mulled over on the weekend. He did not tell Helen and June. There was no reason to unsettle them just yet.

That Monday came quickly and he had an email from Josh. It had been sent Saturday and it requested him for a meeting at eleven that morning.

Jake knocked at the appointed hour and heard, "Come in," from the other side of Josh's door.

Josh was standing at his standing-desk and computer when Jake walked in and as Jake took a seat he turned and put on a fake sad face that was transparently patronizing.

He walked over to the table and said, adding more phony sadness, "Doris and I have looked at your letter and we have decided that you get paid well enough and we have decided to let you go."

Jake half expected this except they were "letting him go" and in a way it was a relief that he would not have to deal with this man and his CFO much longer. His first thought went to his team and his heart sank to his stomach as he had, to some degree, assured them that he would be there for them. They were his responsibility, and he also enjoyed their company and their intelligence and strength, and he would miss that.

"Well, I disagree with your assessment that I get paid well enough for what I do but that will be your problem to deal with. I would like a month to put everything in order and set my team up so they are not left hanging."

"Is that enough time?"

"Yes," was all he said as he thought about having to tell the team.

"We'll send a communication to the agency," said Josh.

Knowing that they would make up some nonsense far from the truth Jake said, "I would like to see it before you send it out." He knew it would say that he had decided to leave and had planned it with Josh for a long time but he did not want it to sound ridiculous. He would have input but he would not backstab the leadership, that was not him. He would put everything in its right place before he left. As his father would say, 'leave the campsite better than you found it, always.'

He would leave this campsite better than he found it but he would also send his own email before he left, which would not contain condemnation but end by saying, "I will miss most of you." This last line would lead to reps calling him just before he walked out the door to make sure that they were not on the list of those who he would not miss. Many people smiled at the note and knew what Jake was saying between the lines.

He headed for his office to think before he told Helen and June. He had not prepared anything to say as they were more important to him than that. He would just speak his heart and then later take them for a final lunch.

Before calling them to his office he thought about the office as a whole. He thought about a united office instead of the one he was working in and getting ready to leave. United we stand divided we fall. Jake thought of his first-grade teacher teaching them about the strength and wisdom of an America that was built by immigrants wanting to become Americans and bringing their skills and knowledge, with enthusiasm, to the great American melting pot. It had made the country strong and safe for both new and old Americans and that was changing. People who thought they were being selfless were actually selfish, and in their selfishness and through their attitude of entitlement they were becoming segregated groups by gender, culture or politics and it was sad. Civilized values were vanishing. Management, like the one he worked for, was paying homage to this for selfish reasons as well, which he found sanctimonious. Jake remembered that first grade teacher holding up one pencil, grasped at either end, and holding it high so the class could see. She had said, "This is what happens when we are not all together as one," and she snapped the pencil in two which startled the first-graders. Then she held up a handful of pencils in the same manner and tried to snap them but couldn't. "And this is how strong we are together." They all understood how important they were to each other that day and how they were all Americans whether their parents came from Italy or Germany, or wherever their immigrant connection originated. No one could separate them; they were one as Americans. He was seeing that shatter along with freedom of speech in the place he now worked and he would soon be happy to leave, but not happy to leave those he cherished as friends and peers. He was simply living in the Age of Unreason filled with grand and hollow platitudes underlined by a collective selfishness and absent of basic human values.

He then picked up the phone and called both Helen and June and asked them to come to his office.

He left his door open and Helen was the first to show up. He was sitting, slouched in his office chair, leaning back and Helen knew something was different as she entered. Then another shadow moved quickly past the glazed glass in front of his office and it was June. Helen was taking a seat as June entered and she too could feel that something was different as it was quiet with no one saying a word.

"Close the door June, please."

As she took a seat he grinned compassionately and Helen could see it.

"What's up boss," she said trying to break the atmosphere and change what she felt was coming.

"I have to leave you both," he said directly and it hit June like a ton of bricks. Her face changed and she looked confused as her jaw dropped. Helen was different, she was expecting this day and shook her head and lowered it.

"I'm not leaving immediately. I'll be here for the next month to put things in order and Helen, I'm recommending you as my replacement. I know you agree with that June."

June nodded her head in sad agreement.

"Helen, you are the best choice they could possibly have and they know that but they will probably look outside too to keep you where you are and load more on you as they look for a cheap replacement for me. They deem both of your salaries high which I don't agree with but that is the nature of the beast we deal with here. I have tried to get you both raises in the past and pushed for the bonus to be partially activated twice, when we came close, but to no avail. I am just telling you this not to beat up on them but to let you know what you are dealing with."

"I've always known," said Helen in a voice which lacked her normal energy, like the wind had been kicked out of her. She was unusually quiet.

"I know you have; even before me you were aware of what we were dealing with. I can only tell you that I have never worked with two better people. You are the best and you made me look good. You will carry on and shine even if, in my estimation, you are not compensated properly. They know what they have in you two."

"You are the best boss," said June still confused with her eyes showing some bewilderment.

"That means more to me than anything else June."

"It's a crime," said Helen showing some degree of anger on her face.

"Listen, I gave them an ultimatum on my salary knowing that they might use it as an excuse to get rid of an old guy and they did."

"An Old White Guy," said Helen with a forced grin. "He also didn't like you getting closer to his reps than he had managed to get."

"Maybe so but this all stays between us. I'm not on a vendetta and this is just life. I don't want to create unnecessary anger in this office but you both needed to know exactly what happened. They will release one of their standard email notices that someone has '...decided to leave and we wish them luck in their new job' except unlike others I will not have disappeared by the time the email goes out."

"But that would be a lie," said June becoming more alert and back out of her confused daze.

"They always lie June," said Helen looking at her.

"It doesn't matter. It's part of the atmosphere here. Don't dwell on it and you both know that in a worse case situation, if things get unbearable, any firm on the street would jump at you both if you became available."

"I've been thinking of it but only at a distance because I wanted to keep working with you," said Helen. "Now that might change."

"Thank you for that Helen," said Jake as June became nervous again by Helen's confession. Helen had become an anchor for June.

"June, I'm not going anywhere right now and if I start to think about it seriously, I will tell you," said Helen noticing June's concern and looking right at her, as she spoke, with deep sincerity in her voice.

"I think we should get out of here today and have a nice lunch someplace. Sound good?"

They went to lunch that day at a restaurant off of Lexington that they considered theirs as they had gone there twice before. The lunch loosened up and relaxed June; and Helen decided, as they talked, that she would leave as well and would have to talk to June about it at some point soon.

At the end of the month Josh asked Jake to stay longer as he could not find the proper replacement and Jake had simply said, "No."

Just before leaving for the last time, Jake stopped into the Chief Operating Officer's office. He had always liked Camille and he needed to give her a proper goodbye by telling her how much he had enjoyed working with her and that he would miss her professionalism. As he was about to leave, he saw a recently hung picture on her wall to his left. It was the bull downtown in Bowling Green near Wall Street but it also contained that new statue of the young girl confronting the bull. He hesitated and asked her, a woman who was not from the securities side of the business and who had no connection to Wall Street, "Camille, is that a new picture?"

"Yes, I just love it."

"Have you thought about it?"

"Yes, a young woman standing up to a bull."

"Well, that's the Wall Street bull as you know and it represents prosperity and she is trying to stop it."

"My God, I never thought of that!"

"Ah, don't worry about it. It's all bull anyway," he smiled and then left.

JOHN D. LOWE

The author once worked in finance, among other things, and now resides in the state of Montana where he has picked up carpentry again, from where he had left off just after college.

www.ingramcontent.com/pod-product-compliance
Lightning Source LLC
Chambersburg PA
CBHW022150170626
46807CB00005B/2151